Praise for *28 Days to Save the World*

"The ventilator project was a game changer from a culture perspective."
—**Mary Barra, CEO, General Motors**

"*28 Days to Save the World* is both a fascinating story of achievement under remarkable circumstances, as well as a practical guide for building company culture. From the incredible story of building ventilators in the first days of the pandemic, to practical guidance for building and leading a company based on culture and values, this book is a valuable read for founders and leaders at companies of all sizes."
—**Eric Starkloff, CEO, National Instruments**

"Dan Purvis delivers one of the most insightful business culture books in these changing times. Set against a backdrop of the life-threatening global pandemic, he graciously reveals how he developed a business culture of honor, customer value and employee well-being to deliver unprecedented results and save lives in America and around the globe. His step-by-step guidance will get you on the path to creating and benefiting from a superior culture in your own business."
—**Dave Wilson, VP Marketing (Ret), NI**

"Colin Powell once defined leadership as 'the art of accomplishing more than the science of management says is possible.' Clearly, different situations require different styles of leadership. If you are a technical entrepreneur who wants to build a business that hires highly skilled knowledge workers to push the frontiers of science to build new products, *28 Days to Save the World* is a must-read. Dan Purvis lays out the blue print for building a culture that can produce outstanding results even in chaotic, rapidly-evolving, crisis situations."
—**Larry Bickle, Director, SM Energy**

"This book resonated with me at so many levels. Whether you own your own business or manage a group of employees or even if you are an entry level employee reporting to a manager, everyone should read this book to help gain perspective on the thoughts that are at the heart of every tough decision. I particularly loved the struggle associated with the conflicting message that arises from preaching work/life balance but needing customer satisfaction at all cost. The common denominator in all things will always be strong culture . . . it is undefeated in my life of experiences in life and work."
—**Ronnie Beason, PhD, Senior Partner, The Colex Group**

"I've already thought of 5 companies that would love to read this book!"
—**Patty DeDominic, Founder, DeDominic & Associates**

"Lots of books touch on the importance of culture, but few (if any) lay out an actionable plan to both distill and implement it as well as this book. I appreciated the realist tone and found more corollaries than I could count to my own experiences and beliefs. I wish 25 years ago I had read this book, it would have accelerated my self-awareness of so much of what just felt right to a younger, more naïve version of me. Dan's authenticity shows throughout the book. Particularly poignant for me was the discussion on principles versus rules and their relationship to high performance. This exact phrase is on a sign that has adorned our company's walls for many years!"

—**David Lashbrook, President, Alicat Scientific**

"From the very start, *28 Days to Save the World* draws you in with a compelling story told in a clear voice. It presented the vision of Great and gives the courage to chase after it. The authors' passions exude from every aspect of the book and they define culture, explain how to identify the culture you want, and then how to implement it within your organization."

—**Katie & Michael Ringer, Co-Founders, Foster Village Houston**

"I've watched Dan "Macgyver" his way through hundreds of situations. We've taught class, traveled, and parented our kids together. I've never seen the man quit. If you can put up a tent in the dark with seven children present, you can lead a team that saves the world. This book shows how those unwilling to accept "inevitability" can make almost anything happen regardless of the resources available."

—**Andrew Hovis, VP Real Estate, Cross Development, Franchise Co-Owner, Children's Lighthouse of Nottingham**

"An inspiring story of how building intentional organizational groundwork creates space to respond in a crisis! Dan gives us a window into growing your vision-driven leadership and collaboration muscles to do world-changing work."

—**Kate Denson, Associate National Director for Justice Programs, InterVarsity/USA**

"Inspiring. Great real-life story about how this highly effective team was built and managed. Demonstrates how a strong team that is grounded with vision and principles can seize opportunities."

—**James Burrows, CEO, Paradromics**

"Companies with a strong culture can weather any storm. Your storm might not look like the global pandemic that Velentium had to contend with, but by building a human centered company, inspired by the example in this book, your organization will be prepared to not only endure, but thrive."

—**Zak Schmoll, Founder & Chair, *An Unexpected Journal***

28 Days to Save the World

28 Days
to Save the
World

CRAFTING YOUR
COURSE TO BE
READY FOR ANYTHING

CAR PURVIS
with Steven Smith

Matt Holt Books
An imprint of BenBella Books, Inc.
Dallas, TX

28 Days to Save the World

CRAFTING YOUR CULTURE TO BE READY FOR ANYTHING

DAN PURVIS

with Jason Smith

Matt Holt Books
An Imprint of BenBella Books, Inc.
Dallas, TX

Matt Holt is an imprint of BenBella Books, Inc.
10440 N. Central Expressway
Suite 800
Dallas, TX 75231
benbellabooks.com
Send feedback to feedback@benbellabooks.com

BenBella and *Matt Holt* are federally registered trademarks.

Printed in the United States of America
10 9 8 7 6 5 4 3 2 1

Library of Congress Control Number: 2022013759
ISBN 9781637741900 (hardcover)
ISBN 9781637741917 (electronic)

Editing by Camille Cline
Copyediting by Michael Fedison
Proofreading by Madeline Grigg and Kellie Doherty
Indexing by WordCo
Text design and composition by PerfecType, Nashville, TN
Cover design by Brigid Pearson
Cover image © Shutterstock
Author photos by Sabrina Casas Studios and Lancia E. Smith
Printed by Lake Book Manufacturing

To Julie & JoBeth,

The joys of our lives

and

In memory of Navor:

It was an honor to spend 28 days working alongside you to combat the pandemic, unaware that the disease we labored together to contain would take you from us just a few months later.

CONTENTS

CONTENTS

Launch: *Culture Lives on Its Own*

Soar

Foreword

Although I genuinely care about helping people and strive to be kind, I must admit I don't always respond to everyone who asks for a meeting. If I know someone has been referred by friends or family, that's one thing. However, if it's a person I don't know, I typically wait and see whether they persist and come back a second time. Relationships, business or personal, can be time consuming. Time is among our most valuable assets and, as most leaders quickly learn, you can waste a lot of time responding to people who aren't committed to excellence. Persistence is a good indicator of a person's seriousness.

So, when Dan Purvis approached me at an epilepsy benefit event put on by LivaNova's charitable organization, I politely left the ball in his court. Dan followed up—gently, consistently—for several months before we were finally able to meet at a local coffee shop. It was clear he was persistent!

During that first conversation, I learned that Dan's son had epilepsy, a condition our company treats. I was immediately interested, not only because our therapy might be useful but also because when I meet people with epilepsy or their family members, I try to help. Having spent years in the field, I can be helpful to them in some situations. But that wasn't the reason Dan wanted to meet with me.

For several years, Dan's companies had worked with Cyberonics, the company that became LivaNova. Dan had watched our Cyberonics team turn around a company that was losing more than $50 million annually and had less than two years of cash remaining. He explained how he'd seen the demeanor of our team members at Cyberonics change as the leadership worked with them to change the company's culture as well as its financials. He wanted to understand how we'd done it.

Before joining Cyberonics, I had the benefit of a seventeen-year career at Boston Scientific during times of extraordinary growth. BSC was a very acquisitive company and at one point completed more than ten acquisitions in a period of a few years. Our BSC leadership team was keenly focused on culture from the time the company was founded by two great leaders, Peter Nicholas and John Abele. As we evaluated each potential acquisition and planned integration strategies, we asked, "Will they become more like us, or will we become more like them?" I became highly attuned to culture and its potential to help or hinder a company in its mission and business success during those years.

From day one upon joining Cyberonics, I worked with the team to reclarify our mission. The initial objective was not aimed at immediate cultural change. This was about the survival of the company, which was, financially speaking, a ship on fire. We had unpaid and thus unhappy creditors, dissatisfied customers, and frustrated team members. Our immediate job was to put out the fires. Fortunately, we had a great product for treating epilepsy that could change lives. We focused the company back on the mission of helping people who had epilepsy, a mission that our revenues and resources could support and accomplish.

During my career, I've seen several situations where individuals, teams, or entire companies become very focused on the money. When the goal becomes personal gain, decision-making and behaviors can change. Those environments often attract certain types of people. As you dig deeper into this book, you'll understand why Dan advises, "Don't follow the money!" Leaders may have a great strategy, but diluting an organization's focus and mission with a message of personal gain can negatively influence its culture and send the company off course. As legendary consultant and author Peter Drucker wrote, "Culture eats strategy for breakfast." Culture matters, and it became a big contributor to our success at Cyberonics.

Over time, as part of refocusing Cyberonics on a mission larger than ourselves, we significantly increased our charitable efforts to raise money for Epilepsy Foundations both locally and, eventually, nationally. We created and formalized a 501(c)(3) charitable organization within the company. It was at one of the many epilepsy benefit events where I met Dan.

Dan intrigued me not only because he was persistent, had a son with epilepsy, and wanted to learn about how we had succeeded at Cyberonics but also because he put his faith and family first. Dan sought me out because he was three years into founding Velentium and wanted to build a company with a dynamic, interactive culture based on collaboration. Not only that, Dan wanted to focus his company on medical devices and organize it around a passion to help people and improve lives. No shortage of resonance and similarities there!

Over my career, I've learned how important it is to embrace continuous learning. There are many ways to pursue continuous learning, including reading books, seeking and providing mentoring, and spending time with mission-oriented people who want to create good and serve a higher purpose among others.

One of the most important lessons anyone can learn is having the humility to learn from others, no matter their relative position to yours. Experience and seniority matter, but that doesn't mean those at the top of an organization have a monopoly on truth, insight, and ideas. So, when someone approaches me asking to have a mentoring relationship, it matters to me what kind of person they are. They're going to influence me just as I influence them. When the person is someone like Dan, I'm going to say "yes" every time I can! The "business stuff" is important—of course we want to do *well* for investors while doing *good* along the way in the business. However, the real staying power in a mentoring relationship is friendship, founded on mutual pursuit of personal and professional growth. The best mentoring relationships are two-way streets. In that sense, the mentoring dynamic is a microcosm of a collaborative culture in a larger organization.

As you'll read in the following pages, whether intentional or unintentional, your organization has a culture. Culture at its most basic level is simply the interaction of people. You can be intentional and work to create and develop a culture that furthers your goals, your mission. Alternatively, you can let culture happen on its own and then deal with whatever happens naturally. That natural development may be helpful, or it may be a hindrance. As Dan said to me recently, "You can try to fight the tide, but the moon is going to win."

When the currents become unpredictable, culture really matters. What you did or didn't do with your culture before the weather changed, before the rip current developed, dictates your capacity to respond. When the storm threatens more than just your group—as in, for example, a global pandemic and supply chain disruption—your cultural preparation enables you to respond to those "out there" who are drowning.

In *Good to Great*, Jim Collins's research found that assembling the right team first is more important than having the right idea or strategy. The right team will create the right culture, continue to recruit the right people, develop the right products and services, and choose the best strategies to win. Ultimately investors win by receiving better returns than those from companies that don't have the right people in the right culture.

The mission and business interests of your organization will thrive with the right people on the team. If you hire the right people for the mission, they will feel an obligation to contribute to the culture and will be energized when doing so. They will rise to the occasion when the culture faces a challenge.

Hal Rosenbluth's insight, shared in his book *The Customer Comes Second*, is that if you take care of your team members first, they will provide exceptional customer service, allowing you to win in any industry. Herb Kelleher built Southwest Airlines on five principles, including taking care of your people, as outlined in Kevin and Jackie Freiberg's book *Nuts! Southwest Airlines' Crazy Recipe for Business and Personal Success*. Success starts with the people and their culture.

The book you're holding now offers something more than those books. *28 Days to Save the World* is more than a great story about a successful business culture. It's the story of an organization whose culture was ready for challenge and triumphed amid a crisis. It's also more than a book of studies and theories about culture. It's an inside look at how Velentium's leaders designed and implemented that ready-for-anything culture, nurtured it, nudged it, and defended it. It's also a practical, hands-on workbook enabling you to design and implement the right culture for your organization.

Where are you with culture?

If this is your first time digging into the potential of culture, buckle up! *28 Days to Save the World* will be your introduction to a whole new realm of effective organizational leadership. Take it slow. Take notes. Don't stop with this book—check out others I've mentioned, others noted by Dan, and embrace continuous learning. This book may be your ticket, but your journey is just beginning!

If you're already familiar with the idea that culture can be designed, developed, and harnessed, I encourage you to read specifically for the practical applications woven throughout the book, but especially in the section wrap-ups. Work through the tools and exercises. Invest your time. When an insight or exercise is particularly valuable to your situation, share it with your team and use it to take your organization to the next level.

Perhaps you're a veteran leader, a culture champion. You know how to leverage culture, and you're here for the story of how Velentium, the small company, helped Ventec, another small company, get up to speed with General Motors. It's an incredible story told from the inside! I hope you enjoy it as much as I did. There may be lessons for you as well in part two. Like I said, seniority and experience don't have a monopoly on truth, insight, or useful ideas.

No matter where you are on the journey of leading through culture intentionally, I challenge you to let this book be the catalyst that propels you to the next level. Maybe reading it will inspire you to go find a mentor, like Dan did. Maybe it will prompt you to find a junior leader you can mentor and be sharpened by in turn. The world needs more people who can lead, prepare organizations for challenge and change, and successfully direct teams to step up in times of crisis.

Next time, I hope it's *your* story I'll get to read.

—Dan Moore
Director, LivaNova
Chairman of the Board of Directors, ViewRay

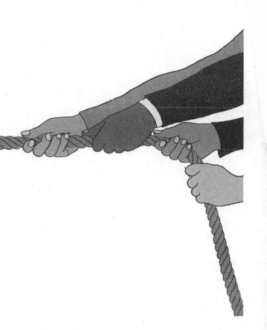

PART ONE

28 Days to Save
the World

Ventec Life Systems' office in greater Seattle. Only three weeks and nine miles away from the first fatal cases of COVID-19 in the United States. In the time since, the number of confirmed cases across the nation has escalated to just below twenty thousand. Two hundred forty-nine patients have died. Hospitals and nations all over the world are urgently seeking new ventilators, and manufacturers are scrambling to find ways to supply them.

Worldwide, fewer than one hundred ventilator manufacturers are in business. Nobody, anywhere, is prepared to mass-manufacture these devices. In a normal year, global demand for ventilators reaches a few thousand units. It is not a high-volume industry.

Yet pandemic response and healthcare experts are projecting an immediate need for tens of thousands of new ventilators. They're saying that without the ventilators, the death toll will be catastrophic.

Over the past few weeks in the United States, a coalition of movers and shakers from private industry, healthcare, nonprofit, and government agencies, put together by StoptheSpread.org, has been strategizing how to address this challenge. State governments and major hospital systems want in. The federal government is determined to provide a solution. Mass manufacturing facilities don't exist, but major manufacturers of non-medical products, like consumer goods and vehicles, are willing to build them. Private funding from deep-pocket individuals has been pledged to ensure emergency ventilator production can get underway immediately, buying time for the bureaucracies to get authorization and approval.

And, approximately one week ago, Ventec Life Systems volunteered to be part of the solution.

Day −6.
Saturday, March 14, 2020.

Tim Carroll is at home in Richmond, Texas, catching up on industry news. He's sipping decaf out of a standard 11oz cylindrical mug with a handle. Tim is very particular about his coffee mugs.

Tim and I founded Velentium together in 2012. It's because of Tim that Velentium is focused on medical devices. Tim started his career working on cardiac devices at Intermedics (today part of Boston Scientific). While he was there, he learned that one of his Sunday school teachers, a close friend, had received a pacemaker. Not just any pacemaker. Her life was now saved by a device made by Intermedics. Out of pure curiosity, they checked its serial number against Tim's records. Sure enough, Tim had personally tested that pacemaker when it was in production.

From that moment, Tim was hooked. Medical devices save lives and improve quality of life for hundreds of thousands of people every day. No other application of his engineering and leadership skills would be quite so satisfying.

In 1998, Intermedics was acquired and its Houston-area facilities were closed.

In 1998, I married Julie, a third-generation Houstonian whom I had met in college. I took an opportunity to start the Houston branch of a New York–based engineering solutions company, and made Houston my home.

Tim came to work for me. He soon transferred our branch's focus to medical devices.

It was during those years that Tim and I became friends. Tim's voluminous mustache highlights a warm smile, the kind of smile that starts in the eyes and moves mouthward, the kind that reveals a genuine love for other people. If Tim says he will help you out on a home project, it means he'll be at your home at 6 AM and will work past dark till it's done. If you tell him about a struggle or hardship in your life, he's going to ask you about it later, because he will remember and he cares. Tim is "Tim" at home and at work—in private and in public. If you get to spend time around him, you'll be better for it.

After twelve years of working for others, Tim and I started meeting for a weekly breakfast at Cracker Barrel. When the Cracker Barrel waitress adds stars to her apron and you celebrate it with her, you know you are a long-timer and a regular. We didn't have to order—the food just came.

One morning over breakfast, I told Tim, "I want to create a culture-forward, family-first company, capable of changing the world."

Tim looked at me seriously. "I think I could run a truly excellent medical device design and development company."

I said, "We can do both, together, and it will be way better than either of our efforts on our own."

And that was the genesis of Velentium.

Fast-forward nine years to March 14, 2020. Fears about COVID-19 causing a global pandemic were now realized. By the end of February, everyone knew for certain that it had reached the United States, and that it was deadly. What this meant for our small medical device company headquartered west of Houston, Texas, wasn't clear.

Velentium had just over sixty people on staff, no outside funding, and slim cash reserves. We'd grown 45 percent year over year since we started, and growth gobbles cash faster than teenagers go through cereal and fast food. We've always been racing to the next milestone, the next invoice, to keep us going and keep us growing.

Now, a pandemic was threatening to hit "pause" on the global economy. Since we design and build medical devices with and for our clients, we are classified as an "essential business," authorized to keep our offices open during lockdown. But the resulting slowdown was going to have repercussions. Social distancing in factories and parts warehouses, adjustments to remote work, would certainly translate into project delays, which would translate into cashflow delays.

Maybe it would work out. The year 2020 was by no means the first time Velentium, like so many other small businesses, had faced a cashflow squeeze. The accordion-like pattern of income and spend, income and spend was a fact of our existence.

But maybe it wouldn't work out. This wasn't your typical business-cycle slowdown. This was unprecedented, worldwide, an existential threat at a scale almost unknown to living memory. The waters ahead were murky, their surface covered in mist. 2020 might be the year that Velentium ran aground and sank.

Like many small business owners across America, I waded into the details of the SBA's Paycheck Protection Program (PPP). I didn't want to. We had always found a way to make it work. But it would've been foolish not to investigate. I also drafted an email to the company expressing my extreme aversion to layoffs. I wanted to commit to making it through together, but still give my team a heads-up that salary cuts or partial salary deferrals could lie ahead. Tim and I were going to try our darndest. But there were no guarantees.

So, here's Tim, reading the news at home on a Saturday morning. He comes across an article analyzing U.S. critical care ventilator inventory, charting current production capacity against projected demand. Tim is surprised and pleased to see that the article features a quote from one of Velentium's longtime clients: Chris Kiple, CEO of Ventec Life Systems. In his quote, Chris offers that Ventec could "ramp up ventilator production fivefold in a 90-to-120-day period," if it had the right kind of support.

Tim immediately fires off an email to Chris. "Saw your comment in *Forbes*," he writes. "We'd love to help!"

Five Years Prior.
March 2015.

We're three years deep into our new company, with just over a dozen people on staff, and Velentium's growth keeps putting us in that same accordion-like state where, even though we have consistent, positive, and growing sales quarter by quarter, we're sometimes stumped for covering upcoming payroll.

It's maddening. The quarterly reports look great. Projected returns are realistic and rosy. Yet we don't have enough in the bank to fund immediate expenses, we don't have enough receivables due between now and that next big outlay, and we don't have any acceptable sources of short-term credit we haven't already tapped. For three years, Tim and I had been working from a spreadsheet of eleven credit cards, personal and corporate, all with different due dates throughout the month, juggling the timing of which purchases go on which cards to keep everything flowing. We've taken out 401(k) loans and home equity loans to supplement our startup capital; those options are tapped. And banks aren't exactly eager to lend to tech startups. We own desks and laptops. Nothing that qualifies as collateral.

On this particular day in 2015, Tim and I were working to close a deal with a potential new client. They had a medical device that was ready to take to market, so they needed a partner to build the manufacturing stations and test systems that would enable them to start mass production. I was due at their office the next day to follow up on our proposal. Everything looked great. The problem was, we needed $50,000 immediately to keep our doors open.

Tim and I worked the numbers around and around, getting nowhere. Finally, I kicked back from Velentium's secondhand conference table.

"Here's what's going to happen," I said. "I'm going to go. I'm going to win the contract. And I'm going to come back with $50,000."

Tim just looked at me. "How the heck are you going to do that?"

I shook my head. "It doesn't matter. It has to happen. So, it's gonna happen."

That night, I got on a plane to Seattle, heading for the very first time to Ventec Life Systems' headquarters in Bothell, Washington.

If you visited Ventec in those early days, right away you'd see a display shelf filled with examples of five different medical devices:

- Ventilator
- Oxygen concentrator
- Cough assist
- Suction
- Nebulizer

In many situations, a standard ventilator alone isn't enough to address a patient's needs. An O_2 concentrator ensures the ventilator pumps the prescribed ratio of oxygen to the lungs. Cough assists help patients keep their lungs, throat, and windpipe clear of buildup, because you can't cough on your own when you're on a ventilator. Suction is like when you're at the dentist's office—it siphons off the extra saliva that people produce when they have an object in their mouths. Nebulizers convert liquid medicine into inhalable mist that's safe to breathe, which the ventilator can then deliver directly into the patient's respiratory system.

When more than one of these devices are needed, they get connected up together on side-by-side hospital carts with a system of cords, hoses, and adapters at the patient's bedside. It's complicated and messy and involved.

From 2013 to 2015, Ventec's team had designed an innovation that fixed all of that: a 5-in-1, multifunction ventilator that integrates all of the functionality of those four peripheral devices into a sleek, elegant machine that goes by the acronym VOCSN (pronounced "*vock-sin*"). It's small and light-weight enough to carry in one arm, and costs less to produce than that assortment of other devices. It's beautifully efficient.

And now, Ventec needed a team to design a manufacturing line to produce a few hundred VOCSNs per month.

Ventilators are sensitive devices. VOCSNs, even more so. Like any medical device, each one has to work exactly right so that they benefit patients in the precise way that caregivers expect. The way to ensure each one is right is by testing them as they're being built—verifying not just the final product, but also key subassemblies at various stages throughout the manufacturing process.

Testing VOCSN subassemblies during manufacturing requires some highly specialized equipment. Ventilators pump a precise mixture of oxygen and other atmospheric gases, moisture, and vaporized medicine into a person's lungs, keep their airways clear, and monitor the content and pressure of each breath. These test systems have to be sensitive in the extreme. One of our tests measures airflow pressure at <.01 PSI with >0.1% accuracy. The afternoon sun shining through an upper window into a climate-controlled factory can heat up a test system just enough to throw off its readings. This is not seat-of-your-pants stuff. The tolerances are very small. Each device has to be right, and your tests have to be able to prove—to the FDA and other regulatory bodies—that it's right. If we win this contract, it'll be Velentium equipment making that guarantee.

No matter what you're manufacturing, a single production line needs the following:

- Inspection stations, where incoming parts are subjected to quality assurance inspections
- Assembly stations, where subassemblies are put together
- Test stations, where subassemblies are tested for proper assembly and functionality
- Analysis stations, where subassemblies that didn't pass testing are analyzed for cause of failure and determined whether to be reworked or scrapped
- Rework stations, where failing but salvageable subassemblies are disassembled, reassembled, and retested
- Final test stations, where the completed device is subjected to a battery of tests that ensure all of its functions are working as expected

As for how all of that breaks down—how many of each type of station, their exact functions, how much of each step is automated, and what the exact workflow of the assembly process through the manufacturing line will be—well, all of that depends on the device being built.

For the VOCSN, we settled on a process in which each ventilator undergoes fifteen automated tests during assembly, plus two different final tests, so that it can be considered safe for humans. Seventeen intelligent test stations to produce one VOCSN. Each of those stations have to be designed, built, installed, calibrated, and qualified for use before manufacturing can even begin.

Engineering a medical device is one thing. Engineering a manufacturing line to mass-produce that device is another. Velentium is one of a very few companies in the world that offers both services. That complementary expertise makes us a uniquely attractive partner for companies in Ventec's position.

When I got to Ventec's headquarters that day, one of the first things I noticed was the sound. It was *weird*. Eerie. From most places in the office, you could hear breathing apparatus at work. Ventilators being put through their paces. Pneumatics forcing air through tubes, into and out of simulated lungs. Hoses being tested for possible leaks. It sounded like two dozen syncopated Darth Vaders lurking somewhere close by, just out of sight. On top of that, alarms and other beeps chimed as the VOCSN's touch screen interface was being worked on or tested.

Dave, Ventec's VP of Operations, took me on a quick tour of the office and then to a conference room. We talked through the proposal and hammered out some last-minute adjustments. At the end of the conversation, he smiled and reached across the table to shake my hand.

"Congratulations!" he said. "Velentium has won the bid."

"Great!" I replied. "That's wonderful to hear. Our terms include a $50,000 advance, due at signing."

Dave blinked, as if unsure whether he'd heard me clearly. "Uh . . . we don't do that."

"Then we don't have a deal." I laid out Velentium's financial situation. "We're going to be fine," I concluded. "We'll be able to get this done for you, no question. But we need $50,000 up front to tide us over into next month, and that being the case, I'm not willing to accept this new work unless we have the cash to guarantee that we can finish it."

"Oookay," he said slowly. "I'll be right back."

He returned with Doug, Ventec's founder. I repeated my terms and my explanation.

Doug listened silently, making steady eye contact.

I finished.

He continued to stare at me.

In silence. For five or six minutes.

Okay, it was probably more like ten seconds. All the while, in the background, I'm hearing the uncomfortable sound of two dozen Darth Vaders breathing somewhere down the hall.

At last he said, "Son, we have a deal." For the second time that hour, a Ventec senior leader reached across the table to shake my hand.

Velentium survived.

Six months into that contract, Doug gave me, on behalf of my team, one of the best compliments of my career. "It's a genuine pleasure," he said, "to have intelligence on the other side of the table." I've never forgotten that comment. It energizes me to this day.

We've had the pleasure of working with Ventec and their incredible VOCSN device ever since. That conversation in 2015 led directly to our involvement with Project V.

Day −2.
Wednesday, March 18, 2020.

Velentium's senior leadership team (SLT) has a strict rule for its quarterly off-site meetings: "No interruptions unless it's a family emergency." But this is a couple weeks into the pandemic lockdown. With available testing extremely limited, most of the definite data we have is on serious cases. So, even though it's not completely clear yet what the true rate of infection is, or how serious an infection is for the average person, we're not "off-site," we're "on-Zoom."

Our meeting began with a discussion of emergency cash saving measures, the PPP loan applications, rolling hours reductions, and contacting current clients to verify whether they would be continuing their engagements with us as scheduled, or postponing.

We interrupted the meeting to take a call from Ventec. In the four days since the *Forbes* article came out and Tim emailed Chris, our two companies had been communicating back and forth regularly. StoptheSpread.org's coalition had also gotten in touch with Ventec, interested in adding as much volume of VOCSN to the anti-pandemic arsenal as Ventec could produce.

At that point, their production capacity was a little over one hundred ventilators a month. They were looking to expand production, and since Velentium had designed most of the VOCSN production line test systems, we would have to be involved. How, exactly, wasn't yet clear. So far, our conversations had revolved around the idea of building an extra production line at Ventec's office in Bothell, plus a couple of lines in Velentium's offices. That would provide enough production capacity to "ramp up production fivefold," as Chris Kiple had proposed to *Forbes*—up to five or six hundred a month.

We all felt strongly that we had to do something. I was haunted by the thought that unless we acted quickly, in some ICU in the very near future, it might come down to your mom, my mom, and one available ventilator.

A big question that had yet to be answered, though, was who was buying. Would it be state governments? The federal government? Direct orders from private hospital systems? Nobody knew yet.

To my mind, the VOCSN was the right device for the need. The more we could build, the better. VOCSNs are particularly well suited to emergency response because that ingenious 5-in-1 design means they're ideal for deployment to temporary hospitals like those that were then being planned for New York's Central Park and numerous empty conference centers and sports arenas in major cities across the globe.

In the absence of available ventilators, New York's then-governor, Andrew Cuomo, was about to approve an emergency experimental procedure called "splitting," which connects a second set of tubes to a ventilator so that two patients can use it simultaneously. Splitting doesn't work well— because of differences in oxygen level needs, lung capacity, and so forth between patients, not to mention the cross-contamination risk—but at that time there was no better alternative. While they waited for new ventilators to be built, hospitals were also converting anesthesia machines, even hacking CPAP machines to repurpose them as emergency ventilators.

There was no time. We needed tens of thousands more ventilators. We needed them a week ago. Every day of delay meant more patients at risk, more patients dying.

Jeff, Ventec's COO, was on the other end of the call this morning. So much was still up in the air: strong interest from multiple parties, a lot of possibilities churning, but no firm commitments of funding, facilities, resources, or plans.

After about five minutes, I said, "Jeff, would it be easier if we were there in the room with you?"

He responded, "We have a war room meeting every morning at eight. You're welcome to attend."

I nodded. "Someone from Velentium will be there tomorrow. Talk to you in the morning."

We hung up the call and had a spirited discussion about which of us would go—Tim, Randy, Mark, Soumendu, or me. We quickly determined that it had to be a founder, someone authorized to make executive decisions quickly in the light of new information and rapidly changing circumstances.

I won. As Velentium's COO, it made more sense for Tim to stay in Houston, to help transition people off of existing projects and prepare the company for the coming shift in priority.

I ducked out of the leadership meeting to find Julie and go for a walk down the neighborhood lane and back.

Julie is my favorite person. Our four kids jokingly complain, "You like her better than *us?*"

"Heck yeah I do!" I say. "If we do our jobs right, y'all are outta here in a few years, but we'll have each other for the long haul!"

Julie is insightful, deep, and cares fiercely for everyone she claims as her own. Being one of "Julie's people" means you *will* become the best, most authentic, healthiest version of yourself. As a twenty-four-year-old, I had no idea that I was lucking into a life mate with the emotional capacity to handle the crazy ups and downs of my professional ambitions. I just liked that she was smart, super cute, athletic, and loved God and the outdoors.

Julie has been through it all with me. Sometimes eagerly. Sometimes begrudgingly. But always there. Never wavering in her searing commitment to "her own."

And so we walked. And talked. At a time when all non-essential travel, even locally, was prohibited or highly discouraged, I was about to get on a plane. A plane headed into our country's COVID-19 hot zone, where the first deaths had just been confirmed. The extent of the risk I was about to take was wildly unclear. As a former physician's assistant, Julie understood the situation better than most.

After a few minutes, our conversation fell silent. I knew she was processing.

Our steps shifted the gravel beside the road that led back to our house. Muffled noise from the occasional car drifted in from beyond the neighborhood.

After several long minutes, I broke the silence. "Babe, you know I have to do this."

Two hours later, I kiss Julie on the forehead before heading out for the airport. She's weeping, unable to raise her head to look at me.

Ninety minutes later, I'm on a plane.

Most of the seats are empty.

Day –1.
Thursday, March 19, 2020.

I'm at Ventec, in the war room meeting. I'm going to be here all day as we lay out a plan, timeline, and costs of "increasing production fivefold," moving from one-hundred-plus ventilators a month to five-hundred-plus per month. The tentative plan is to kit out additional factory lines in Seattle and convert Velentium's factory space, as well as a portion of its lab and office space, to create new lines in Houston. Ventec clears a desk for me and we get to work.

Later that afternoon, Jeff stops by my desk. "Hey. There are some people coming from GM tomorrow."

"GM? As in General Motors? Why?"

"I don't know. I guess we'll hear what they have to say."

"Mind if I come as a fly on the wall?"

"Sure. We start at 7 AM."

Day 0.
Friday, March 20, 2020.

It was 6:30 AM. GM's people were due at 7. I found a seat at the conference table in Ventec's boardroom and waited.

Phil, Steve, Ron, and Jeff from GM arrived. I offered to bring everyone coffee while Chris, Joe, Shan, Mike, and Jeff from Ventec handled introductions. As the meeting got underway, we went around the room describing our roles.

When it was my turn, I simply said, "Hi. I'm Dan from Velentium, and we handle the test systems."

By seven thirty, it's clear that General Motors is thinking big.

Real big.

Thanks to StoptheSpread.org, they've been in talks with multiple sources, including the federal government, to get ventilator production moving on a massive scale. GM's goal is to retrofit an automotive factory into one capable of producing ten thousand ventilators a month to meet national demand. That's *twenty times bigger* than the "big-time" ramp-up we were planning just the day before.

There's no question that GM knows how to build stuff, but they build cars, not medical devices. Both kinds of manufacturing are highly controlled, quality assured, safety critical. Yet they're subject to different regulations, different standards, different processes. Even though the fundamentals share a lot in common, you can't build a ventilator the same way you build an SUV. Does GM know how to build *this* stuff?

At the same time, our two medical device companies were inexperienced with mass manufacturing at this scale. Ventec and Velentium together had fewer than two hundred staff combined. Although Velentium had supported mass manufacturing for other large clients before, in-house manufacturing for both of us meant a few hundred units going out the door each month. GM plays in a whole different league, and it was going to take real effort to get everyone on the same page. We needed a new playbook.

"Why don't we show you the assembly line," someone suggests. Minutes later, most of Ventec senior staff is back at their desks to get caught up on this new development, and Ventec's quality manager is leading a facilities tour.

As the tour enters the manufacturing area, Ron, one of GM's procurement engineers, notices the incoming parts storage and begins grabbing components. "Is this everything you need to build a ventilator?" he asks me.

"Don't touch those!" the quality manager exclaims from the front of the tour. "Every component there is inspected and catalogued during receiving. Each step of this process is traceable and controlled, by law."

Everything about Ron says "no nonsense." He strikes you as a guy that has led a lot of people through a lot of tough spots. Ron is ready to make things happen, and here he is being told not to touch things?

"I have a team of seventy buyers who will be on a conference call in two hours, ready to start sourcing everything we need to build ten thousand of these per month," Ron shoots back. "In the next forty-five minutes, I want a disassembled ventilator on this table. I want to see every single part we need. We are going to find them. And we're going to start finding them in two hours."

Tour over.

Project V begins.

For the rest of the day, we took the GM team through production logistics for the VOCSN and started to brainstorm scaling them up a thousandfold. What's the assembly process? How long does each step take? How much margin is needed for failure management? How often would a manufacturing line require downtime for maintenance, and for how long? How big was the physical footprint needed for a single line, including test stations, assembly stations, inspection stations, rework stations, and final test stations? To reach ten thousand completed units every thirty days, how many jobs per hour (JPH) do you need to complete? How much was this going to cost, and which of us was responsible for which part of the effort?

Twelve hours later, I found a moment to get my bearings. *Has this all really happened since six thirty this morning?*

I called Tim to get him caught up. "Things are way different now. I'm not really sure what is going to happen or what our role will end up being. But I can tell you this with certainty—*something* is about to happen. Something really big."

Day 1.
Saturday, March 21, 2020.

G M's team had flown to Bothell from Detroit on a private plane sourced by StoptheSpread.org. And now, for the next several days, they were commuting from our hotel with their knees at their ears as all five of us squeezed into my little rented Mazda. I apologized every time. Forty-eight hours before, I'd had no way of knowing we'd wish we had a much larger vehicle.

By the end of Saturday, we were starting to arrive at a workable plan. It looked like "Project V" was really going to happen. I had created a massive spreadsheet that let us calculate test time, product needs per month, allotments for failed units and failed testers, shift training, shift changes, and so on. Once the team had all the right inputs and the spreadsheet neared its final form, there was no arguing with the results. It was just math. If we wanted to scale production that much that quickly, the factory was going to need a lot of test systems fast.

Half of every step in the manufacturing process is making sure that what was just put together works. By function, test systems represent half of the plant.

Laying out the whole job on this spreadsheet revealed something thrilling and terrifying: our little company, with its staff of sixty-five, was about to be responsible for 50 percent of this new ten-thousand-unit-per-month factory.

After two days spent gathering the information and optimizing the spreadsheet, I finally stopped and just stared at what it was telling me. Ten thousand ventilators per month was going to require 141 test systems. In normal times, it was seven months' worth of work. We were only going to have one month to get it all done.

I called Tim again. "Forget manufacturing," I told him. "We are about to be completely overwhelmed with test systems alone. It is going to take everyone we have and many more—like double our current staff. GM needs our systems up and running before manufacturing can begin. We're the only ones who know how to build them. We need to start ordering parts for these test systems immediately. And we need to onboard another sixty-five people right away."

Tim and I talked over how we should proceed. We don't have a signed proposal yet, and not only that, with so many moving pieces it's not even clear who our customer would be. Who is buying these test systems? Would it be Ventec again? General Motors? A federal agency, perhaps FEMA or HHS?

People are dying. We don't have time to wait for financial guarantees. But to get this done, we have to start buying parts and equipment and hiring staff immediately. Yet just days ago, we had been filling out the application for a PPP loan and considering furloughs.

Tim and I decided to move forward on faith, trusting that Velentium would be taken care of financially. We directed our engineering teams to start prepping bills-of-materials (BOMs) for Ventec's factory test systems, reverse engineering and documenting the few test systems that our people didn't design. We sent those BOMs to our purchasing team so they could start placing orders. Within hours, we made five figures' worth of purchases, all of it at risk.

Our purchasing team was rapidly overwhelmed. With so many businesses in lockdown, especially Houston's energy industry, we start recruiting friends, neighbors, and temp workers to augment our existing staff. We keep expanding our engineering team as more and more Velentonians get pulled from existing projects and reallocated to Project V.

It all starts here, on Day 1, and it just keeps accelerating. Nothing about the project is finalized, we have no assurances, and even though we can't afford to take the risk, we also can't afford to wait. As far as anyone knows, the nation's future may just depend on it.

Day 2.
Sunday, March 22, 2020.

Sunday morning, I got to the Ventec office to find that Phil and Ron from GM and Chris from Ventec had arrived early and were already deep in logistics discussions.

"Why does this thing have so many d*** parts!" Ron exclaimed in a moment of frustration. "What if we just built Vs instead of VOCSNs?"

The conversation quickly morphed as we considered the merits of manufacturing VOCSNs or a stripped-down version that would be ventilator-only. The reduced-feature model would require fewer parts and could be built and deployed faster, with less risk of complications and delays during assembly, and would cost less, but would be less versatile in ICU deployment.

It was Phil who proposed the solution. "Why don't we just equip the factory to build both? Two separate sections, with lines dedicated for each model?"

Chris readily agreed. The total quantity of ventilators built wouldn't change, but the amount would be split between the stripped-down model and the full-feature model. Each would require its own set of dedicated production lines.

Yesterday, I was swimming in logistics. Today, in the last twenty seconds, one of the largest projects in the history of Velentium had almost doubled in size.

My head spun. At that moment, I knew two things for sure:

1. We were in for way, way more than we'd originally volunteered for.
2. The timetable for getting it all done wasn't growing. It was shrinking.

If we didn't move quickly, we would drown.

The cost to participate was also tallying up rapidly in my head. We were still in the early exploratory phase of proposal development—not even close to a contract. Yet we had to start spending money immediately just to stay relevant. GM was already doing exactly that. They didn't have a contract either, and they had started ordering parts yesterday. But they're GM—one of the world's largest corporations, with massive cash reserves. That is not us. Not by a long shot!

Over the next several days, we would order $2.4 million in test system components, many of them custom, non-returnable. We would pull almost our entire staff over to Project V, and we would start hiring. We would begin to receive components, analyze build cycles, generate documentation, and assemble test systems. We would nearly double our head count, jumping to 110 staff in a few days. We would bring aboard two other engineering firms as subcontractors. All without receiving a purchase order.

In the final two weeks of March 2020, Velentium would commit to spend more than 30 percent of its entire gross revenue from 2019 on Project V.

If we didn't get a purchase order, we would drown.

Day 3.
Monday, March 23, 2020.

Two of our mechanical engineers, Tim and Ryan, joined me at Ventec HQ. Their task was on-site analysis of the VOCSN test systems, followed by remote education and familiarization for the staff back in Houston. It had been five years since we turned these systems over to Ventec; most of our team had joined Velentium since then.

Tim and Ryan photographed, documented, and started building out BOMs for each system on a shared server. In response, staff in Houston and elsewhere created what came to be known as the "bird-dog list." Anyone could put in a question about the test systems, and Tim and Ryan would go track down the answer and create a central reference guide for the engineers.

This central reference point became the backbone of the project planning and proposal development that Tim Carroll and I were doing alongside several other senior engineers. Jason, a longtime Velentonian who had worked on the original Ventec project and was their point-of-contact for ongoing support work, was integral to this process. Tim reached out to subcontractors—Moore Controls, located near us, and Oasis Testing, based well north of the city—to get supporting estimates.

As the big picture started to come into focus, the need for information and understanding became more detailed and granular. Tim organized operations management, assigning each of the seventeen different test systems a designated "system owner" whose job was to know that system down to the specs of its smallest screw, make the final call on any decisions pertaining to that system, such as acceptable component swaps driven by supply chain issues, and ultimately be responsible for keeping construction of that system on schedule. We had people documenting every aspect of the system, from updating build instructions to quality verification.

As each hour passed, more and more Velentonians were reassigned to Project V. With about two dozen project managers and engineers collaborating, we hammered out a proposal in less than forty-eight hours.

Day 4.
Tuesday, March 24, 2020.

Monday night, I had stayed up all night finalizing our proposal. I delivered it to Phil first thing Tuesday morning.

A good friend of mine, Chris, is a leader in GM test engineering. Years ago, we'd worked at the same company together, and we'd been in touch quite a lot over the past couple of days. Later, after the proposal had been signed, Chris sent me an email. "No pressure," it read, "but I may have bet my career at GM that you come through on time."

It turned out that when GM's purchasing team saw our proposal, they took it to test engineering to review, asking, "Can anyone else do this?"

Chris was among those who reviewed the proposal. His feedback? "Sure. I can get you the names of five other companies that could bid this work. Any of them could do it. But it would take them six months, because this is an impossible schedule. The only company in the world that has any hope of hitting this timeline is the one that designed and knows these systems."

Day 5.
Wednesday, March 25, 2020.

I stayed up all night, again, putting together the master build and delivery schedule for the test systems, the one that would guide Velentium's next month of activity.

We got back a signed proposal—the precursor to a purchase order, not yet a financial commitment—hours before I flew back to Houston.

Back in Houston, operations had ramped up immensely. With most of our other projects on hold, volunteers from our Boulder, Colorado, office had flown down to help. We'd broken down cubicle walls, cannibalized desks, and rearranged furniture, converting most of our office space and R&D lab into test system assembly stations. We'd set up remote collaboration points, with VPN connectivity and cameras aimed at physical equipment so that system owners in Bothell and at the ventilator factory, location yet to determined, could collaborate with their teams in Boulder and all four Houston locations, or vice versa.

It was abundantly clear that our first big problem to solve would be parts procurement for those 141 test stations. The urgency of the schedule, plus the widespread disruption of the global supply chain, equaled enormous logistical challenges.

Ordinarily, Velentium procurement was handled by a three-person team. If you factored COVID-19 out of the equation, our team would have no trouble sourcing the components for an order like this. Under normal circumstances, estimated lead times of six to eight weeks for specialized parts would have been an acceptable piece of the project schedule. Under normal circumstances, we could afford to split up the ordering process over several weeks, starting with the longest-lead parts and working down the list from there.

Project V had none of this normalcy. Each of the 17 different types of test stations requires an average of 86 unique components, ranging from 11 different components for a relatively simple receiving station to 167 kinds of parts for the most complex. In total, we needed almost 1,000 unique parts, plus over 150 different common components and tools.

Early responses to our procurement efforts were not encouraging. With so many people unable to work from their offices and warehouses, lead times for the longest-lead components were being estimated at double or more what's typical. We needed overnight or same-day shipping on every order, right when delivery times appeared to be least predictable. Even Amazon's fabled two-day shipping for in-stock items was being estimated at five to ten days. Anything that had to cross a national border on its way to our receiving facility risked being held up indefinitely. And since we didn't yet have a purchase order in hand for the project, some larger suppliers weren't eager to open a new account or raise an existing credit limit to accommodate us.

Yet we had to source these parts as quickly as possible. Some items had to be custom-manufactured and calibrated. Others, off-the-shelf parts, were needed in volumes higher than were available at any single location. That meant tracking down individual warehouse inventories, talking to upper management in each supplier's organization to get strings pulled, lining up a series of alternative suppliers, and coordinating with the engineers in charge of each test station on any shortage-driven design changes.

Our purchasing team was working from a shared spreadsheet with two dozen tabs—one for each test system and then some others for common parts, new additions, and tracking. We started buying on Day 1, but our system owners were still determining the list of parts that would be needed. This multi-systems BOM wasn't static. The engineers were clarifying details, making design changes, identifying and swapping alternative components in and out of the spreadsheet based on parts availability and other needs. It was simply too much to keep track of with a purchasing team of three.

How do you recruit reinforcements for a purchasing group, all working remotely on a complex and error-prone shared tool, to buy things off of a list that isn't finalized yet, on a timeline where delivery looks impossible, with limited credit capability, to help save the world?

Well, at about half an hour till midnight on Day 4, I started scouting for more hands.

With so many people across the country unable to do business as usual because of social distancing and stay-at-home orders, it seemed a fair bet that I knew folks who had extra time on their hands and would be willing to help out. Given the nature of the challenge, I knew I needed to recruit people who wouldn't accept "no," or "I'm sorry, there's nothing more I can do" from potential suppliers. That meant people who understood the challenge, knew the value of persistence, were creative problem-solvers, good with people, and were not intimidated by risk.

My first call that night was to a neighbor, Steve, an executive of a Houston-based company. "Are you working from home or going into the office? When you are home, do you have any downtime? Can you help? Would you help?"

Steve said yes! Encouraged, I kept reaching out whenever I could find a few seconds that night and throughout the following day. Then, out of the blue, another Houston-based executive, Lanny, sent me a text:

> Checking to see how you guys are holding up?

I texted back,

> Wanna help? Mike Pence was talking about my project from the White House yesterday. I could use you on the phone. Ventilator manufacturing text.

> Really??

> Yeah. No kidding—this is legit.

> Sure! Give me twenty minutes.

Soon enough, Steve and Lanny had my corporate credit card details and were working with Paul, our CFO, to buy things as fast as they could off of the shared-access spreadsheet.

At its height, this spreadsheet was being actively worked on by as many as fifty people at any given time: purchasers, receivers, engineers updating their purchasing needs, managers, and buyers. Nine of them were Paul's newly recruited purchasing team. This team stayed in continuous contact with one another, the build teams whose systems they were buying for, and the team that was receiving purchased items into inventory. They talked by phone, Zoom, Slack, and spreadsheets, from about 6:30 AM until 10 PM for almost two weeks straight. Their job was to figure out who had the parts we needed, who we needed to talk to in the supplier's organization to get that part ordered and expedited, and to make it all happen while maintaining the accuracy of our spreadsheet and keeping it continuously up-to-date.

Twenty-eight days later, when the dust finally began to settle, we calculated that the affectionately dubbed "Friendly Neighborhood Purchasing Team" had sourced over 37,000 parts. The cost of each item ranged from $0.01 to $2,759. Vendor invoices ranged from $79,028 to a mere $2.62. To reach us, components traveled distances of less than a mile and from as far away as 7,000 miles. Thanks to the dogged persistence of Paul and his team, we were able to dialogue directly with executives at dozens of suppliers to get accounts opened and orders expedited. Paul tracked down senior managers in airline and shipping companies, manufacturing facilities, and retail distributors who had the vision and the authority to override internal policies and circumvent bureaucracy to reprioritize, redirect, and expedite orders, shipments, flights, trucks, and people.

Procurement at Project V's scale and timetable was impossible.

The Friendly Neighborhood Purchasing Team did it anyway.

But purchasing was only the first unprecedented challenge of the process. Shipping parts to Houston and shipping completed test systems to the factory was a major concern. We needed everything to move immediately, as soon as it was available. Every hour mattered. We reached out to UPS, and after a few false starts, I soon had the cell phone number of the person in charge of our four-state region (Texas, Oklahoma, Arkansas, and Louisiana). If you're wearing that brown uniform in any of those four states, you work for Deryl. I explained the situation, and Deryl sent the head of UPS Houston to find out whether we were the real deal. That division head and his nine-year-old son showed up on Sunday morning and found a whole factory of people working their tails off to save the world.

Immediately, our relationship with UPS changed. They committed to support Project V at a level I had never seen: They rearranged their carefully planned delivery schedule. Every morning at 7 AM, the first truck out of the Stafford facility in Southeast Houston headed straight to our factory. We got our 10:30 deliveries at 7:30 AM—an extra three hours daily that made a huge difference.

But that's not all. They told us exactly what the final deadline was for overnight shipment. And I mean the final deadline. The real one. Not "You have to have it ready for pickup by 7 PM," but "You have to have it at George Bush Intercontinental Airport by 9 PM." They cleared the way with the airport authorities so that we could drive a private vehicle directly to the loading docks.

Guess who drove that vehicle? Many days it was Julie, especially early on. One time with a build running late, Julie made the run because it was raining and she has the competence and confidence to drive fast in Houston through the rain. Lots of other drivers don't. Driving in the rain here is needlessly dangerous. Between the build delay and the traffic-plus-weather delay, Julie had to drive right through the commercial access gate and directly onto the tarmac to the plane with airport security trailing behind, sirens blaring, to make the drop.

UPS flexed their schedule *and* the standard operating procedures of one of the world's biggest airports to enable us to use every last minute of the day to build test systems.

Even that was not always enough. Specialized workshops all over the country were making us custom parts. We got a call from a supplier one day who said, "We can't make the 6 PM delivery deadline. But we've got people willing to work around the clock on this, and we can make 6 AM."

Well, the reason for the 6 PM delivery deadline was that the daily UPS shipment left at 7 PM, and we needed that part the next day. If we didn't have that component on that plane, it was going to be delayed at least twenty-four hours.

We didn't have twenty-four hours.

But we did have my personal trainer, Seth. Lockdown had severely disrupted my ability to make it to the gym for our training sessions, as it had for most of Seth's clients. Seth had a lot of time on his hands. So, I called him.

"How'd you like to be a private courier for a few days?"

That night, we sent Seth to an airport hotel near the shop where the custom component was being built. At 6 am, the vendor delivered it to him there at the airport. He got on a red-eye back to Houston, and we had it in hand before 10 AM.

Seth was thrilled for the adventure. Which was great because it turned out that vendor was not alone. Everyone, and I mean everyone, was scrambling around the clock to get parts sourced, built, and shipped. For Seth, "a few days" turned into "a few weeks" of flying all over the country, keeping crazy hours, picking up critical custom components hours before they could have shipped by conventional means, and getting them to their destination that much sooner.

It was pretty hair-raising, especially in the first week. One of the parts we had to send by courier was an artificial lung. It's not as sophisticated as it may sound—essentially a large-diameter PVC pipe, sealed and instrumented with a bunch of wires connecting a variety of sensors to the test system. I don't know exactly what that artificial lung looks like on X-ray. "Homemade bomb" comes to mind. Hoping that Seth would be able to fly with it, Tim's wife, Stacy, handwrote a detailed note to TSA explaining exactly what this wired-up piece of PVC was and put it into the luggage next to the lung. Her efforts got the lung through security and successfully to its destination!

Seth wasn't the only one. Pretty soon, our CFO's two oldest sons, Chris and Daniel, took on courier roles as well. So did our accountant Jessica's husband, Barry. He had asked how he could help, and since he's a pastor, I figured he might know someone willing and able to fill another open courier need we had. Barry responded, "Oh, I know the perfect guy for that. It's me." And off he went! Without our couriers, we would have fallen days behind.

So much for shipping, the second unprecedented challenge of Project V. The third challenge was receiving.

Under Tim's direction, well over half of our manufacturing facility was devoted to receiving incoming orders, sorting the inventory based on which of the seventeen different types of test system each part was earmarked for, and inspecting it to make sure the part matched the order and hadn't been damaged during shipping. Shipments arrived continuously, seven days a week, from seven thirty in the morning until ten o'clock at night.

The variety and quantity of incoming parts was massive. New boxes would arrive before we were done sorting through the previous box. Thirty-seven *thousand* parts. Each of which had to be sorted and inspected manually.

"I feel like we all work for a hardware company," Tim quipped on our company Slack channel, "and it's our first day."

The fourth major challenge to solve was personnel. We were badly short of people in every aspect of operations. But this was the one challenge where the fallout of pandemic lockdowns actually worked in Project V's favor. With global demand for energy at an all-time low, Houston's oil and gas industry had slowed to a crawl. Projects were on indefinite hold. Thousands of workers had been laid off or furloughed. Many of them were people experienced in logistics, shipping, and flow engineering. As one of our subcontractors put it, "If we can design high-pressure systems for 30,000 PSI and beyond, we can absolutely adapt to work on low-pressure systems."

Tim put out the call to his network and got tremendous response. Interviewing was continuous. When a candidate's first question was about pay, we immediately moved on. We were going to pay well, but we didn't want people signing on for the paycheck. We needed more buy-in than that. We hired people who wanted to help save the world.

Most of our sixty-plus hires were independent contractors. However, engineering companies who primarily served the Houston energy industry had time on their hands, too, so we contracted a couple of subcontractor shops as well. We wanted builds going on in multiple locations, so that if we had a COVID outbreak at any one facility, the others would be able to isolate and keep working.

Days went by in a blur. Days of frenzied activity and ordered chaos. Days filled with major recruiting and purchasing efforts, logistical gymnastics, and builds underway. Nathan, one of our system owners, likened the experience to "sprinting down a pier, at night, in heavy fog. While trying to build the pier. And there are piranhas in the water."

Twelve-hour days. Sixteen-hour days.

Still no purchase order.

Days 6 and 7.
Thursday, March 26, and Friday, March 27, 2020.

The day after GM accepted our proposal, and it looked like everything was moving forward, a press statement and a couple of tweets from the White House threw everything into question. The federal government had been planning to authorize the production of tens of thousands of ventilators through Project V. The exact number kept changing, but some reports earlier that week had put the estimate as high as one hundred thousand. However, after learning how much that quantity would cost, the Trump administration balked. As the government canceled its plans to announce a ventilator deal, then-President Trump lashed out directly at GM and its CEO, Mary Barra, on Twitter.

"As usual with 'this' General Motors, things just never seem to work out," Trump tweeted. "They said they were going to give us 40,000 much needed Ventilators, 'very quickly'. Now they are saying it will only be 6000, in late April, and they want top dollar. Always a mess with Mary B. Invoke 'P'."[1]

Everyone with direct knowledge of the project knew that the accusations of heel-dragging and cost inflation coming out of Trump's White House were unfounded. I was right there with GM's team. The commitment, the energy, the raw speed, and the scale of everything they were doing was unlike anything I had seen in my twenty-five-year career. And it was a goodwill effort. GM did not profit from Project V—they undertook the entire project at cost.[2]

We tried to reassure each other that the tweets and White House statements were just posturing, a negotiation tactic. But that didn't necessarily mean that the project wouldn't get called off for political reasons.

Internally, Mary Barra issued a calm, "stay-the-course" directive. Her message was clear: Don't worry about it; just keep going. Ignore what's being said and keep going. We will find a way to make it work.

Nevertheless, I was terrified. On Thursday night I went to bed, not daring to look Julie in the eye. I didn't want her to see my fear. We'd bet the company's future on this. Not only that, but we had gone to extraordinary lengths to get extraordinary efforts from our suppliers, founded on the idea that Project V was officially part of the nation's emergency pandemic response, that it was really, truly, happening. If it collapsed now, not only would it ruin us as a company, it would ruin hundreds of relationships and impact hundreds of other companies as well. Velentium's passion to change lives for a better world had taken us right to the brink of making our biggest impact ever . . . or our most disastrous mistake ever.

On Friday, GM and the federal government reached an agreement, settling on thirty thousand ventilators and a ninety-day delivery schedule. Our manufacturing facility would ultimately produce many thousands more, for private hospital systems and governments around the world, but the federal government's initial purchase made it possible to create a ventilator factory at the necessary scale. That thirty-thousand order enabled Project V.

Immediately after the agreement was signed, Trump invoked the Defense Production Act. Due to its timing and language, the gesture was more symbolic than practical, but it came in handy several times for Velentium's purchasing team. Informing domestic suppliers that our orders were subject to the Defense Production Act allowed them to prioritize us, reroute inventory, and, in a couple of cases, coax reluctant managers into action. It was one more way to leverage the world of engineering supply shops, warehouses, and parts factories to move fast in spite of lockdown, and we needed all the help we could get.

It also got our couriers expedited through transportation security. The National Guard was supplementing TSA, enforcing travel restrictions, and assisting with COVID screening. Barry deplaned once and was swiftly ushered into a very long, sternly enforced line. He stepped right back out of line and presented our Defense Production Act letter to a National Guard member. The guardsman swiftly saluted him, thanked him for his service, and sent him on his way. On a separate occasion, Seth was transferred directly via black SUV from one plane, just landed, to his next plane, about to take off, to ensure he wouldn't miss his connection.

The agreement signed, GM announced the base of operations for Project V: a shuttered automotive factory in Kokomo, Indiana. I spread word to my soon-to-be on-site team and booked a flight.

Day 13.
Thursday, April 2, 2020.

Phil from GM called me, stressed about the next day. His team was on the hook to provide weekly updates on a conference call with numerous federal agencies, including the White House, and the first call was scheduled for tomorrow.

"You're killing me here!" Phil said. "Got to get these test systems in place. You're falling behind."

"Phil, you know exactly what our status is," I replied. "We're moving as fast as we possibly can. The systems are coming."

He was quiet for a moment. Then, "What should I tell the White House when they ask why you're late?"

Without thinking, I blurted: "Tell them to call me!" Then my brain caught up. "I mean it," I added. "I'll brief anyone you authorize me to talk to about our status."

"Okay," he said.

Day 14.
Friday, April 3, 2020.

GM's purchase order "finally" arrived. Under normal circumstances, fourteen days is a completely reasonable, even rapid, turnaround for issuing a PO. On this project, fourteen days felt like an eternity.

GM's PO was, by far, the largest single order Velentium had ever received. And I rejected it.

On the follow-up conference call we had immediately after swapping emails, I explained why. "This PO calls for complete delivery of the entire order in two weeks. That's literally impossible. My purchasing team has critical test system components on order that have six-week lead times under normal circumstances. We have fabrication shops that custom-build specialized equipment volunteering to work around-the-clock shifts, 24/7, to cut those lead times in half, because they understand the gravity of Project V. For the off-the-shelf stuff, supply chain problems are going the other direction. Lead times have quadrupled. Stock is depleted around the world. Everyone is racing to build ventilators and other critical medical equipment right now. Global shipping and customs inspections are delayed or shut down. Manufacturing times are extended as companies move to limit employee exposures and allow for social distancing in factories." *Two weeks?* Literally could not be done.

GM got it. They were sourcing parts for the ventilators at the same time that we were sourcing parts for the test systems that would enable those ventilators to be built. They were encountering the same set of challenges.

"Okay. What should the delivery date say?"

"It should say, 'Continuous delivery as soon as available,'" I dictated. "And add this: 'Once per day, at any time of GM's choosing, Velentium CEO Dan Purvis will brief anybody GM chooses on current project status.'"

I could hear the frustration with this abnormal contract term bleeding through the line. "But that's not a date!"

"No, it's not," I agreed. "But it's how it has to be." Then I brought up the second item of concern. "We also need $1 million up front."

"That's not what we do."

"I don't care," I said. "It's how it has to be. We're not a giant company with a vast credit line. We've bought close to $2 million for this project already, on faith, and we're not done buying everything required. We need $1 million immediately so we can pay down our credit and keep going."

All those times working through accordion-like financial challenges, lining up credit card due dates against receivables due dates, learning to be creative with contract terms and bold enough to ask for unusual consideration?

They'd been practice. Practice for this.

Day 16.
Sunday, April 5, 2020.

A team of Velentonians, including Alberto, David, Matt, and Mark, preceded me to Kokomo, working alongside factory renovators to prepare for our equipment and test systems as they began to arrive, and working remotely with Houston-based teams to get the systems ready. Each system had to be built, tested, and prepped for shipping in Houston, then reassembled, calibrated, and validated as factory-ready after reaching Kokomo. I flew out to join them late Sunday night—my birthday. Stowaways were slipped into my suitcase: Stuffed animals from my youngest son, which I posed and photographed enjoying hotel amenities to text back home every few days. A sealed envelope from my daughter marked "Open the day after you arrive," which contained an invitation to a daddy-daughter dinner once I got home.

I had spent the past ten days in Houston more or less glued to my laptop and my phone, often on two or more calls at once, for at least fourteen hours every day. My family was stuck in lockdown, but we didn't see much of each other. Julie was part of a small team of volunteers delivering breakfast, lunch, and dinner to each of our build sites, every day, as well as making airport runs to catch that last UPS flight out every night. I ate at my desk, working until eleven, then going out to play midnight basketball with my oldest boys on our driveway. We'd play for an hour or two, make a fast-food run, hang out, then crash hard. While they slept till midmorning, enjoying the circadian rhythm shared by teenagers the world over, I was up again before the sun and back to project coordination. It was a sweet, intense, and exhausting time, during which Julie and I barely saw each other. But the best way for me to love my wife during this season was to spend every bit of time I could loving my kids. I wasn't sure how I was going to carry that on from Kokomo, but I was determined to find a way.

I went to Kokomo partly with the intent of providing on-site accountability. In the unlikely event that the extreme pressure we were under might tempt the production crew to "pass" ventilators that were failing our tests, or any other ethical dilemma, I didn't want my engineers to have to be the ones to stand up for *Honorable*, Velentium's foremost core value, without backup. Thankfully, that scenario never happened. Instead, I spent my time acting as a program manager, keeping our team of about twenty—Velentonians, plus engineers from Ventec and GM—unstuck as we assembled these manufacturing lines. My career began in test engineering, and although the circumstances were wild and extreme, it was fun to dive back in and do hands-on engineering work again.

While there, I listened to the audiobook *Freedom's Forge* by Arthur Herman. Herman lays out the wartime production effort that enabled Allied victory in World War II. It was a massive multi-industry, multi-company initiative . . . also led by GM. I felt it was important to understand the heritage of the company I was serving. GM has decades of culture supercharging the help that they are providing the country today. Knowing that that effort was part of their history, their legends, their culture helped me understand the perspective behind the pace and potential of Project V.

I also played point on keeping us reminded that we are all human. I wanted our people at their best, which requires peak nutrition and sufficient sleep. Sleep we could not have. We worked from 6 AM to midnight for a week. On a couple nights we "knocked off early," meeting in the hotel lobby at eleven thirty for a round of beer before turning in. David even set up a cot against the back wall of our conference room and slept at the factory a few nights, unwilling to sacrifice the extra forty-five minutes it would take to get to our hotel and back. Sufficient sleep was not for us. But we could have nutrition, so I bought everyone in our sector lunches and dinners of lean meat and green vegetables every day. We worked like mad, rubbed bleary eyes, and lost weight despite the terrible schedule due to sheer adrenaline and the high-protein, low-carb meals Velentium provided.

Test systems started arriving from Houston. The first one showed up the same day I did. Every day, with every UPS and private courier shipment, a few more would arrive. GM was still renovating, getting ready for mass production, and constantly receiving shipments of ventilator parts. It was a real challenge to make sure deliveries for our test systems didn't wind up getting routed to GM's ventilator receiving and inspection crews and delaying our test system install.

Every hour mattered.

Day 19.
Wednesday, April 8, 2020.

At the heart of every VOCSN is a subassembly called the metering valve. The metering valve regulates how much oxygen is in the air the ventilator delivers to the patient, ensuring the mixture matches the level the physician prescribes. As with other critical components, metering valve function is tested at the subassembly stage to make sure it's working correctly. Our test stations first calibrate the valve, then verify the calibration. This takes time! Out of the seventeen tests performed on each ventilator during manufacturing, this one takes the longest. To keep overall production from bottlenecking at this point, we built extra metering valve test stations. That way, the factory could compensate for the extra time required using extra test system capacity and keep overall production running without bottlenecks.

But we had a problem. Due to parts shortages, the flexible tubing we'd been sent, intended to connect the metering valve test system to the metering valve, was slightly narrower than it should have been. The narrower tubing was affecting the calibration and causing false failures. The results were very close, but still just outside the tolerance limits. And when it comes to medical devices . . . especially those that are going to pump air into human lungs . . . "very close" is not good enough!

We figured out that swapping out the tubing for slightly different sizes would correct the airflow measurement. That was the good news. Even better news was that these were parts we ought to be able to get at any plumbing supply store.

I should mention that these test systems had just arrived in Kokomo, along with a bunch of others, and we were setting them all up overnight so that the first manufacturing shift could get started at oh-dark-thirty the next day. It was a few minutes after 8 PM. Nearby stores were already closed for the night.

That was the bad news.

This exact situation was my Project V nightmare. The supply chain issues we kept running up against, combined with the speedy responsiveness we needed from hundreds of vendors who just weren't used to moving this fast, made me continuously dread that the entire manufacturing effort would grind to a halt because we couldn't get some common $2 part from wherever it was to where it needed to be. So, 36,999 parts in the right place and we still can't ship a ventilator because we're missing part 37,000. *We can't let this happen. We can't!*

I mapped a route to the nearest hardware supply store, a Lowe's, and dialed the store. Thankfully, someone answered.

"Can I please speak to the manager?"

"Sir, we're closed for the night."

"I understand. But this is a matter of national importance. Can I please speak to the manager?"

I laid out the situation while sprinting to my car. He told me that their registers and books were already closed and the business day was over, but offered me a solution. "Get here as soon as you can," he said, "and we'll figure out a way to do it by the time you find what you need."

He met me at the front door and let me in. We hit the plumbing aisle and loaded up with $120 worth of tubing, fittings, and any related parts and tools I thought might possibly help with the night's work. Then, he wrote down the SKUs and quantities of everything I took, along with my credit card details, so that the store could process the sale during the next business day.

We got the parts back to the factory, and the swap worked exactly as predicted. Problem solved! Our total delay was less than two hours, and we made it up by morning. All thanks to a night manager at Lowe's who could've said, "No, we can't do that," but chose instead to stay late, figure out a workaround, and accommodate a low-dollar customer after hours because he got the message that this wasn't your typical parts supply run.

Day 23.
Sunday, April 12, 2020.

I got my kids on a video call for a virtual Easter egg hunt through my hotel in Kokomo, early Sunday morning. My camera was pointed at a blue egg, resting on the bedspread. It was up to them to give me instructions. What did they want me to do?

Inside the egg were a couple of clues—a room number and a riddle to the location of the next egg. My team had given me permission to stash an egg in each of their rooms, and my kids started sending me all around the hotel to track down the treasure hunt. The grand prize was back in my hotel room—an Xbox that I could use to play games with them late at night from the hotel. A way to continue the midnight basketball tradition we'd started what felt like months ago, but in reality had been less than ten days.

The next day, Day 24, Monday, our team had decided that we had sufficient numbers and were well enough on top of things that, instead of everyone working eighteen hours each day, we could give ourselves a break by splitting into two twelve-hour shifts. The early shift would work six to six; the late shift, 2 PM to midnight. Which meant that each of us in Kokomo could once again, at last, find a little bit of time to spend with our loved ones while we were still awake, albeit remotely.

Against the odds, against expectations, against all the inertia of a world in lockdown, Project V was truly coming together. Ventilator production had begun.

Day 28.
Friday, April 17, 2020.

General Motors delivered its first shipment of new ventilators—to Franciscan Health Olympia Fields hospital in Olympia Fields, Illinois; to Weiss Memorial Hospital in Chicago; and to FEMA.

To enable Ventec and GM to ramp up ventilator manufacturing to the level required, in less than one month, Velentium had sourced, assembled, documented, verified, and supplied 141 more of the automated test systems we had created with Ventec five years earlier.

To succeed,

- We recruited and onboarded over sixty contractors—mostly oil-and-gas techs who were let go due to the shutdowns and the dramatically reduced demand for energy production—which more than doubled our existing staff.

- We reinvented our procurement process, working closely with suppliers—themselves impaired by stay-at-home orders, restricted travel and shipping regulations, and global lockdowns—to source components from inventories housed all over the world, and to build anything that wasn't already on a shelf.
- We tracked down senior managers in airline and shipping companies, manufacturing facilities, and retail distributors who had the vision and the authority to override internal policies and circumvent bureaucracy to reprioritize, redirect, and expedite orders, shipments, flights, trucks, and people. When traditional logistics couldn't make the deadline, we flew our own couriers around the country.
- We built, verified, documented, and shipped, over and over, with daily team meetings often the only recognizable constant in twelve-, sixteen-, even eighteen-hour days of continuously changing activity riddled by Zoom meetings and calls to and from personal cell phones at all hours of the day and night.

We shipped the first test system to Kokomo just four days after receiving GM's purchase order.

Between late March and late August, under GM's leadership, Project V retrofitted a shuttered factory in Kokomo, Indiana, and built thirty thousand critical care ventilators for the U.S. Department of Health and Human Services. The first two shipments of new ventilators were delivered just twenty-eight days after that first face-to-face meeting in Seattle. A third shipment went out the day after.

Over the next two weeks, our team brought the last few production lines online. Once all the lines were operational, the factory could produce a new ventilator every seven minutes.

In non-pandemic conditions, every ventilator saves an average of ten lives.

"Whenever I hear that end-of-line bell ring," one Ventec technician told me, "I just tell myself—there's another ten people saved."

And in seven more minutes, I thought, *it's going to ring again.*

Maybe, just maybe, we helped save the world.

PART TWO

Crafting Your Culture to Be Ready for Anything

Why Not You?

Volunteering yourself, or your team, is scary. And potentially humiliating. Through hundreds of small, mostly insignificant experiences peppering our childhood and early career, most of us have been conditioned to avoid raising our hands. Our instincts were trained for inertia. *Stay seated. Don't rock the boat. Don't draw attention to yourself. Wait to be called. Wait to be picked.*

My inner monologue is ever primed to feed me a stream of "good" reasons for sticking with the status quo. But over the years, I've learned something pivotal: that inner monologue isn't speaking with my True Voice.

When I see something that gets me fired up, the script in my head plays out like this . . .

True Voice: "Someone's got to do something about this!"
Other Voice: "Calm down. What's it got to do with you? It's not your problem. Don't stick your neck out."

I've coached myself to speak to both voices when this happens: "*Why not me?*"

Now, maybe there are good reasons why it should not be me. But I've got to at least ask the question.

The Other Voice wants me to play it safe. It wants to keep me from stepping into opportunity, challenge, and adventure. Asking "*Why not me?*"

gives my True Voice permission to take center stage. It silences the continuous noise of the Other Voice. Asking *"Why not me?"* flips the script so that I begin thinking and working toward action.

How do I know it's time to give the Other Voice the cue to step aside? I've learned to recognize the three false messages that the Other Voice uses again and again. They are Imposter Syndrome, Fear of Failure, and Comfort. These are the forces plotting to keep us right where we are.

False Message #1: "You're not capable of that."

Maybe you feel like a fraud. Maybe you are absolutely certain that if anyone looks closely enough, they'll realize you have no business being where you are, doing what you're doing.

This type of self-doubt is called "Imposter Syndrome." Lots of people experience it—including famous, highly accomplished people you'd think would be immune. Bestselling author Neil Gaiman relates that he was once feeling out of place and underqualified at a gathering of noteworthy people from the sciences and the arts—writers, inventors, musicians, technological pioneers. People who'd contributed to making it better to be human.

While he was there, Gaiman happened to find himself in conversation with another man named Neil. To Gaiman's surprise, the other Neil confided that he, too, felt like an imposter at this gathering. He felt his contribution, his work, didn't make par.

Momentarily astonished, Gaiman also felt reassured. Because:

The other Neil was Neil Armstrong.[3]

I love this story. It shows that feeling like an imposter isn't a trustworthy feeling—it happens to everyone. Think about the contestants on Fox's celebrity-contestant show *The Masked Singer* who describe how freeing it feels to perform anonymously, without the pressure to live up to their own well-established professional personas. Many are Grammy-level musicians who secretly wondered whether it's truly their talent or simply the inertia of past fame that's been carrying their careers.

Imposter Syndrome is a very real, very difficult challenge to overcome. I've resigned myself to the reality that it may not ever go away. Even after wading out time and again to take on projects that are slightly out of our depth, and always finding a way to swim instead of sink, Imposter Syndrome still rears its ugly head. But here's the kicker:

Imposter Syndrome is lying. You can prove him wrong.

False Message #2: "That will never work."

Perhaps you consider yourself a realist: you know that your Fear of Failure is entirely legit. Optimists like me don't call such people "realists"; we call them "pessimists." Realists like them call optimists like me "dreamers." My favorite realist is Julie, my bride of more than twenty years. She calls my optimism "deferred disappointment."

My mentor, Larry, once told me that 75 percent of being a leader is making a decision in the face of extreme ambiguity—and then doing whatever is necessary to turn that decision into the right decision. Decide. And then make it happen. And the best trait to assure that it does happen is not talent . . . it's not intellect . . . it's not charm. It's stubbornness.

The organizations and initiatives that succeed are not necessarily led by the smartest, the luckiest, or the most well-resourced people around. I'm living proof! Successful organizations are led by stubborn people. People who are willing to go where the problem is and find a way to contribute. People who bring others along with them, and who successfully transmit their own tenacity and determination to their followers.

Marc Randolph, Netflix's co-founder and first CEO, has this to say about stubbornness in his book, *That Will Never Work*:

> I knew that our idea was good. It might not happen now, but it would one day . . . When it comes to making your dream a reality, one of the most powerful weapons at your disposal is dogged, bullheaded insistence. It pays to be the person who won't take no for an answer.[4]

Stubbornness! In my opinion, the number-one factor for success. And it's entirely in your hands. Dig in and decide that you will not fail. The bulldog wins because the bulldog grabs hold and doesn't let go. Nothing more complicated than that.

Fear of Failure keeps us from volunteering or tempts us to self-sabotage with half-hearted effort. Better to play it safe, to save an "out," to claim "I really didn't care." Commitment makes us vulnerable. Fear of Failure convinces us that we'd rather fold than bet all-in when success isn't guaranteed.

Fear of Failure is lying—just like Imposter Syndrome. Failure happens, but you don't need to be afraid of it. If you are stubborn enough to keep working the problem, keep learning from your mistakes, you'll learn, you'll grow, and you'll emerge more capable than before.

False Message #3: "You're fine—this is good enough!"

Maybe you've got a good thing going right now, and you don't want to jeopardize it. Why would you? It's comfortable in the nest. In fact, if your nest comes with enough autonomy and cashflow, it might not even occur to you to consider leaving.

When I turned in my two-weeks' notice to go start Velentium, my peers at my former employer thought I was joking. *Why would anyone quit a dream job?*

In many ways, the move made no sense. I traded low-risk employment for high-risk entrepreneurship, no debt for lots of debt, and day-to-day peer interaction for isolation at the top.

Was Velentium worth that trade?

Absolutely.

Nests come in many shapes and sizes: from steady employment, to a settled family, to an organization or team that's doing "good." Any situation that feels stable, sustainable, and comfortable can become a nest.

Nests are safe. Nests are good. For a season.

The trouble with nests is: they coddle us into believing we don't need to fly.

Do I need to learn how to fly? How will you know if you don't ask?

It isn't in our nature to wake up when we feel a little too comfortable. To build muscle, you must tear it. To become flexible and agile, you must stretch. To learn to fly, you must flap—and you will fall.

Good may be good enough for most people. But you're reading this book. If you're in a good situation, you feel content there, and want to stay that way, you should seriously consider putting this book down. Once you start asking "Why not me?"—once you catch a vision of Great . . . Good won't be good enough for you anymore.

As you begin stretching your wings, clumsily hopping and flapping at first, your goal must be chasing something Great, not escaping something bad. I didn't leave the nest because it was bad. Neither will you. I left because I dreamed of something better. Something Great.

TAKE THAT FIRST STEP

When you ask "Why not me?" you quickly find yourself staring down an unmarked trail on a foggy morning. The number and nature of the steps between you and your destination? Unknown. The challenge looks endless and daunting. But there's a secret: not all steps are created equal.

The first step is the hardest. It's terrifying. And it's lonely. When you take that step, when you start asking for something different, when you start working to create something new, many around you who are content with "good enough" will resent, resist, and reject you.

To keep going, cultivate your True Voice and tune out the Other Voice. You know you're not better or more deserving than others. You're just braver, maybe more foolish, certainly less complacent. Having a Good Thing is no longer good enough for you! You're headed to Great. And when you blaze a new trail toward Greatness, you improve our world. You have my sympathy—and my heartfelt gratitude.

In the blockbuster movie *The Fellowship of the Ring*, two of the characters—Samwise Gamgee and Frodo Baggins—are crossing a farmer's field near the borders of their hometown, early in the film. At the edge of the field, Sam stops. "This is it," he says. "If we take one more step, it'll be the farthest away from home that I've ever been."[5]

Not only do Sam and Frodo take that next step . . . and the next one, and the next one . . . they end up traveling across the known world, on foot, carrying the unimaginable burden of a deadly superweapon that can only be neutralized at a heavily guarded location behind enemy lines, under continual threat of capture, torture, and death, with little outside help and often nobody to rely on except each other.

If you know the story, you know that their grueling, epic journey ultimately ends in triumph. But it all began with that one step.

After that first, seemingly impossible step, the second step is not as bad. By step five, your focus is now on the excitement and the energy you get from creating something out of nothing. By step one hundred, you're on pace for a long run. By step five thousand, running has become second nature, and you're miles ahead.

Feeling less like an imposter. Less vulnerable to Fear of Failure. And farther than ever before from the comfort and safety of Good.

But many steps closer to Great.

SPEAK REALITY

That meeting with GM and Ventec on March 20, 2020, Project V Day 0, was a big deal. But it was also nothing more than the latest step in a years-long journey of Tim and me learning to volunteer ourselves and our company. Through constant practice, volunteering becomes second nature. That meeting was the fourth or fifth time that week Tim and I had volunteered Velentium for Project V.

Seth Godin, podcaster, speaker, corporate trainer, and bestselling author of business books like *Linchpin* and *This Is Marketing*, explains that although "it's a cultural instinct to wait to be picked," you first have to "reject that impulse and realize no one is going to select you . . . then you can actually get to work."

He continues,

> Once you understand that there are problems just waiting to be solved, once you realize that you have all the tools and all the permission you need, then opportunities to contribute abound.
>
> No one is going to pick you. Pick yourself.[6]

After asking "Why not me?" you have to follow up by declaring your role, your place in the story. That's where everything starts. You have to speak that reality to make it real.

That sounds paradoxical, so let me explain.

There are things you know you're capable of, but you've never done. Put that hunch to the test by stepping into the arena. Declare your role out loud. Publicly. You'll work harder, faster, smarter, and longer at proving yourself right because you've declared it.

This truth plays itself out in all kinds of ways. Have a crush on someone? Tell your best friend, and you're more likely to ask your crush out. Want to run a half-marathon? Start telling people you've signed up—better yet, ask them to show up to support you on race day—and you'll be more motivated to train. When the training gets hard, you'll think of the people you told and you'll keep running.

Declaring what you will make real is huge. You've put your mouth where your heart is, and wagered your reputation. Speaking reality creates discomfort. But over time, like a bodybuilder going for a personal record, or an orchestra musician aiming to move up a seat, you'll learn to enjoy the feeling because it means you're improving.

Most importantly, speaking reality reverses your psychology. The Other Voice gets drowned out as your whole being shifts into gear to make your True Voice's declaration happen. The glass goes from half-empty to half-full. You've moved from having promise to making promises.

Promises you'll work overtime to keep.

WHY NOT YOU?

Some of you reading this book are like me. You desire to accomplish something Great. In quiet moments, an impulse seizes you. An idea that sends chills down your spine. You're itching to be part of something bigger, to help right wrongs, to make life better for someone, better for society. To build something with staying power. Something with legacy.

Cultivate that impulse.

If you do, you will change. Your friends and family will notice differences in what you value, how you spend your time, what energizes you. Life will get harder, and lonelier. And it will be worth it.

Why not you?

I think it should be you. I hope you'll decide to stop accepting the world as it is. I hope that, instead, you'll start making promises and taking steps to go after something Great. And I know that you'll be able to do it, because you'll understand the power of culture.

Someone's got to save the world.

Why not you?

Culture Forward

Before COVID-19 disrupted the world, I'd planned to write a book called *Culture Forward* about the power of organizational culture. Velentium's years in business had already demonstrated the difference it makes in the workplace. But Project V proved just how valuable culture really is. The years we spent hatching, nurturing, and launching our culture made it possible for our little company of sixty-some people to step up and successfully join this massive pandemic response effort. If our culture had not been ready to guide and sustain us in time of crisis, we would have failed. But because it was ready, so were we. Ready to help Ventec and GM achieve the impossible.

I've seen that culture can:

- Reveal the right path in a crisis,
- Tap into your team members' inner motivation,
- Unite leaders and followers,
- Compel action in "for such a time as this" moments,
- Enable you to step up to global challenges, and
- Catalyze deep connections between people inside and outside your organization.

How does it work? That's the focus of the rest of this book.

But first: *Why* does it work?

Well, before my explanation will make sense, we need to acknowledge that the Big Enemy every leader has to face down is Inertia. The power of the status quo. The gravity of how things are.

You and I live in a world resistant to change. That means we live in a world resistant to entrepreneurs, go-getters, independent thinkers, initiative-takers, pioneers, shaker-uppers, and anyone with ideas and guts.

A world resistant to leaders like you and me.

That resistance manifests as logistical challenges, personnel and personality challenges, competence challenges, cashflow and debt challenges, management challenges, and strategic challenges. In themselves, each of these challenges is very real, and must be faced and fought. But collectively, they're all just symptoms of Inertia.

Resistance to change is human. It might be in our nature. It's definitely in our nurture. Existing conditions shape us, and because we're used to them, we're subconsciously invested in upholding the status quo. It's basic. And it gets expressed through culture.

That's good news. If the resistance is cultural . . . then culture can overcome it.

I lead a relatively small organization. At any given time, there are over four hundred million organizations like mine across the globe, battling inertia. Working to overcome the resistance. But it sure ain't easy. Statistically, of the six-hundred-thousand-plus new businesses and nonprofits that will be started next year in the United States alone, half will never see a fifth anniversary.

If you are

- starting a new venture,
- stepping into a new leadership role,
- concerned about surviving an upcoming business cycle, or
- contemplating a scale-up to the next level,

and if you're anything like me, then one of the questions you lose sleep over is: "How can we ensure that we're in the half that makes it?"

I repeat: one very big piece of the answer is *culture.*

WHY CULTURE?

For the purposes of this book, culture is that intangible "third thing" that arises when you and I (and any number of other people) are in each other's presence for a long enough time. It's the effect we have on the way we behave, talk, think, and work. It's part atmosphere, part relationship, but mostly *shared identity*.

When two or more people interact regularly, a subtle negotiation takes place as we all try to figure out who "we" are, how "we" do things. Through a succession of exchanges, most of them unspoken, we reach consensus. To quote Seth Godin again, that consensus takes shape as *"people like us do things like this."*[7]

In the vast majority of social situations, from "impersonal" corporations to nuclear families, the consensus of the tribe is almost never stated outright. We negotiate it, we learn it, and we learn to recognize it, instinctively. We adhere to it almost blindly, never giving it much overt thought except whenever we or someone else does the wrong thing. Tribal expectations exert an invisible influence and inertia. When someone goes afoul of it, the violator is either brought in line or ejected from the tribe.

Culture happens. If not developed by design, it *will* develop by accident.

Culture happens because people are hardwired for belonging. Belonging requires a set of agreements about the whys and hows of behavior. As social creatures, humans are so adept at figuring this out together, we don't have to explicitly talk it out to arrive at a shared identity.

Culture happens in every organization, large and small. In every group of friends, household, and church. In the back room of every grocery store, in the kitchen of every fast-food franchise, in the locker room of every sports team, in the third-grade classroom of every elementary school, right now, a culture is being negotiated. Reinforced. Perpetuated.

Shared identity is powerful. It may be the most powerful driver of human behavior on the planet. It reinforces norms and motivates extraordinary effort from individuals.

So, here are the billion-dollar questions every leader should confront:

Can I afford to let the most powerful driver of human behavior go untapped?

Can I afford to let it take shape by accident?

Can I afford to let the culture in my organization be a mishmash of expectations and behaviors imported from outside relationships, previous jobs, childhood experiences, sports teams, service organizations, military units, or social clubs?

No!

To win this race, leaders have to shrewdly identify the best traits available and breed them into a champion that can dominate. A champion worth staking the organization's future on.

Because staking everything on culture is what every leader does.

A lot of them just don't know it.

WHERE TO START?

One of the dilemmas of being someone with ideas and guts, of having the drive to start something and the stubbornness to stick with it until you succeed, is that you could just pick something random and you could probably make it work. Rather than found Velentium, I probably could've made more money owning a Smoothie King franchise. The past decade would've been a lot easier, too. But not nearly as interesting or as satisfying. Smoothies are delicious, but smoothie-making just doesn't grab me. And if I don't connect with that product on a deep level, how could I convince my staff or customers to care? How could I build shared identity around something that doesn't excite me?

The best way to pick the whys and hows that will define your organization's shared identity is to first figure out who *you* are. Once you've honed what you're about, the whys and hows become clear. At that point, not only do you have clarity but you develop the emotional amplitude to connect dozens and hundreds of others to the cause. You'll have capacity to spare—energizing not only yourself but them, too, through all the tangible challenges that lie ahead.

THE ROAD AHEAD

This is not a book about how to "create" a culture, in the same sense that it's not a book about how to design a car. This is a book about how to identify the culture you want, and then implement it. It's a book about driving your organization to the places that matter, using culture to map and fuel your journey. Culture isn't a one-and-done, set-it-and-forget-it thing. If you create a great culture on paper, but aren't effective at putting it into practice, it won't matter how stunning your mission statement, brand slogan, or corporate values are. Pretty soon your organization will be back in the same deep-worn rut that everyone else is, moving slowly down the road well traveled. If you're moving at all.

In the chapters that follow, I'll show you:

- How to shape your inner drive into a force powerful enough to effect world change,
- How to channel that force, focus it onto the right problems, and translate it to your team, and
- How to recognize and volunteer your team for challenges and opportunities that will unify them and spur their growth.

I'll use real-life stories to illustrate these points, many from Project V. But the lesson that should become clear isn't that the Project V partnership achieved something few people believed possible because of some superheroic ability. Not at all. With the right culture, any organization with similar technical know-how could have stepped up to the task.

On Day 0 of Project V, Velentium volunteered for a journey that rapidly grew in scope far beyond what outsiders expected our company would be able to handle. We knew differently. Like everyone else, we had no idea that COVID-19 or Project V were headed our way. But we had deliberately crafted a culture that was suited to opportunity and challenge. That's something any organization can do.

Let me show you how.

HATCH

The Culture Core

More than Air

DON'T FOLLOW THE MONEY

What makes you tick?

Think about the things that really excite you. Things that make you smile, no matter what. Things that get you on your feet, hands in the air. This is personal to you. There's no right or wrong answer. What makes you tick?

What makes me tick is best told in stories. You've read some of those stories already—and when it comes to Velentium, there are so many more—but even though leading a business is a big element, there's a whole family side as well. There's the moment I ascended the steps in a Kazakh orphanage to make our sons our own. Watching the Astros eleventh-inning comeback in the World Series with my eight-year-old boy. Walking into my bedroom and finding my dog sleeping, somehow, with all four paws straight up in the air, comfortable as can be.

Your true passions, big and small, are what make you tick. Passions aren't right or wrong. Other people can't validate them. They aren't up for debate. They just *are*. Your passion is whatever gets you out of bed in the morning, whatever lifts you from the inside out.

I ask new hires about their passions regularly. Our recruiting team asks it when screening candidates. Never have we ever heard anybody answer: "Air."

Why not, though? Air is pretty important. Vital, even. Without air, six minutes from now you would be dead and so would I. Air sustains us. When we can't get enough of it on our own, someone or something else has to help us breathe, or we'll die.

But even so, air doesn't make us tick.

When it comes to for-profit companies, leaders often act the exact opposite. Asked to state their purpose or reason for existence, many say something like, "to generate great returns for our shareholders" or "to maximize ROI and drive revenue growth." In a word: money.

But money doesn't make a company tick. Money is what a company survives on. Money is the air of a company. It's not the reason your company gets up for work every morning—not even in the most mercenary of organizations. It may seem like everyone there is chasing dollars, but I guarantee you that every individual is chasing those dollars for a reason.

If your organization is a charitable nonprofit, this point might be a little more obvious. You might struggle with not emphasizing revenue enough, or with the inherent tension between fundraising and charitable work. We'll talk more about that over the course of this chapter.

The point is, the discrepancy that exists between *air* and *passion* for a person is the same one that exists between *money* and *passion* for an organization. Maximizing quarterly returns, smashing projected sales or fundraising targets—these are nothing more than ensuring the air supply that enables your organization to keep doing great work.

Air is everywhere. Opportunities to generate revenue and earn a living abound. Unless you're in a severely restricted labor market, there is zero chance that the reason your staff show up to work each day, at your place, is just to make money. Air is motivational only when people aren't getting enough of it. When we're breathing easy, our goals elevate, our mood changes. But air can only go so far. Once air is present, true satisfaction is tied to passion.

That's not to say that money doesn't have a part to play. It does. "*Money talks*" and "*Follow the money*" are not empty phrases. Organizations communicate what matters to them with their wallets. When money moves, a message is sent. That monetary message either reinforces or undercuts everything you say with words. Like air, money really matters. But money isn't anybody's *why*. It doesn't inspire true passion . . . or provide true satisfaction.

But because money is easily measured, every leader of every organization is constantly tempted to assume that revenue plus reserve is a "good enough" proxy for everything else.

That's a trap.

Don't follow the money.

Real success comes from harmonizing the culture-cashflow tension.

CULTURE-CASHFLOW HARMONY

To assess the strength of an organization's culture, simply watch what happens when cashflow and culture are at odds. When the customer demands a result that means keeping staff on-site through the weekend, but the culture promises consistent hours and work-life balance, do you tell the customer no and risk losing the account? Or do you tell your people to work Saturday and risk losing your staff? If you think you might lose staff either way, do you pick cashflow and hope your people understand? Or do you pick culture and hope your customer understands? Which one wins?

This is a book about the power of culture, so you might think that I'm going to tell you that culture should come first, every time. I wish I could. But the truth is, just as I can't live without air, culture can't survive without money. Passion energizes you, energizes your team, but money provides the means to pursue that passion. Managing that tension is no easy feat. Upholding your culture is a matter of identity. It's how you prove your trustworthiness to staff and clients alike. Drop the culture ball, and you're exposed to the "soft" threats of being unable to meet interpersonal commitments. Drop the cashflow ball, and you're exposed to the "hard" threats of being unable to meet financial commitments.

Hurricane Harvey hit Houston in August 2017. Thousands upon thousands of people were suddenly without a place to live, all their possessions ruined, their worlds turned upside down. At the time, Velentium had fewer than twenty employees and contractors. We told our staff to go out into their neighborhoods and help. If somebody's home has flooded, help them get the stuff out of their home, get drywall stripped out, get that home drying so mold doesn't begin to grow. Check on all your family, friends, neighbors, check on their houses. Tell us where there's need. And we will come alongside you and help. Don't come to work—go help.

Our leadership team decided we would continue to pay salaries during this time. It seemed like the right thing to do. But instead of being just a few days of getting people back on their feet, Harvey cleanup, even for just those folks our few staff were connected with across the city, stretched out for several weeks. I watched as our bank account drifted dangerously close to zero, wondering how we were going to hold it together. The project delay fallout caused by Hurricane Harvey nearly drove Velentium into bankruptcy.

Come the last day of October, Julie was walking around our home saying goodbye, because we'd leveraged our home for startup capital and were about to have to put it on the market and sell a controlling stake in Velentium to a bailout investor. She was scared. I was traumatized.

I had thought we'd done the right thing, standing by our decision to be generous and care for our people as people in the face of extreme need. Tim and I felt like we needed to tough it out during this crazy, unprecedented event. But the next day, we were going to pay for that decision by giving up our company . . . and my home.

Yet that evening, at 5:27 PM, I got a call from a customer . . . in response to a proposal . . . a customer who then placed the largest order in the history of the company.

Halloween night. One day before our self-imposed deadline for listing our home.

I called Julie. "Hon, you're not going to believe this . . ."

I could practically hear her head shake over the phone. "Being married to you sure ain't easy, Purvis!"

Will things always work out like that? Probably not! After that experience, I would never advise running out of air for the sake of culture. In fairness, that's not what I thought we were doing. We made an open-ended commitment and it had a long tail of unanticipated repercussions. What I do know is that we resolved to do this thing in the midst of Harvey for the community and for our staff, declaring that things have got to work out because we are the kind of company that stands by its people and the people they care about. And, miraculously, it did work out. We survived. Ever since, because of that experience and its stories, we've enjoyed a level of strength and resilience for difficult moments that we never would've had if we hadn't chosen to put our passion for changing lives for a better world in front of everything else.

Project V also demanded an intense juggling act of culture and cash-flow. With a global economic slowdown looming, we had no choice but to step up to this opportunity. It could easily have been the only new work we got for months. Before GM joined the project, it looked like a relatively small project, a typical engagement for us from a financial perspective, with the extra cultural satisfaction from getting to fight COVID-19 directly, plus the extra cultural risk from asking staff to work and travel during a pandemic. After GM joined, the scope grew and the timeline accelerated so fast that choosing to keep up and contribute meant putting the whole company at risk. Two million dollars in purchases would've sunk us if the project had fallen through. Even if we'd somehow found a way to survive the financial loss, the amount of goodwill we would have burned through probably would have spelled the end for Velentium.

If Project V was a high-wire juggling act in the big tent, then all the "business as usual" leading up to that moment of intensity was us practicing the fundamentals. If we hadn't been putting our money where our mouth is all along, we wouldn't have had that environment of trust that let us double our workdays, double our staff, demand twenty-eight days' worth of weekends and then some, send staff out on open-ended travel, massively expand and max out our credit with suppliers, and deliver on our promise.

Investing in culture benefits your bottom line. You'll see the proof in staff engagement and retention, in customer satisfaction and referrals, in brand reputation and market share. You have to have healthy financials to make those investments. But if you get too preoccupied with the organization's financial health, as so many leaders do, you'll neglect its cultural health.

Learn to breathe, but don't stop there.

With each breath, live for what makes you come alive.

WHO ARE YOU?

To intentionally design and nurture your organization's culture, you've got to figure out who you are as a company. What is it that really excites the collective *you* as an entity?

The easiest way for leaders to build deep, defining, identity-level passion in their organizations is for that passion to mirror their own.

When you realize your passion, when you start talking about it and pursuing it, the reaction you'll often get is a head-tilt and people scratching their chin in confusion. *"How in the world can someone be passionate about that?"* And if that confusion and pushback doesn't throw you off, doesn't make you stop caring about that thing, you know what you've found is real.

As I write this, Julie is retaking organic chemistry in our home office. For fun. And that gives you a hint about what makes Julie tick. She went to med school and became a physician's assistant because she's energized by the complexity and wonder of the human body.

When Tim and I founded Velentium, we knew we had to describe our joint passion right from the beginning. And we kept coming up with different ideas that didn't quite land. You may have a similar experience when you work through the exercises at the end of this section.

Tim and I kept circling around this statement: "Changing lives for a better world."

That statement *is* the two of us. It's a perfect fit. But it sounds corny, trite, and broad. So we tossed it and kept trying other phrases, but we kept coming back to that one. Eventually, we embraced it. And we've made it work.

Why did the Passion statement matter so much to us? Because it's the first and most important filter in our decision-making. All of it. If an activity will change lives for a better world—not just our clients' lives or their customers' lives, but our staff and their families' lives as well—then that activity stands a good chance of being right for us. It fits. We can justify it against the passion. If something we're considering wouldn't better those peoples' lives, we're going to say "no" to that opportunity.

It's common for people encountering Velentium to observe, "There's such energy around your company." Our company is built on the passion of its founders. Our passion attracts others who share the same passion. If a candidate doesn't share the passion, they're not a good fit and we don't hire them. We're energized to work here together because we all carry this same shared passion. It's why we show up every day. And it's why we were willing to step up in the face of extreme need, despite the risk and the sacrifice.

When you've met the child, the neighbor, the teacher, the veteran, or even your own grandson whose life or quality of life is sustained by a medical device you helped bring to market—all of which have happened to people at our company, by the way—you never forget it. That memory sustains you through the paperwork you dread, the nights-and-weekends-and-still-impossible deadline, the last-minute supply chain collapse, the difficult relationship with the unreasonable client or vendor. Working on something you're passionate about, side by side with people who share your same passion, energizes you in a way that no paycheck or profit margin ever could, no matter how big.

TIME FLIES WHEN

Have you ever gone to that dinner party with a date that you didn't want to attend? The one where everyone present is all of your date's old friends, and you don't know anybody?

You go along anyway, and a couple hours and a few drinks later, you're having the time of your life. Why? If you look back and analyze it, well—those drinks probably helped. But what really made the difference was discovering that one or two or three of the other guests have similar interests to yours. Next thing you know, conversation is effortless. That's the power of passion. I might not know you at all. But if you wanna talk about Astros baseball . . . or adoption . . . or shaping an organization's culture . . . you've got a friend for life in me.

What are those conversation catalysts for you? What subjects instantly turn a stranger into a friend?

I had breakfast the other day with a friend of a friend named Joe Bob. Joe Bob has served on the boards of multiple companies, including as chairman of a Fortune 500 company, since 2012. Up until a certain point in our breakfast, he was just a potential source of advice, perhaps a mentor for me.

But then, there came a point where I asked myself, *How can I convince this guy to join my board?*

What prompted that moment? It came when I casually asked if he was married.

Joe Bob lit up from ear to ear, and said, "Jeanie and I have been together since high school."

Right then, I knew we had a connection. It wasn't what he said. It was the passion behind how he said it. I'm passionate about successful marriages, because they're difficult and rare. And I'm pretty crazy about Julie.

Given his career experience, Joe Bob clearly had the aptitude and experience to be Velentium's chairman. But when we connected over a shared passion, I began to recruit him in earnest.

He agreed, and officially became our chairman just a few weeks before we finished writing this book. That's passion at work.

Passion is easy, once you know it. You don't have to work at it. And the surprising thing is, people connect with *your* passion. Not with "passion" in the abstract: your passion. Your natural excitement is what's contagious. That's the energy you're inviting people to share. Don't hide it or downplay it—send it up like a signal flare! Look for the spark it ignites in others, and invite them to join the excitement.

AND YOU SHALL RECEIVE

When you see how to make the world a better place, some way to improve a situation or ease the life of someone experiencing suffering, it is good and right and OK to ask for participation from others. Whether your "ask" is for a person's time, career, financial investment, or charitable donation, as long as you're honest about what you're asking for and why, your request is justified. It's justified because your passion is worth pursuing, and because you're going to pursue it using any and all resources given to you. If you're truly passionate about something, don't apologize for it. Just ask. If the passion doesn't connect with the other person, they'll say no. Think of your ask less as a request and more as an attempt at passion-matching. If they say no, they're not rejecting you; they're saying, "*It's not a passion-match for me.*" And that's okay! Now you know to ask someone else.

Similarly, when someone says yes, they're not accepting you because you've made a good argument. It's because they already share your passion; hence they're thrilled to go on this journey with you. So ask! The other person cannot join their story with yours until you ask.

For nonprofits, your passion is what you're about. There's no confusion on that point. Your passion is your greatest asset, and when you share it with more people, together, all of you have more power to effect change in the area you all care about most. And the only way you'll discover more people who share your passion is by asking.

I have several friends who direct charitable nonprofits. When they have a financial need, they know they can ask me. I don't always say yes. Sometimes I can't. Other times I don't share their passion for this particular request. It doesn't offend them when I say no, and it doesn't offend me when they ask. In fact, I'd be disappointed if they didn't ask.

When you lead a passion-driven organization, nonprofit or for-profit, you might start to feel that the cause should speak for itself. *If other people know about us, they'll show up.* That's a common misconception. And an even more common way to avoid your discomfort with asking. People might care deeply, might even long to get involved, and yet will hesitate to join. Why? Because everyone likes to be asked. We like to be invited. We want to be offered the right to become part of the story. We long to receive the gift of being needed. Whether it's volunteer hours or career hours, a charitable donation or a job change, most people aren't bold enough to knock on your door and say, "I like what you do; I want in." But everyone appreciates it when you open your door and hold out an invitation to make the world better.

So get past your hesitancy and your hang-ups and get practical. You can't pay the electric bill, serve the customer, or implement that solution with nothing but passion. People who share your passion *want* to help. And you need the resources and expertise and, yes, the passion they'll bring to the effort. But you have to ask. Be bold. Is your passion worth it? Yes? Then it's worth it.

When the passion at the office matches our life's passion, we don't have to manufacture energy and enthusiasm when we go to work. Work is us being us. Consequently, the hard days are not impossible. And the good days are fantastic.

It also means that when the organization has to do something difficult, whether interpersonally or professionally, it's possible because everyone has already agreed that it's worth it. Maybe none of us anticipated this project specifically or that schedule specifically. But on a fundamental level, the whole team believes in why we do what we do. At a passion-driven organization, your work aligns with the passion and the passion is deeply meaningful to you.

UNLEARN WHAT YOU HAVE LEARNED

Set this book down and grab your journal or a notepad. Write down what you're most passionate about. Even in private, if you've developed the habit of downplaying, apologizing, making excuses, or keeping quiet about your passions, you might find this challenging. That was my experience for many years. Certain passions are socially acceptable. My passion for competitive sports? *Plenty* of support. But my passion for a great marriage, or adoption? As often as not, crickets and awkward comments.

If you're having trouble defining your passion, keep reading. We're about to offer some techniques for recognizing it. But, before we get to the exercise, let me caution you. If you can't figure out how to bake your passion into your organization, it might be time for a new organization. It is *not* time for a new passion. The passion that you have in you . . . is part of you. It's there to stay. And it's awesome. It's so powerful. When you unleash it within an organization, every ordinary day includes something great. Plus, it helps build your resources and financial return, which you can then reinvest and double down on doing what you truly care about.

Look for your passion. You probably already know, subliminally, exactly what it is. But getting out of your own way is often challenging. Why? Because we've heard from early on that what we're passionate about is not practical. We've been told repeatedly, "You can't be like that in the professional world." But before you entered the "real world," what did you get most excited about? Look for your passion through the eyes of your inner ten-year-old. You may have less trouble finding it there than you do as the adult that you are today. In the naïveté and innocence of childhood, there is a natural inclination to dream big. As a ten-year-old, what thrilled you? What filled you with wonder? Did you prefer to spend time alone, or with people? Were you fascinated with how things worked, or were you eager to use those things to accomplish other things? When you encountered a challenge, did you stop and seek advice, or prefer to try tackling it yourself? There are no wrong answers. Questions like these will help you get a glimpse into what's innately "you."

Check Your Scopes

There are two types of passions. Let's call them macro and micro. Macro-level passions are about grand, global problems and opportunities. Micro-level passions are about changing one life at a time.

They're not opposed to each other. They may even be tackling the same issue from different angles. But depending on your personality, you may be drawn to one way of framing the challenge over the other.

Macro: Telescoping the Big Picture

These are the big problems and big ideas of our world. When you think about passion from a macro perspective, it's things like, "end world hunger" or "alleviate climate change" or "achieve universal literacy" or "peace in the Middle East" or "a loving home for every child." It can be focused globally or on one geographic region, one nation, one demographic, or even one neighborhood. Whatever it is, it's a big idea that matters deeply to you. Animals matter. Farming matters. Forests matter. Urban design matters. Diplomacy matters. Eradicating disease matters. Hospitality matters. Ending unemployment matters. Laughter matters. Whatever it is, it's at the level of the big grand scheme of things.

Do any of those fire you up, or bring to mind something that does? If so, you've got your first clue to where your passion may lie. If a fundraiser calls you from one of the groups that represents something that you are deeply passionate about, suddenly it doesn't feel like a spam call. You're excited to take that call. For our family, there's a group called All God's Children International (AGCI). It's the organization that helped us adopt our two oldest sons from Kazakhstan. If AGCI calls, I don't roll my eyes and hang up. I want to hear what they've got going on.

And in that, there's a hint about my passions: orphans, both in the U.S. and abroad, matter to me. Also, there's a clue to the passion-discovery process: your life story informs your passions, whether macro or micro.

Make a list of significant moments in your life. They don't have to be watershed moments necessarily—events that you didn't get to follow up on, but that still linger in your memory and make you wonder *"what if?"* can hold clues to your passion. If a moment moved you deeply at the time, it's worth exploring.

Micro: Magnifying Lives One by One

These spotlight the transformation of a single life. Micro-level passions are about the impact on one person at a time, about someone living out a powerful, relatable, repeatable story that inspires imitation and gives you hope. What is the story that grips your soul?

Whenever you encounter this story, in any form, something within you jumps to its feet and starts applauding. You experience that feeling of, *Yes! That's what I'm talking about!*

Think about the movies that you enjoy. Think about the movie that you think is the greatest movie of all. What are the themes in that movie? Is it an underdog story? Is it grit and determination? Tremendous athleticism? Wilderness survival? A team coming together in loyalty and common cause? Wrongs righted, justice served? Soul mates getting a shot at happiness? Growing up? Healing?

One of my favorite movies is *Miracle*, about the U.S. Olympic team in 1980 and its coach. It's a movie about a guy facing insurmountable odds who puts a very big dream and a huge goal on his shoulders and refuses to give up until it's done. I love that. I love the idea of someone saying, *"Enough is enough. It's time for a change, and I'm going to make sure it happens."* Then, rallying lots and lots of people around that vision for change despite intense opposition, and making that change happen to create good. I love that. I'm literally getting chills just thinking about it.

Another greatest movie of all time for me is *The Shawshank Redemption*. Despite being mistreated, unjustly imprisoned, and abused, Andy Dufresne figures out how to stick it to the bad guy even when he's completely powerless. He finds a way, and he comes out victorious. I love that, too! Stick it to the bad guy!

What are your top stories—in movies, in books, in life? On your sheet of paper, write down the stories that really inspire you, and next to each one, place a couple of bullet points describing why they made your list. They won't all be fiction. Some of them will be stories from your history, your family, your friends. Some will be stories from current events, biography, historical events. Any story counts, as long as it stirs you deep within.

Putting It All Together

Now you've written down the macro concepts that you like. You've also listed out the individual stories that you like. When you feel like the list is pretty much complete, look at what the entries have in common. Work to identify your three or four deepest, most consistent passions—not just what they are, like "chocolate" or "team sports," but what it is about them that gives you energy. What is it about you that resonates with each of them?

When I went through this exercise, I came up with one resounding theme over and over again: I like to elevate things. It could be my backyard, which is being renovated as I write this. It's always my children, who are brimming with limitless potential. It could be a business that's being revitalized under my care. It could be a new client who's been treated poorly by their previous vendor. Whatever or whoever it is, I like to take things and elevate them—to build, to create, to make things better.

Your passion could be completely different. I have a friend so passionate about a country western band that he became their chief fan roadie. He and his wife traveled the country going to shows. Hey—if that's your passion, go find a way!

When you think you've figured it out, take it to two close colleagues and two loved ones who know you best. Explain what you're doing and try out the phrase or phrases on them. Get some feedback. Do they agree? Does the phrase capture what gives you energy? Does it describe what you're all about?

Work through the feedback, then let the results marinate for a month. Come back to it after four or five weeks and see if it still feels right. Tweak until it does. When it's ready, you'll know it. You'll feel it. You'll recognize yourself in it. And you won't feel like something important has been left out.

"Okay," you might say. "I think I've found my passion—but I have *no idea* how to carry it into the work I do."

So, you've put in the time and thought. But you're not quite sure how to make "chocolate" the passion of your accounting company. Let's explore that.

I'll start: "*Why is chocolate your passion?*"

Perhaps you'd answer: "*Well, it tastes good.*"

"*Why are you passionate about 'tastes good'?*"

"*I feel good when I'm tasting good things. The world kinda . . . stands still.*"

"*Why would you want the world to stand still?*"

"*Because this crazy life of mine is spinning too d*** fast!*"

(I'm not a fan of cussing, but when your inner voice starts dropping expletives, you know you've touched a nerve and are getting somewhere!)

"*So the taste of good chocolate gives you a momentary retreat, a little bit of peace, during which everything slows down?*"

"*Yeah—I guess so.*"

Looking at chocolate through that lens, I'd say you are passionate about order, simplicity, peace, and serenity. Is there a way that your accounting firm could pivot to incorporate those ideas? Maybe change something about how you do customer service, rethink some internal processes, or shake up your reporting cadence and communications expectations . . . all inspired by chocolate?

My passion for people has been in me for as long as I can remember. For years, I worked in engineering for others. But when we started Velentium, Tim and I went back to the core of who we are with the desire to make that central to our company. I'm passionate about improving people's lives. Tim is particularly passionate about doing that through medical devices. So we found a way to express what we care about through our work.

We have a client currently who is very difficult. I'd be happy not to work for them anymore. But the engineers working with them came to me and said, "Please find a way to let us see this through. We believe this product will change lives for a better world, and even though the working relationship is difficult, we want to make sure they succeed." So we kept trying. That's passion at work.

FIRST STEPS TO PASSION ROLLOUT

To build shared identity, your passion must enter the life of your organization, and be nourished like a living thing. It's a good contagion, a symbiont, entering and altering how your team talks through challenging situations and makes judgment calls. It shapes your workplace stories. Guides your processes. Gives life to the organization's legends.

Passion does all of this because you, the leader, take action.

Your first action is to introduce the passion to the organization. Remember this mantra: *Simple isn't easy, but simple is worth it.* Before your passion can generate shared identity, you must be able to express it in a short, easily memorized phrase.

If you're founding the organization, you can build this into the starting package and it becomes part of onboarding. If the organization is already established, you'll need to introduce it over and over again. Express the passion statement. Explain its new role in how you'll be doing things from now on. You cannot overcommunicate passion.

Then, find ways to put the statement in front of every team member's eyes, all the time. Email signatures. Office wall art. Monitor displays. Custom swag. Update your website. Build a new marketing campaign around it. Saturate the organization to the point where people memorize it accidentally, without ever trying to.

Then, teach the passion. Find a new way to highlight it during each all-hands meeting. Use it to describe how and why the organization is doing each thing that it's doing. Breathe life into your passion by showcasing it with real stories about real people. Passion is human.

And if you find yourself struggling to figure out how something the organization is doing furthers the passion, take a long, hard, careful look at that thing. If the organization can't find a way to do that thing with passion and for passion, and it isn't absolutely essential for the organization to function, you shouldn't be doing it at all.

WE KNOW WE HAVE TO DO THIS

When Tim and I opted to take on millions of dollars of risk to support Project V, before we had assurances that the project would actually happen or that Velentium would definitely be involved,

- and before that, when Julie and I had that first conversation about the flight to Seattle that led to Project V,
- and before that, when Velentium's senior leadership team agreed that a founder should take the risk of traveling during the early unknowns of an escalating pandemic,
- and before that, when Tim read the *Forbes* article quote and reached out to a friend and client in need,
- each time, although the path ahead was anything but clear, our next step was *always* clear.

When your passion is simple, following your passion is simple.

You need money to follow your passion. If cashflow is a problem and the organization is struggling to breathe, your job is to survive. The organization needs a financial ventilator. The question is, what do you do after you've recovered? When the ventilator is no longer needed . . . then what?

If your organization is following the money, that means everyone there is also following the money—for the sake of dozens, hundreds, or thousands of individual passions that have little to nothing in common with the organization's activities, nothing in common with the hopes, cares, and motivations of their colleagues. Your people might not want to be mercenaries, but that's how they're compelled to act, because a money-first organization forces a mercenary identity onto its staff. Passions are splintered. Identity is shallowly shared. In big and small ways, all day long, the mercenary organization undermines itself and struggles to find its way.

The passionate organization knows where it's going, why it's going, and how it's going. It knows which activities and projects are "us" and which are "not us." And it's made up of people all pulling in the same direction, rooting for the same outcome. A team who cares about breathing because they know what each breath makes possible.

Principles over Rules

One Saturday early in Project V, I was on the phone with one of our engineers with a question about the next day's tasks. Boy, did I get an earful.

"I didn't sign up to f***ing work on Sunday! Is this what it's going to be like from now on?"

"Do you mean during this project, or at this company, forever?" I asked.

"This company. Forever."

"H*** no! But it's absolutely how it's going to be right now. This is a global emergency. The passion to change lives for a better world, starting with you and the rest of our team—the passion that says go home after putting in your forty, and flex that forty around the needs of your family—just got temporarily reversed. We're the only people who can do this work. That means right now, the needs of every family in the nation are getting prioritized over your family.

"My expectation right now is everything you've got. Sixteen-hour days. And if you're going to lead a team, I expect that you will expect the same from everyone working with you.

"If you can't do that, that's okay. You still have a job, and you can still be on the team. But you can't lead the team.

"Why don't you take the rest of today off. Go home, sleep. Think about it. Then call me this evening and tell me what you decide."

DAY NINE

> Ummm, I'm gonna need you to go ahead come in tomorrow. So if you
> could be here around nine, that would be great, mmmk . . . oh oh! and I
> almost forgot. Ahh, I'm also gonna need you to go ahead and come in on
> Sunday too, kay.[8]

The terrible boss's lines from *Office Space* have become iconic, the perfect quotes to express the sins of corporate management culture. Gary Cole's character represents everything that well-meaning bosses everywhere aspire not to be.

Office Space heralded an emerging trend toward recognizing people as people, human, not just cogs in a machine. That trend came to be labeled "work-life balance," and while I'm all for the principle, I don't like the label.

Velentium emphasizes "work-life *fit*," not "balance." We know that there are going to be times when staff have friends or family who need them. You'll have to leave early to get to your kid's game, or come in midmorning after running your spouse to an appointment, or skip Monday to help your best friend prepare for a career shift that's gonna take them overseas. Hence, that week, you can't work as much. Other weeks, a thorny challenge or a tight project deadline will demand extra from you: late nights, maybe even weekends. Both situations, considered as stand-alones, are *un*balanced. Yet, as a mutual dynamic, each must square with the other to create a good fit between your work and your life. Anything less than a good fit is unsustainable. And because those situations are by definition unpredictable, we've never made rules to govern them. Rules are too inflexible. Rules would inevitably punish a staff member who just needs to be with a grieving family member, or prevent someone from working ahead one week in order to flex later. Instead, we tell everyone to proactively own their schedule, talk with their manager, talk with their team, and work it out. Make promises. Keep those promises. Do right by your colleagues, your clients, *and* yourself and your family. Make it fit.

During Project V, we discovered firsthand why the workweek ends at day six. When you're going flat out, you either take that break or your body will take it for you. Despite, or maybe because of, all the adrenaline, the pressure, and the thrill of doing work that matters on an impossible deadline, you periodically find yourself unable to think, unable to focus on simple tasks or solve simple problems. Sometimes you act out of character in surprising ways. Like swearing at your boss's boss's boss over the phone.

People have different tolerances for how long they can give 100 percent without a break. We found that nobody lasts past eight days. Sometime on the ninth day, if not sooner, you hit a wall. It's kinda like the wall that marathon runners talk about. We all experienced it early on, before we figured out the pattern and established a rotation.

My nine-day wall moment was when I almost got myself ejected from the Kokomo factory for forgetting to wear safety goggles one too many times. I'd made a run to get lunch for everyone on the floor, and when I brought it back in, I left those blasted goggles in the car.

"Don't let it happen again," a GM safety overseer admonished me, as if I were a child. "Or I'll kick you outta here."

I felt bile rising in my throat. Struggled to get a completely outsized emotional reaction under control. He was in the right. He was doing his job, with passion. The rule he was enforcing was not just important, it was non-negotiable, imposed on our activities by OSHA. My intention was to comply, same as him. And I had just brought lunch with the intention of serving him and his colleagues, hoping to provide a little ten-minute bubble of calm amidst our relentless drive to save the world.

He didn't need a tongue-lashing. *I* needed a nap. A very long nap.

Maybe then, I wouldn't forget my goggles in the car.

RULE BLOAT

When organizations begin, it's typical to have few rules defining how staff are expected to behave and how work is expected to get done. But as organizations gain experience, more and more rules tend to get created. Each new rule added is a reaction to a specific situation, the outcome of a lesson learned. Lots of rules indicate the organization's breadth of experience.

Lots of rules also indicate a loss of good faith. Lots of rules signal that leadership doesn't believe that staff will do right and act right without explicit instructions.

Lots of rules may indicate organizational senility. Where rules exist, critical thinking doesn't have to. The hard part is done—now just follow this rule. Don't question it—we've already been through this; don't make us repeat ourselves. It's like bowling with bumpers. If you don't already have the skill to bowl strikes, the bumpers eliminate the incentive to learn. Just put enough force on the ball to get it down the lane, and you're basically guaranteed to knock over a bunch of pins. In the same way, lots of rules disincentivize creative problem-solving. Just follow the established procedure, and nobody can blame you if things go wrong . . . or inefficiently . . . or fail to satisfy the customer.

For many people, that system of rules creates a sense of safety. They think of their work primarily in contractual terms. *If I jump through these clearly labeled hoops as prescribed, I will remain in good standing at my job, and my family will continue to receive a paycheck.*

For other people, the lack of trust and flexibility implied by lots of rules is demoralizing. Depressing, even. *I'm not free to exercise my best judgment here. My team can't experiment with better ways of working. I see a problem I could jump in and fix, but there's so much red tape I'll never get permission. If I take initiative, I'll get in trouble.*

For people who like to *think*, not just *do*, this is a major deterrent. Top problem-solvers won't stay in a role they feel that "anyone" could do by reading a recipe and doing exactly what it says.

As organizations add more and more rules over time, they gradually attract people who like having rules to follow. People who want to keep their head down, do the job, and know with certainty whether they've done it "right."

Over the same period, the rule-bound organization gradually repels the independent thinkers, self-starters, step-up-and-take-ownership people who enabled it to survive and thrive during the organization's early days. You remember them—they're the people who like to:

- Fully engage with their work, then go the extra mile for the sheer enjoyment of it,
- Think about how best to get things done,
- Pioneer new processes and workflows, and
- Take risks and accept responsibility for the sake of innovation, better results, and greater efficiency.

There's an energy around the office in the early days, a sense of possibility, a can-do attitude, and best of all, a mental alertness and creative acumen that seems to fade as the organization matures.

We've been told that this is part of the natural cycle of organizations. That the people who lead and succeed in those nimble, edgy early years aren't the same people who can create success at scale. But what if that's not the whole truth?

What if the overburden of rule upon rule, each one apparently reasonable, each one created to respond to actual experiences, is draining and driving away your top performers . . . and enabling average performers to survive in their place?

And it gets weirder. Because as you think back, you might remember some meetings or memos where *your top performers asked for more rules*.

A situation happened. Or was foreseen. And your all-star contributors proposed new rules to address the issue.

But if lots of rules is a problem for attracting and retaining top performers . . . including the very people who suggested some of the rules . . . what's really going on?

Rules proliferate for three main reasons.

1. Making Rules Feels Like We've "Done Something"

Rules make us feel powerful. Rules make us feel in charge. Rules make us feel like we've done something. However, *rules are lazy*. They fixate on the first detail that would have prevented one uncomfortable situation from taking place and treat that situation like a universal problem, without considering unintended fallout. And when the fallout creates a problem, guess what: it gets addressed by a new rule!

Life happens. And by that, I mean bad stuff happens. It's a given. In your organization, things will go wrong. But let's back up a little bit. What makes "bad" bad? I think it has a lot to do with how we interpret expectations.

We are all creatures of habit. We like routines. We like consistency. We like reliable. We want things to "just work." Unfortunately, things rarely "just work." Even when they do, they rarely stay that way for long. But if we change our expectation for what's normal, if we expect things to be wrinkly, things not to be quite the same as we envisioned, then, when things really, truly do go wrong, we're better able to recognize them as problems. And since we haven't gotten bent out of shape over expectation mismatches, we still have the emotional bandwidth to respond well. It's the clutter of our expectations that often blocks our ability to perceive what's actually going on.

Typically, instead of calibrating our expectations for a broad range of what's acceptable, people react emotionally to anything and everything that isn't happening *exactly* the way they pictured. A few months ago, I was at an Entrepreneurial Operating System conference where attendees were encouraged to *respond* instead of *react*. To insert our will, our self-discipline, and our best selves between the circumstance and our response.

But a disciplined response runs counter to my instincts. Somebody pulls in front of my car and BAM!—immediately on the horn. Shaking a fist in anger. A kid disrespects me and BAM!—immediately yelling. My will over yours. I'm in charge here.

We do it all the time. We allow our emotions to take control. And that is why so many companies have so many rules. Almost every rule has an emotional situation behind it. A conflict behind it. A couple of names involved in that conflict. Someone did something unexpected, maybe dropped the ball or made a bad judgment call under pressure, and the consequence of that event felt awful. It shook up the workplace. Reliability was shattered. Dependability flew out the window. Schedules were shredded. Instead of planned work, there was chaos, cleanup, and damage control.

Nobody wants that. And it feels great to be able to tell yourself, *That bad thing will never interrupt our stable routine again, because we made a rule.*

Even though, deep down, *you know* it isn't true.

2. Making Rules Feel Effective

In your organization, people are going to want rules. Why? Because of "them." "Them" equals "not me." "They" are people who "I" think need to be brought under control. Because I don't have the authority to remove them, and I also lack the time, resources, and training to coach or mentor them. Hence when someone does something annoying, my go-to request becomes, "Please put some handcuffs on them and keep them from ever doing that again."

But just because something bad happened doesn't mean that you need to put a rule in place.

In fact, issuing a new rule doesn't even guarantee that the bad thing won't happen again. Nor that the person causing the problem won't do a different bad thing that nobody has thought of a rule for yet.

Rules are carrots and sticks; carrots and sticks are tools for getting a stubborn animal to do stuff it doesn't truly want to do. Rules create an "us" vs. "them" dynamic between leaders and contributors.

I've rented Airbnbs where, everywhere you look, there is a sign telling you what you can or can't do. *Don't put towels here. Please don't touch this. Owners only. Coffee maker procedure* . . . It drives me nuts! Someone renting me a house should trust me to be able to figure out how to use a toaster. I co-own a home. My wife and I run a household together. I think we can probably manage a weekend getaway without causing property damage!

And yet, I know that each of those signs is there because a guest behaved badly. The guest did something stupid, or took advantage, and those experiences gradually tempted the host to cross the line from hospitality to control freak.

And do all the little notes and signs help? My friends who host Airbnbs themselves say no. They say "problem guests" ignore the signs and come up with new ways to violate the social compact between guests and hosts.

They say the solution is not to create more rules.

It's to attract better guests.

3. Making Rules Feels Leaderly

The main problem with rules is that they apply to everyone, all the time. You can't say, "Hey, if you are a dingbat, this rule is for you." If people have to opt in to follow the rule, nobody will follow it, because no one thinks that they are the dingbat. Numerous studies have shown that 80 percent or more of all people think they are "above average" at a given thing. That'll apply to "are you a dingbat?" too.

Same with opt-out rules. *Are you smart? Then this rule does not apply to you.* That's not how rules work. They apply to everyone. And if you suggest that certain rules don't apply to everyone, you've created another problem: the Haves and Have-Nots. You're brewing envy, resentment, and bitterness.

When a situation doesn't fit a rule, your staff faces an identity crisis. Either:

- Follow the rule, and hope that the mismatch to the situation will turn out to be Somebody Else's Problem, or
- Use my best judgment.

If I choose the second option, I put myself in conflict with the core identity of the rule-bound organization. If I'm part of an organization founded on rules, and I don't follow the rules when I have a good reason not to, what am I? A renegade? A maverick?

Whatever my self-conception becomes, I'm now defining myself *against* the organization, rather than *as part of it*. Some of my energy gets siphoned off to manage the conflict. Like a tire that's a couple degrees off perpendicular to the axle, I experience extra wear and tear psychologically. I feel like I did the right thing, but I'm concerned that my decision won't be supported by the organization. And since the organization is governed by rules, there's no basis for reconciliation. We can't appeal to a common understanding of "who we are" to judge my choice. Worse, we can spend a lot of energy discussing it, but at the end of the day, we won't have a process that will help us navigate future situations that also don't fit the rules. All we'll have is a judgment about what happened this one time, plus some new rules that tell everyone what to do if that exact situation happens again. And the rules just keep growing.

All of this becomes a massive energy and attention sink. An absolute distraction from your passion and your work.

Leadership is not about managing nitty-gritty details, controlling situational dos and don'ts. Leaders need to stay focused on pursuing the grand passion of the organization and shaping that passion into shared identity by translating it into vision, values, and principles to guide decision-making.

Leadership is not about:

- Overarching rules reacting to specific situations,
- All-hands rules to rein in one individual, or
- Bureaucratic procedures that limit our ability to serve our customers and make our day-to-day work less elegant, less adventurous, and less satisfying—for us, and for those we serve.

So, instead of a bunch of rules, here's what I would suggest: everywhere possible, opt for principles over rules.

PRINCIPLES OVER RULES

Principles are how you communicate: "We are *x*, therefore we do *y*."

Principles ensure that your actions reinforce your identity. Some rules, in some situations, can do that, too. But only principles ensure that your actions and your identity remain flexible enough to cope with unforeseeable challenges.

Principles are proactive, anticipating and clarifying the unknown. When you lead with principles, principles lead you to certain knowledge: *We know we have to do this.* Why? Because *this* is what we're about. Principles are tools for winning people over to the organization's shared identity.

Principles allow leaders, and every generation of staff or volunteers that signs on, to reach a pre-agreement about what the organization values most, and how each person should behave if they want to be a part of it.

Moreover, because behavior is best supported by character, principles imply who each staff member needs to be or become in order to stay on. If I know the organization values a trait that I'm weak in, I can expect that over time I'll need to grow in that area if I intend to stick around. Maybe I'll need coaching, mentoring, or counseling. Maybe closely observing my longer-tenured peers and imitating them will be enough. But when an organization shows by its lived-out principles that it values something, over time, I must conform to those same values. Or working here won't be a good fit, and I'll move on, before I'm asked to leave.

Principles shine a light down the path ahead, illuminating my future with this organization in a way that a bunch of rules never could.

Rules put me in my place. Principles help me find my place.

Deriving Principles

Cashflow is the air in your engine. Passion is your fuel and your compass, providing energy and defining direction. Principles are your headlights. They reveal the terrain ahead: telling you how to steer, clarifying your next move.

Velentium's guiding principles begin with the passion—Changing Lives for a Better World. From the passion, we derived a set of values that prescribes *how* we'll go about changing lives and bettering the world. To identify those core values, Tim and I worked through an exercise we got from an Andy Stanley leadership seminar. You may not have heard of Andy, but his leadership skills are impressive. He's the founder of a once-small nonprofit organization that grew over fifteen years into what is now an eight-campus, forty-thousand-person megachurch in Atlanta, Georgia.

The Values Exercise is pretty simple. It helps if you have two whiteboards, or two giant notepads, or a couple of shared digital spaces your leadership team can all be dialed into.

On the first whiteboard, each person lists their heroes. If "heroes" feels like too weighty of a word, you can think about it as listing "people you admire." The name doesn't have to belong to someone you consider a role model in every aspect of their life to make the cut. It just has to be someone who exemplifies a quality you greatly respect.

The names you put on this first whiteboard can belong to anyone. People you know. People who are famous. People from history. People from fiction. Batman? Beyoncé? Simone Biles? Yes. Herbert Paul Brooks Jr., that hockey coach played by Kurt Russell in *Miracle*, or Denzel Washington as football coach Herman Boone in *Remember the Titans*, or college basketball coach Mike Krzyzewski? Yes! The good wizard Gandalf from *The Lord of the Rings*? Clever witch Hermione Granger from *Harry Potter*? Captain Picard of the USS *Enterprise*? Yes, yes, and yes. And what about:

- The janitor from your middle school
- Your neighbor
- Your kid's baseball coach
- The guidance counselor from your high school
- Your university tutor or advisor
- Your professional mentor
- Your spiritual advisor
- One of your in-laws (Hey, some people marry into *great* families!)

All yes. Teddy Roosevelt, Marie Curie, Toni Morrison, Scipio Africanus, Simón Bolívar, Mother Teresa . . . anyone you admire enough that you find yourself thinking about them, studying them, seeking to imitate them. Put 'em on the list!

OK, now turn to that second whiteboard. For every name that is on the first whiteboard, answer this question:

"Why is that person on the list?"

It's fine to verbal-process through what it is you admire about them. This is an exercise for your whole leadership team: let them help you clarify and distill that admirable quality or qualities down to one-word traits or very short phrases.

- Decisive.
- Calm under pressure.
- Bold.
- Wise.
- Morally courageous.
- Visionary.
- Loyal.
- Focused.
- Shoulders risk AND responsibility.
- Keeps promises.
- Tells it like it is.
- Generous.
- Sees people as people.
- Underdog.
- Team player.
- Maverick.
- Giving.
- Poised.
- Sees the humor in serious situations.
- Thinks well of others.
- Total badass.
- Always looks for a bright side.
- Trailblazer.
- Good gambler.
- Faces facts.
- Competent.
- Says the right thing.
- Honest, no matter the cost.
- Shrewd.
- Master negotiator.
- Elevates others.
- Realist.
- Vigilante

Pretty soon, that second whiteboard is full of all the traits that make your heroes your heroes.

And now comes the tough part. If you could have it all your way:

1. What characteristics would define your coworkers?
2. What would characterize the experiences of your customers, those you serve?
3. If news reporters and TV anchors started doing stories about your organization, what would you want them to report as your stand-out qualities? How would you want to be known?

With these questions in mind, go around the room playing "Kill, Keep, or Combine?" with each trait on your list, one by one. Are any of them not a good fit for the purpose? Suppose one of the things you admire about Batman is his vigilantism, his willingness to take the law into his own hands. But you're not here to form the next Justice League. Other traits on the list—like maybe "Decisive" and "Morally courageous" and "Competent"—do a better job of describing characteristics applicable to your organization. So you vote to kill "Vigilante" and it gets crossed off the list. (Sorry, Batman.)

Next, maybe you decide that "Calm under pressure" and "Poised" can be combined. In the discussion, you realize that "Poised" helps you tease out some nuance to what "Calm under pressure" means to you. Maybe it's not only the ability to think clearly during a crisis that you admire. Maybe it has something to do with a person's demeanor as well. Thinking, communicating, and acting calmly, with focus, aren't enough. It's the ability to radiate that calm and that focus to others that you admire also. And "Poised" helps you capture that whole idea. So you strike through "Calm under pressure" in favor of "Poised."

As you go on, you'll find it gets harder and harder to make the case for killing or combining traits. That's where "keep" comes in. You'll isolate these ideas, grouping them with greater precision, figuring out what the top-level trait is for each set of traits you combine. You'll realize that some of these traits are not top traits for the team, not critical to the identity of your organization, and you'll cross them out. But when neither action seems possible, you'll vote to keep that trait.

Eventually, you'll make it to where every vote is to "keep" the remaining traits on the list.

But there's a problem. You still have fifteen traits on the board. Your aim should be five or fewer traits. Remember the mantra: "Simple is not easy, but simple is worth it."

So take a break. Then get back at it—kill, keep, and combine. This is how you discover, collectively, who you are. Who you'll strive to be.

Who you'll hire.

How you'll work.

How you'll stay on course through ambiguity and hostility.

Why you'll make tough calls.

Why you'll stand by them.

How you know "this is us—we do things like this" and "this is not us—we don't do things like that."

How you'll know when it's time to make a change.

How you'll know when to fire someone, and why.

A few years ago, Ben Horowitz, co-founder of Opsware and the venture capital firm Andreessen Horowitz, published a book called *What You Do Is Who You Are*. It's a collection of case studies on leadership and culture, and its title is spot-on. What you do flows out of who you are, and who you are flows out of what you do. Over time, an organization's collective behavior always drifts toward the path of least resistance and short-term incentives. And the path of least resistance, the most convenient short-term reaction, will always be to add more rules. Soon, your organization's core defining behavior will be creating and policing rules. And the only people you'll be able to keep on staff will be the people who are unwilling or incapable of thinking for themselves.

Principles over rules is how you stop the drift.

PRINCIPLES IN PRACTICE

Let me give you a framework for evaluating the circumstances that will inevitably hit you. Something in the coming weeks is going to be less than ideal. Maybe even severely screwed up. When it happens, ask the questions in the graphic on the following page.

I bet you can already see that principle-based responses are way slower and less immediately satisfying than rule-based responses. They don't feel as good because the results take a while. You don't get the endorphin rush of saying, "ENOUGH! Nobody EVER does that again!"

Governing with principles takes hard work, patience, and trust. Applying principles takes time. Teaching principles delegates decision-making power. Principles over rules is slower, messier, harder, and . . . *waaayyy* more effective in the long run.

Through principles, you can mentor genuine character change. Not just enforce external behavior change, but actually cultivate shifts in what people desire. "Heart change." Change that transforms your organization from the inside out.

I'm a principles-over-rules guy, 100 percent. But it's just like my diet and exercise regimen: It is hard work. It demands consistency. And it only pays

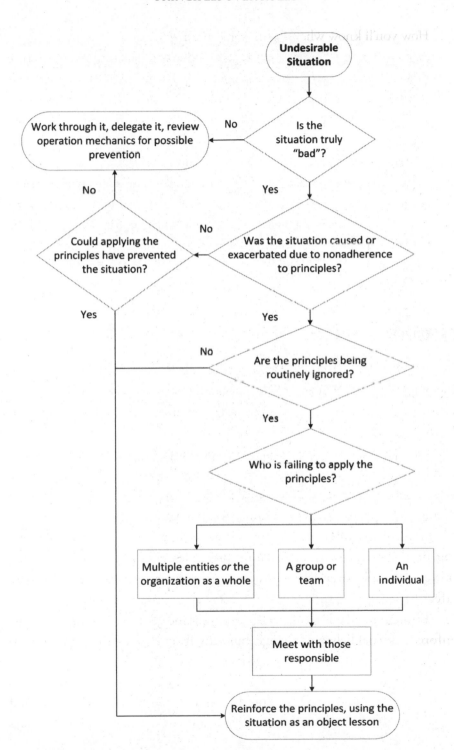

off in the long run. If you take a five-year perspective, principles over rules will save you extraordinary time and effort. But in the short term, principles take way more effort than adding another rule.

Worth It?

When considering a new rule, if it's not one that you're required to have by law, like "personnel on the factory floor must wear PPE at all times," here are helpful questions to ask:

- Is this rule going to guide, inspire, and support my top performers?
- Will this rule promote more productivity out of my number-one person on this team?

If the answers are *Yes*, then lay down the law and make that rule. Proclaim it proudly and declare its worth from the rooftops! On the other hand,

- Is this rule going to police, cajole, or babysit the problem-causer and others like them?

If that's the case, STOP! Do not add that rule! Only add rules that support your principles!

Example one: A manager walked by the desk of one of his direct reports, who was playing solitaire on his work-issued PC. During the management meeting that week, it was proposed that standard-issue games, including solitaire, be disabled on all company laptops and a new rule be created to ban playing games.

I immediately vetoed the proposal. If we had made that rule, we would have taken a step toward becoming an organization that polices how people spend their time. But do we really care how our staff spend every minute of their day? No. We care that they keep their word to the customer and to their teammates. We want staff to work however they work best—which most likely includes taking mental breaks during the workday. If they choose to spend that break time playing solitaire because that's what they find refreshing, that should be their prerogative. On the other hand, if they're falling behind or failing to communicate proactively about their workload, then we have an actual problem. Either way, banning solitaire isn't going to help. And it would have set an untenable precedent, forcing us over time to make rules about all kinds of situations that, ultimately, have nothing to do with our passion, our values, and our goals.

Example two: Years ago, as the division head for a multimillion-dollar corporation, I once took a call from the CFO about a $10 pen on my expense report. I kid you not. To this day I'm not sure what upset me more about that call: that division heads were apparently not allowed $10 of discretionary spending . . . or that the CFO was personally policing expense reports. That brief phone call between the two of us cost the company far more than $10 in lost productivity—and made me think seriously about leaving. Yet it happened because someone, sometime, had a made a rule.

SPRING-CLEANING

Every spring at my house, we go through the garage, which tends to accumulate all kinds of crap. I don't know how it happens. Maybe the birthday parties where the kid comes home with that obligatory bag of favors. Maybe it's our own kids' birthday parties where we had leftover obligatory bags of favors! Maybe it's extra trips to the sporting goods store, plus extra trips to the home goods store. Whatever it is, the garage steadily fills with junk until we make time to clean.

The emotional release that happens when walking out into a clean garage is subtle, but it's heavenly. Every year I find myself asking, "Why didn't we do this a long time ago? Why have I gone five months without parking in the garage?"

A few years ago, Julie decided to take on gig work as an independent Realtor. Part of her job entails touring homes and helping people catalog everything they have to take out of their house so it will show well. Sometimes the sales process takes a while, and the sellers live in their sparsely populated home for a few weeks or months. And you know what they invariably say?

"Man! Why don't we live like this all the time?"

A simplified, straightforward, clean, put-together home is a delight to live in.

A keenly principled, bureaucracy-sparse, rules-light organization is a delight to work for.

Rules Audit

It's time to do a rules audit of your company. Time to spring-clean the processes, meetings, procedures, and rules in your company. What is happening that shouldn't happen? What is scheduled that shouldn't be scheduled? Let's clean it up and get it out.

As you embark on this process, you'll find that a lot of superfluous rules and processes that you want to get rid of have names attached to them. You're going to cancel a meeting—and there is a person who runs that meeting. You are going to change the process, procedure, or rule—and there is someone who oversees and implements and QAs that activity. You're going to stop tracking certain metrics—and there's somebody who for the last three years has been collating those numbers every week. So, before you begin, remind yourself that the person who is attached to that item is perfectly capable of not being attached to it. It is OK to clean house. Their supervisors can find something better for them to do. But people are creatures of habit. If you remove the things they've built their routines around, they will feel unsettled, and they may get upset.

Just to be clear, I'm talking about cleaning out meetings, rules, and processes, not the people performing them. Removing people is a different topic altogether, which we'll get to later. Auditing rules has to do with how the organization requires things be done and why. Is it truly necessary? Does it add value? Could it be stripped down to an essential core, with the remainder downgraded to a recommendation or helpful FYI? Do it!

BAD APPLES AND PRINCIPLE VIOLATIONS

Our house is one of twenty on an older street in our area. Suburbia has grown up around us, but turning down on our lane still breathes a little of that "out in the country" feel. And with that comes, every so often, a little more contact with wildlife. Not always the pleasant kind.

A few months ahead of spring-cleaning one year, the garage started to smell. We looked for the source many times, couldn't find it. It was driving us crazy. I put out poison to stop the smell-generator, but the smell did not go away. It wasn't until the full-scale spring-cleaning that we finally found a rat that had chewed its way into a storage bin and died inside.

Once we got the carcass out, and cleaned the bin, the smell was gone . . . but it took days to identify all the camping supplies and sporting goods that were ruined or needed repair or additional cleaning because he had chewed through the camp chairs, eaten sleeping bag stuffing, pooped in the golf club bag, and on and on.

It reminded me of the old saying: "One bad apple ruins the whole barrel." It's a reminder to be vigilant, because rot from one apple so easily spreads to the others while they're in storage. The longer rot goes unchecked, the longer it will take to identify and repair the damage.

The same is true of principle violations. They must be dealt with. Swiftly. In *What You Do Is Who You Are*, Ben Horowitz observes,

> Culture is not like a mission statement; you can't just set it up and have it last forever. There's a saying in the military that if you see something below standard and do nothing, then you've set a new standard. This is also true of culture—if you see something off-culture and ignore it, you've created a new culture.[9]

Letting principle violations go unaddressed causes rifts to form between what the company says it cares about and what behavior is actually tolerated. Before long, tolerance gets interpreted as unspoken encouragement. That gap creates cognitive dissonance, encourages hypocrisy, makes all your hard work to nurture a passionate, values-driven workplace come across as mere lip service. Unaddressed principle violations are how you let your culture get destroyed. You must take action. If you don't, your top performers will. Some will leave. Others will first try to take matters into their own hands, burn out, and then leave.

Again, I'm not necessarily talking here about firing violators. I'm talking about addressing specific situations where principles were violated. Removing people is one option, but rarely, if ever, a first resort. Decide in advance which principle violations call for:

- Immediate firing
- A simple one-on-one conversation
- A confidential review with all involved
- A short-term retraining and accountability process
- Long-term mentoring between the violator and another staff member who "gets it"

In the vast majority of cases, the best way to address principle violations is with mentoring and coaching. A quick note about the difference: Mentoring puts qualities and skills into you—stuff you didn't have before. Coaching draws out of you and into play the best of what's already within. You'll need to mentor *and* coach your leadership team. Leadership needs to mentor and coach your management team. Management needs to mentor and coach your individual contributors. All to train your organization to live by principles over rules.

Your goal is total buy-in across the whole organization. Which is easiest to achieve if you start small and develop organically, always recruiting with culture in mind and constantly reinforcing it internally so it stays top of mind.

Total buy-in is *impossible* to achieve if you let principle violations slide. Buy-in proliferates when you create and tell stories about living out your principles.

Years ago, the company founded by my mentor, Larry, hired a new office manager. That office manager started implementing some practices imported from their past experience at previous companies. Companies where bureaucratic rules and other behaviors and policies had evidently fostered a culture of distrust. In keeping with that past experience, the new office manager started locking the office supply cabinet.

That's not the way things were done at Larry's company. At Larry's company, the culture relied on trust. When you act like, "I trust you to do your job, you trust me to provide the supplies you need to do your job, and I trust you to help yourself to whatever you need without being excessive or wasteful of company resources," you don't actually have to spell all of that out with a bunch of rules. Locking the supply cabinet was a violation of this principle of trust. And once Larry realized it was happening, he knew he needed to do something about it.

Could he have sent a memo? Yes. Could he have asked for the key? Yes. Did he? No.

He brought a hammer to work.

Larry knew that the culture had been violated in a noticeable way that impacted lots of people. That meant a big, grand, message-sending gesture was needed in response. A gesture that said, *We are not that kind of company.*

Memos and keys are not the stuff of legend. Hammers can be.

Larry took the hammer to the supply cabinet and explained to those nearby what he was about to do, and why. He then whaled away at the handle until he broke it off. And he ordered that cabinet not be fixed or replaced. He wanted its slightly damaged, now-unlockable doors to serve as a reminder that, in this organization, we don't obstruct people. We trust them to get their job done.

When Larry later left the company, they presented him a going-away appreciation plaque listing his many accomplishments. Mounted to that plaque was . . . you guessed it—the broken metal handle from the supply cabinet.

I'm sure his company still talks about that day. I've told the story at my company. And now you're hearing about it! Why? Because your passion and your values are living things. They enter and permeate the life of your organization—its language, its processes, and above all, its stories.

When someone does something to uphold the culture, by pursuing the passion or exemplifying the values, talk about it! Honor that culture-affirming decision and action.

When someone does something that erodes the culture, do not fail to act. If the action violates the culture in a big way, respond in a big way. If the action violates the culture in a small way, respond in a small way. But respond. Make an example of anything that reinforces or threatens the culture.

At Velentium, our guiding principles are encapsulated by three values:

- Honorable: We do Right for Right's sake
- Results[++]: We do the job and then some
- Humble Charisma: We strive to be people that other people want to be around

When it comes to violations, our values are listed in the order of importance. Honorable is on top. If you willfully deceive a customer or colleague, we're done. Anything else, we can work with. All of our values are trained, mentored, coached, peer-reinforced, endlessly discussed. We trust that everyone in our organization will grow into them and get better at them over time, becoming adept at applying them to new and unfamiliar situations. When violations occur, as they inevitably will from time to time, those closest to the situation (both leaders and peers) consider what is needed to address that violation, including correcting any consequences that resulted from it, and any accountability that may be needed to keep everyone growing in the right direction going forward.

And yes, sometimes the "bad apple" that has to be dealt with is a person. A person who has to go.

Several years back we hired a guy—let's call him "Aaron"—whose project manager summed up his first two weeks as "miserable."

"He's got a side business," the PM explained. "He's working on that at his desk while missing deadlines."

I brought Aaron into a conference room with another PM, and asked that PM to brief him for transfer to another project. The second PM, having heard about this guy, protested that he didn't want him. "Humor me," I asked.

So, for twenty minutes, the PM laid out the project on a giant whiteboard, explaining its technical aspects and what needed to be done. I stayed in the room, listening. I knew nothing more about this particular project than what I was hearing now, for the first time, just like Aaron.

Aaron listened in silence, taking no notes, and asking no questions. When the PM finished, I asked if he understood the project, invited him to ask any questions. He asserted he had all he needed. So then I told the

PM to erase the whiteboard and proceeded to quiz Aaron on everything I could remember.

He couldn't answer a single question. He hadn't engaged at all. It appeared he either didn't understand what was needed, or didn't care enough, to contribute. Time to clear a desk and show him the door.

Around the time we let Aaron go, we hired several other folks, including someone we'll call "Brent." Brent started well, but over the course of six or eight months, Brent slowly but steadily fell behind on his work. He would take long breaks during the day, often on his phone but not usually on calls. Sometimes he'd work odd extra hours. Several staff members reached out casually, offering support, but he politely resisted.

None of that was ideal, but neither was it a huge cause for concern. We expected that things would improve over time, or Brent would leave on his own. But then, Brent fabricated some test results and signed off on a project milestone . . . *before* the equipment we'd ordered to perform the test had even arrived at the office. Hoping to avoid internal oversight, he bypassed the review process and sent the results directly to the client. Fortunately for the project, the results he fabricated were implausible. Concerned, the client reached back out to Brent's PM.

Brent broke down in tears when confronted, citing how far behind he felt, work pressures, family pressures. If he'd brought up any of that stuff sooner—if he hadn't resisted attempts to help—we could have found a way to make it work. But by showing himself willing to deceive—not just his colleagues, but our clients—he'd violated Velentium's first value, Honorable. So Brent had to go.

By now, I was directly involved in the situation. I called our client's CEO and personally apologized, explaining what had happened and the steps we were taking to address them. Those steps included "making it right" for free: doing the testing for real, correcting the documentation, and taking on the financial consequences of full responsibility for what Brent had done. It also included a sizeable refund of what we'd invoiced on the project so far, to cover the client company's expenses for time spent uncovering and correcting the deception. "I hope that's acceptable to you," I concluded. "If it's not, you tell me what else needs to happen to make this right between our companies. As you know, one of our core values is Honorable, and another is Results⁺⁺. We take those values very seriously. We will not accept anything less from ourselves."

It was expensive. It hurt. But it was the only way back to Honorable.

In these Bad Apple situations, everyone is watching you. They are hard. They hurt. They are a huge opportunity to reinforce your principles.

When you remove a Bad Apple, whether it's

- an unnecessary meeting, process, or rule,
- a stated policy or a common practice that no longer aligns with your principles, or
- a person who isn't capable or interested in living out your principles,

your organization surges forward with fresh energy. Top performers are heartened to know that you're serious about what defines this place, that you'll act boldly, and that you'll pay the price to keep the organization pursuing its passion, according to its principles. You're not going to let the pursuit of passion get diluted by a bunch of bureaucratic rules, and you're not going to compromise on your principles because of fear or fortune. And they will respond with joy, with renewed enthusiasm for the work. Because they recognize that your organization is different. Your organization shares their passion *and* their values, so it's worth devoting themselves to.

So resist rules. Shun them. When rules show up, examine them critically and clean them out regularly. Let other organizations be slowed by rules. Yours is spurred by principles. Find them. Proclaim them. Identify yourself with them. Base your decisions on them. Defend them. And they will reveal the road ahead, speeding you on your way.

Slow—Fast—Slow

SLOW

For some people, the message they need to hear is, *"Get off your butt and get something done."* But most of the time, that's not what people like us need to hear. Our message is quite different: *"Slooowww dooowwwnnn."* Slow down!

The most valuable thing that you can do for your organization is think. I learned this from a friend who sold his company for $50 million. He said the biggest contribution he makes is coming up with the next idea, the next strategy, the big-minded thing that's going to get the organization out of a bind. What's our next key hire? The next key fire? These things don't come to your mind when you're rushing, hurrying, checking off boxes, keeping plates spinning, task-juggling, or living under the tyranny of the urgent. Slow. Down.

Being deliberately slow is hard for people like us. We didn't get to where we are by being slow. We got to where we are by kicking everybody else's butt. By getting ahead. By making sure that our results were better than everyone else's. We got to where we are by moving fast. And then, there were a million details to take care of, just to keep the business going, and not enough hands to do it all. That meant we had to step up. We worked nights and weekends, seeing hours we maybe hadn't seen since shift work or college all-nighters. We sacrificed time with our families and friends.

And even though we've maybe been able to ease back on the crazy hours as growing cashflow allowed us to bring on more staff, it's really, really hard to get out of that mode of go, Go, GO!

But you're a leader. And more than leaders *do*, leaders *lead*.

That doesn't mean you don't do stuff. You still charge from the front. From time to time, you'll flex your skills and prove that you're capable of stepping right back in there with the best of them. But as your organization grows, that will not be the best use of your time. Your resources. Your brain. Your position.

The best use of *you* is to think. It's up to you to look ahead and come up with those strategic ideas—ideas that then send others into motion, more than they send you into motion. Get comfortable with the mindset that what got you to this point is not going to take you to the next level. Learn to be okay with doing less and thinking more.

If you can't, you need to seriously consider whether your strengths and personal comfort zone align with your title and your goals. Are you here to do the work yourself, or are you here to organize a team to do the work? Within your organization, have you claimed a role that you're not willing to grow into? It's not bad to step back. It is bad to hang on stubbornly while refusing to grow. Which do you want more—to keep doing the day-to-day work you love, or to build an organization capable of accomplishing more than you can manage from your own desk? The choice is yours, but you can't have both.

Lead with Review

You've identified your passion. You've identified your values. These are your core principles. Now it's time to support them with a critical practice: the practice of continuous review.

What does this look like? It looks like letting your organization operate as normal; observing; and then disciplining yourself and your team to thoroughly and thoughtfully review what occurred.

Every project.

Every activity.

Every time.

How did it go? What worked? What didn't work? What would we do again? What will we never do again? How do we feel? Did we enjoy it? Was it easy? Was it easier for us to do than for our competitors?

Yes, you can codify review as a procedure. A rule. You can tie it to project closures, milestones, metrics, management objectives. And you may have to—perhaps to comply with external standards or contract terms. Perhaps simply to ensure that people do it.

But an organization that pays lip service to reviews, checking boxes because leadership says it must, is not enough. What you must establish is *a culture of review*. Your people must welcome review, must be eager for review. You want them seeking feedback regularly. And feedback must be captured in a lightweight, easy-to-use framework—a repository of experience and insight, accessible to all.

Organizations only achieve this if reviews are used exclusively as a tool to improve processes and reward good decisions, never to lay blame and punish bad decisions. You really only have two options here. Either you'll make staff feel safe, supported, and enriched by reviews. Or you'll incentivize them to exaggerate the good stuff and minimize the bad stuff.

Here's an extreme example: In an analysis of communication failures that contributed to the 1986 *Challenger* space shuttle explosion, professor Dorothy Winsor pointed out that what happened was, tragically, also pretty typical. "Research has repeatedly shown that bad news is often not passed upward in organizations . . . even when bad news is sent, people are less likely to believe it than good news."[10] *Challenger's* deadly launch showed how problems with culture lead to problems with communication. Engineers issued clear warnings about the possible loss of human life due to O-ring failure as early as six months before the fatal accident, yet the critical message was so diluted in transmission across business units and up to top decision-makers that it failed to prevent disaster.

Establishing a culture of review requires you, the leader, guiding and safeguarding the new process until it takes hold. It's like planting a new grove of trees. When the saplings are small and tender, they're vulnerable to wild animals like rabbits, groundhogs, and deer grazing on them. So they're protected with these little biodegradable tubes until they've grown.

But when they're taller, their trunks aren't strong enough yet to withstand high winds, nor are their roots strong enough to keep them upright in loose soil. So they're staked with guide ropes to ensure they'll grow straight. Then, after a few years, the stakes come out and the tree grows strong on its own.

Same goes for reviews. People who have little experience of review-positive cultures may feel a strong temptation to cast blame over stuff that could have been done better. In a review-negative culture, where reviews are used to evaluate personal performance, our instincts get conditioned to withhold information or, worse, to blame someone else to draw negative attention away from ourselves. This simply doesn't work. A review is only as valuable as its participants are honest. But the desire to be honest can be fragile. Blame must be kept out of the culture of review. Keep the focus on *what* and *how*, not *who*.

Harvard Business School professor Amy Edmondson explained the importance of psychological safety to a culture that embraces review in her book *Teaming*:

> Psychological safety makes it possible to give tough feedback and have difficult conversations without the need to tiptoe around the truth . . . it produces a sense of confidence that the group won't embarrass, reject, or punish someone for speaking up.[11]

University of Houston professor Brené Brown, who uses her research in vulnerability, shame, and empathy to coach organizations in how to become more effective, urges leaders to "calculate the cost of distrust and disconnection in terms of productivity, performance, and engagement." Brown sums up a key takeaway from her research like this: "Leaders must either invest a reasonable amount of time attending to fears and feelings, or squander an unreasonable amount of time trying to manage ineffective and unproductive behavior."[12]

Getting the human side of pro-review culture right is hard enough, but that's not the whole challenge. The review process itself can easily become onerous and burdensome. Many who've worked in companies with a dedicated quality assurance division have experienced this. A bureaucracy can grow up around complex management systems. Tools meant to serve our work become overdesigned to the point where the organization needs specialists to operate them. Participating in reviews becomes so burdensome that people learn to shun them, doing everything they can to avoid them.

That's no good either. It's like a grove of top-heavy trees, grown without guide ropes, all leaning at crazy angles. They can only grow like that for so long before they get tangled up, branches die and break, and tipping trees start to domino. And if that's what people are used to, they will bring that perception into your organization and they'll resist review. They'll need to be shown that things are different here.

It's up to you, the leader, to set the tone for reviews and protect your people from blame. Model nothing but curiosity, continuous learning, and a passion for improvement.

It's also up to you to keep the tools for reviews from bloating into bureaucracy. Capturing those lessons requires a formal system, but that system is only useful when it's lightweight. It has to be robust enough to pass audits for whatever regulations, standards, and contractual obligations apply to your organization—but no more. Don't overengineer compliance.

Listening to Understand

Because you're so involved, you're going to be very familiar with your organization's review practices, tone, and tools. As you go through that process over and over, you will start to notice the organization's operating fabric has loose threads. During reviews, you have the opportunity to learn something you might never notice otherwise. But you'll only take advantage of that opportunity through attentiveness and curiosity, commonly called active listening. Active listening is intensely powerful. But it takes calm, solitude, and silence ahead of that meeting to put yourself in the right frame of mind to listen and explore. Unless you slow down and get yourself into the right headspace, you won't even notice the loose threads you should be tugging. You'll overlook them completely.

An early pioneer in the study of organizational culture and its impacts is Larry Senn, founder of the Senn-Delaney Leadership Consulting Group. Senn-Delaney emphasizes a tool they call the Mood Elevator, which helps leaders recognize the quality of their thinking and current state of mind.

"Listening to understand" is the highest form of listening, above other listening postures such as "Listening for how it applies to me," "Listening to judge or evaluate," and "Listening for a chance to speak." *Listening to understand* entails "being fully present" as well as "hearing beyond the words."[13] And, according to Senn-Delaney's decades of experience in the field of management consulting, that's just not possible unless we're operating from the top of the Mood Elevator: feeling curious, appreciative, content, grateful, in good humor.

When the unexpected happens around your company, lean in. Be curious! Embrace agitation! Be open to new experiences. Be present in the moment. Explore with intent to listen.

This is easiest face-to-face and in-person, and it's important for all kinds of communication, not just reviews. That's why we encourage everyone at Velentium to prioritize in-person over videoconference, videoconference over phone call, phone call over anything text-based, like email. The more difficult, controversial, or potentially contentious the conversation might be, the more important it is to proactively choose a communication medium as high on that list as you practically can. The more present you are for the conversation, the easier it is to be open and listen.

These aren't skills most of us are naturally good at. But you don't come up with good questions—let alone uncover good answers—if you're always moving fast. If you operate every day as if you already know what comes next, or as if you can't afford to think about it, you'll miss things you'll wish you hadn't.

Are you fighting to make it through each day as fast as you can without crashing? Are you locked into your plans with no time or attention to spare for anything that isn't a catastrophic emergency?

Or, have you built margin into your schedule? Have you disciplined yourself to respond with openness and curiosity, even when you don't feel those feelings in response to disrupted expectations?

STEADY YOURSELF

What you talk about is what you focus on. What you focus on is where your attention goes. And wherever your attention goes, there your energy goes.

To reap the rewards of a culture of review, you first must cultivate a strong sense of self. Not just your own self, who you are, but also a sense of the organization's "self." This, again, gets back to passion and principles. Because the organization's passion reflects your passion, and its values were born out of your values, you are deeply connected to your organization. As you initiate changes that maintain or bring it better into alignment with the passion and values, as you forge ahead to the next big thing, you will again encounter resistance. People inside and outside the organization will question, opine, comment. They'll throw expressions of disappointment, disapproval, and confusion your way. A strong sense of self—who you are, what this organization is about—is how you keep that rudder lashed to the heading you've chosen. Without a strong sense of self, you'll let contrary winds influence your direction. You'll let crosscurrents of comparison to the past, comparison to other companies, comparison to other leaders, push you steadily off course. And the faster you're moving, the farther off course you'll be when you finally realize what's happening.

Take your time. Slow down. Take deep breaths. Often.

COUNTDOWN TO SLOW DOWN

10. Get outside often.

There's something about nature that does amazing things for our creative selves. And whatever your organization is, as the leader, you need to be creative. Maybe it's creative about management structure. Maybe it's creative about pivoting your strategy. Maybe it's creative about ways to communicate vision, or values, or passion. But you need to be creative. And nature just helps.

Reading Steve Jobs's biography was what finally gave me permission to go take a walk. Jobs was famous for walking with people during meetings, but I really struggled to get there. Why do I have a problem with "interrupting" my workday and taking a walk? Because it's not something I did on my way up the ladder. And why not? Because I didn't ever see other leaders doing it.

Be that leader. Show your organization that getting outside is a good thing. In good weather, have meetings outside. If you can manage it, create workspaces that allow for interactivity with nature: Make sure your Wi-Fi reaches the patio. Lease an office near a park. Model calling in to meetings from your backyard or the kids' playground or a walk around your neighborhood. Get people outside!

9. Get comfortable with discomfort.

A culture of review is a culture of introspection. A culture of introspection hurts, because you'll be looking honestly at things you're not doing well. But you know what else hurts? Lifting weights. Showing up for spin class. Living on a healthy diet. I could go on and on. Some things that hurt produce great results. So get comfortable with discomfort, and lean into review. Don't turn a blind eye to hard sights. There's no benefit to sugarcoating. No benefit to dancing around the subject. Just accept it for what it is. Call it what it is. Live it as it is—and get better.

When people resist your scheduling of that review time with them, force it to happen anyway. And then show them that in this organization, reviews are safe and effective. We're here to learn, to strategize, to evolve. Not to punish. Our focus stays on processes and outcomes, not people. Encourage critical, collaborative introspection.

8. Schedule time away.

I mean extended time. Four hours or more. For me, pre-pandemic, this happened on airplanes all the time. To this day, I think somebody could make a lot of money if they just re-created the first-class cabin, complete with food service and a dedicated restroom, that you could check into around the corner from the office. And the only caveat is, once you check in, you can't leave for four hours and you can't get mobile phone service!

Why are planes so great? Because they force you into a time of uninterrupted thought. With COVID-19 severely restricting travel, I've had to proactively create those times. It isn't easy. And once again, there's something psychologically difficult about giving myself permission to reserve that time. But put it on your schedule. Add a recurring four-hour block to your calendar for multiple days each week. And then spend that blocked time doing the same things you might do on an airplane. Disconnect. Get out a notebook and journal your thoughts. Turn off your phone, your email, and hone in on something that takes deep focus.

7. Periodically, pull your leadership team out of the office.

Get away for a daylong planning session together. Repeat this each quarter.

When we started out, this was a very scary step for me. Think of all the billable time we're losing! Think of the travel costs! Think of all the emergencies that might happen while we're gone! All kinds of different excuses as to why it shouldn't happen. Now, they're my favorite workdays of the year.

Off-site meetings aren't just about brainstorming. They're also about review and analysis, and about growing together as a leadership team around new ideas, new tactics, and new strategies. And the sooner you establish the right rhythm for your leadership team to briefly disconnect from the daily bustle and think together, the better your organization will be.

6. Don't let this just be a business thing.

Take the same kind of time away with your family.

Most of us look for best practices and key strategic edges in our business, but don't apply the same level of wisdom, desperation, creativity, action, and thoughtfulness to our family life. Yet it's the family life that is most important. You can always start another organization. It's way harder to start another family . . . and way easier to lose the one you've already got. Invest in them, nurture them, cherish them. The tether and tension of those relationships will stabilize and accelerate your leadership.

Devoting time and attention to your family is hard. We're driven by fear. We're driven by a need for success. We're driven by a sense of duty. We're driven by all kinds of things that seem to tell us that spending time with our family is something that we'll do "tomorrow." Yet somehow, tomorrow never turns into today.

Recently I took an informal survey and found that Julie and I talk more one on one in a week than most. It seems like the average couple talks about two hours a week. We talk about two hours a day. Does it make us slower? Yes! That's the point. It's infinitely harder to achieve calm, to be curious, to listen, to find Slow, when you're suppressing stress from your relationships at home instead of leaning into and working through it. By being connected to your family, you will find more effectiveness, more creativity, and more productivity in your work life.

5. Wait.

If something doesn't feel right, hit "pause" and keep thinking. Don't rush. Short-term results are not nearly as important as having your core identity solidly aligned. Strategy, tactics, and activities should click with your passion and values. If you're feeling forced into something, it is perfectly OK to say, "I'm sorry, but this is going to have to wait."

Early in our marriage, Julie and I were intrigued by an Orlando time-share. Then we got to the pricing section and found it was an order of magnitude more expensive than I expected.

I said, "No, thank you."

They came back with, "This deal is only available today."

I said, "Well, great. In that case it's definitely a no, because at that price point, if you won't give me time to think about it, I'm not going to do it."

They said, "You are going to miss out!"

I said, "You're right!" And we left.

And you know what?

We have never looked back and wished that we had bought that time-share.

Velentium has had several companies approach us, interested in some manner of joint venture. As we've grown and become more well known, that has happened more and more often. When the proposal is strong, my response is, "That sounds interesting! Let's do some joint projects together, and see how it goes." What I've found is that about 90 percent of those venture deals just evaporate—they never turn into real work. Clearly, our companies weren't ready for a joint venture. Velentium currently has no formalized joint ventures, but there are several companies with whom we may be slowly progressing in that direction through joint projects, and maybe they'll turn into something. If they do, that will be fantastic and exciting. Rushing into those decisions, no matter how strong the business case appears, would be unwise. Go on some dates before you get married!

4. Breathe deeply.

Our bodies are conditioned for fight or flight. When circumstances are tense, fight or flight will happen inside your body. But humans are capable of controlling those instincts. You'll want to develop your ability to circumvent that initial response. Because if you're like me, fight or flight most often shows up on my tongue. And when it does, before I know it, I've said something that I cannot take back.

The best way to interrupt that impulse is to train yourself in bodily responses that treat your fight or flight response for what it is: It isn't truth. It isn't your "best self" manifesting. It's biochemistry trying to hijack your higher cognition. So, try this: When you feel fight or flight—heart rate picking up, face getting warm, a desire to lash out—cultivate a habit of deep breathing. Try it right now. Breathe in for five straight seconds. Now breathe out for ten seconds. It takes a bit of concentration, doesn't it?

That fifteen seconds gave your emotional and mental systems a chance to process through what your body has already started reacting to. Not long enough? Repeat it!

Learn this technique. It will save you again and again. Just the other day, it saved me from saying something unkind when, in a recent review meeting, we realized we'd prematurely credited ourselves with $400,000 we had yet to receive. Deep breathing enabled me to respond calmly.

Over time, with practice, you can interrupt your natural bodily tendency to reach for fight or flight and rewire yourself to breathe deeply instead. It won't always happen automatically—but sometimes it will! And you'll be a calmer, more measured person.

3. Learn how to make yourself scarce.

Communications, scheduling, and meeting tools are great. But who's in charge of them? Are you in command of your own tools? If a block of time is open on your calendar, who is authorized to book it? If someone emails, texts, or instant messages you, do you let yourself be interrupted by a push notification? Do you feel compelled to put your current task on "pause" to read the message? If the phone rings, are you able to ignore it?

You're not alone. Georgetown University comp-sci professor Cal Newport points to research by Stanford communications professor Clifford Nass:

> Constant attention switching online has a lasting negative effect on your brain . . . Once your brain has become accustomed to on-demand distraction, Nass discovered, it's hard to shake the addiction even when you *want* to concentrate.[14]

Many of us have worked jobs where there was an expectation of constant availability. If a call went out for someone to jump, we won by being first to fire back "how high?" We got to where we are by making ourselves essential. Now, as leaders, we win by establishing a different rhythm and setting different expectations. Elements of what we're now essential for can only get done if we make ourselves scarce.

Part of the challenge is psychological. Part of it is expectation management. And part of it is managing our tools.

According to Jason Fried and David Hansson, co-founders of Basecamp and co-authors of *It Doesn't Have to Be Crazy at Work*, "Modern-day offices have become interruption factories." They list numerous examples—as I'm sure you could, too—adding, "When someone takes your time, it doesn't cost them anything, but it costs you everything. You can only do great work if you have adequate quality time to do it."[15]

This meshes with a paradigm coined by Paul Graham, co-founder of Viaweb and Y Combinator. He calls it "Manager's Schedule, Maker's

Schedule." The Manager's Schedule generally operates in one-hour blocks of time, where the task you're doing (or the meeting you're attending) changes every hour. But the Maker's Schedule requires blocks of half a day or more to really focus and get into flow. When you're producing something ambitious, you are "by definition close to the limits of your capacity."

> When you're operating on the maker's schedule, meetings are a disaster. A single meeting can blow a whole afternoon, by breaking it into two pieces each too small to do anything hard in.[16]

When you're an individual contributor, or a manager, you'd think it would be easy to tell which schedule you're on. But functionally, things are rarely so cut and dry, especially in small organizations, where everyone wears multiple hats. Most managers also function part-time as individual contributors. Leaders, especially leaders whose job includes review and strategy, function in both capacities as well.

In his definitive book on how to focus, *Deep Work*, Cal Newport proposes that "shallow work"—things that don't require a lot of effort to engage with, like attending meetings, answering emails, and returning phone calls—should be batched together so as to leave blocks of at least four-plus hours available each day for intensive, ambitious, attention-demanding work. Fried and Hansson have a low opinion of the shared work calendar, calling it "one of the most destructive inventions of modern times,"[17] but Newport shows how you can put it to productive use: block off your "deep work" time to signal when you're not available. Fried and Hansson also suggest blocking off some weekly "office hours," as college professors do, to signal when it's okay for others to interrupt you.

Train your mind. Own your tools.

Ben, my head of sales, loves scheduling focused meetings when we need to discuss complex topics. With him, and with any key staff I need to speak with fairly often, I've found the best way to reduce ad hoc meetings is to schedule a single, predictable meeting that recurs on a regular cadence. So, whenever any of those contacts requests a meeting, my first response back is always, "Is this so urgent that it can't wait until our next regular meeting?" Guess how often the answer is "Yes." Not very often!

We have a company Slack, but instant messaging doesn't work for Jason, my co-author. Being continuously available interrupts his focus and makes him less efficient at the work we hired him to do. He knew that from day one, but it wasn't until after reading *Deep Work* that he gave himself permission to put up a permanent status message on Slack. It reads, "Urgent? Call or text. Important? Email." By process of elimination, that signals that anything you send him on Slack must not be urgent or important. He'll see it eventually, and he'll respond. But it may take a few hours, or even days. And if you really need to interrupt him, he's given you clear instructions for how to do it.

Learn to make yourself scarce. If you don't, you'll never be allowed to slow down. You'll be constantly kicked back into high gear by RFAs (that's "Requests for Attention") and tiny emergencies.

2. The magic word is "No."

Fried and Hansson argue eloquently in favor of "No":

> When you say no to one thing, it's a choice that breeds choices. Tomorrow you can be as open to new opportunities as you are today.
>
> When you say yes to one thing, you've spent that choice. The door is shut on a whole host of alternative possibilities and tomorrow is that much more limited.[18]

Anytime you're asked to do anything, your default response must be "no" until you're convinced that "yes" is the best response. But many of us, myself included, have conditioned ourselves to respond the other way around. Once again, this is because we got to where we are by saying "yes" when asked, or even without needing to be asked. Then, results were our most precious commodity. We won by trading time for results.

Now, attention is your most precious commodity. And because you are the key decision-maker, the guy to convince, the gal whose word is law, demand for your attention from within your organization will trend sharply upward. The more your organization grows, the more RFAs you'll get. And all the outside requests? From school, community, church, neighborhood, and all the other organizations that will increasingly want to do business with you? Those don't slow down either. Yet your attention remains finite.

As Fried and Hansson put it, "No is no to one thing. Yes is no to a thousand things."[19]

Say no. A lot. And don't feel bad! You don't have to be a jerk about it. There's no need to burn bridges, or even settle for being coldly polite. Let your enthusiasm be as loud as your "No."

"What a great opportunity! I just don't think that's a great fit for where I'm at right now. Thanks for asking."

1. Cultivate a habit of solitude in silence.

Spend at least ten minutes a day alone, somewhere quiet. No devices. No TV, radio, music, podcasts playing. If quiet isn't possible, use white noise.

If you keep your bathroom uncluttered, the master bedroom shower can be a great place to start. And when you get good and comfortable with that, level up by reclaiming other space. Another room in the house, your backyard, a conference room at the office, your own car. No media playing. Just the quiet of your own thoughts.

Cal Newport unpacks the importance of letting ourselves be bored:

> Efforts to deepen your focus will struggle if you don't simultaneously wean your mind from a dependence on distraction . . . gird yourself for the temporary boredom, and fight through it with only the company of your own thoughts. To simply wait and be bored has become a novel experience in modern life, but . . . it's incredibly valuable . . .
>
> To succeed with deep work you must rewire your brain to be comfortable resisting distracting stimuli.[20]

You've got to slow down.

Your role requires it.

Your organization desperately needs it.

Because the time to act fast is coming.

And without the deliberate practice of *slow*, you won't be ready for *fast*.

FAST

Ever watch a feral cat hunt?

At first, it seems like the cat is wandering around. Sniffing things, looking here and there, generally interested in the world.

Then, something catches its attention and it goes into stalking mode. It gets low, slinks through the grass. Every step is steady, deliberate, slow, and smooth. Eyes never leave the target.

Then it explodes into motion. Muscles come together and the cat surges forward. Leap, sprint, dodge left, feint right, and *pounce*.

Survival secured.

That's how this works. Once you've established a rhythm of slowness, you'll find that your organization, yourself included, has the ability to make decisions and act on those decisions faster than any of your competitors. Your culture of review, your culture of slow, leads to decision-making that is fast. Your assessment of whether or not to chase an opportunity becomes so rapid, it looks instantaneous to outside observers.

You'll ask:

- Are we passionate about that?
- Does it mesh with our values?
- Can we execute on it?

And when you get those three answers—*yes*, you'll move like lightning.

Have fun with that. You'll blow people's minds. Because you've taken the prep time to develop your core—through attention, iteration, and review—your response time is unbelievable to people accustomed to "business as usual."

Here's the secret. When your organization is small and still trying to get on its feet, you've got to chase every opportunity that comes within your sight. It's at this point that you will feel, very strongly, that you don't have time to slow down and think. You'll feel that strategy and tactics are a luxury you can't afford. And that's exactly where your feelings are mixing you up. The more your survival depends on speed, the more you need to invest in slow.

Think about the cat. It doesn't run around the whole time it's hunting. It *conserves* energy and *observes* its environment. It works to attain a *favorable position* before unleashing that burst of speed. If it doesn't see a good target, if it can't get into position, it doesn't waste energy on a frantic chase. That's how it survives.

How do I know this works? Because in the early years, we made it our goal to take a call from a potential client, return that call, visit or at least virtually meet that client, take copious notes on every interaction, write the proposal, and return that proposal to the client . . . all before any potential competitors returned the first phone call. And we did it! Over and over again. We got on planes and met clients face-to-face at their own offices within days of hearing from them.

That philosophy of rapid-response remains the basis of our sales cycle even now. And it's only possible because, during our rhythms of Slow, we do the work necessary to support those critical bursts of speed when the time to move Fast arrives.

Fast happens easier when you have history. And it doesn't have to be *your* history. Studying past success, and even past failure, helps enable Fast. That's why you're reading this book!

You get to Fast when you've done the research, done the thinking, had the conversations, and made the critical decisions before the critical moment. So when that moment comes, you have nothing left to hesitate over. Just act.

A few years ago, I went to a buddy's bachelor party, and the bachelor party included a skydiving trip. If his best man had sprung that on us as a surprise, I don't know what would have happened. I don't know if I would have gone! And if I had gone, there's no way I would've been "in the moment," in flow, attentive to what was happening. I would have been out of my mind with hesitation and anxiety. But since I had a few months' advance warning, I was able to prepare myself mentally. And when the moment came to fall out of an airplane . . . on purpose . . . I was able not just to act on it, but to enjoy it.

This is not a new idea. It's a key principle behind almost all preparedness training. You do safety training and emergency drills when there's no emergency, so that when an emergency arises, your people can act like they've seen it before—even though they've only seen practice examples. It's not about knowing intellectually what to do; it's about being so well practiced that nobody has to think about it.

It's a key principle in self-defense. There's the iconic example from *The Karate Kid*, where the arm and wrist techniques "paint the fence" and "wax on, wax off" turn out to be muscle-memory conditioning. Outside the silver screen, self-defense training goes way beyond that. You practice techniques for escaping and disabling an attacker who has ahold of your clothes, your hair, your wrist, or even your neck in a chokehold. You practice them over and over and over until they become second nature, and if someone ever makes an unwanted move on you, the training takes over faster than the speed of thought.

It's a key principle in deliberate practice, the discipline underlying great musicians and great athletes. You may be acquainted with this concept thanks to Malcolm Gladwell's popular book *Blink*. When you train the right way, when you practice the technique properly, you're able to perform under pressure.

Without Slow, you won't know whether Fast was truly fast, or just a frenzy of activity. Anyone can generate a whole lot of rushing around, but you can't know whether it was the right play, or even a good play, unless you've done the right prep.

If you've done all the slow work, including exercising the discipline of saying *no*, then when an opportunity presents itself that is a good fit, you can immediately say *yes*. In the face of opportunity, you're ready with fast decisions, fast execution, fast people, fast teams, fast iterations. Attention to process makes you fast. It takes years to collate the experience your organization needs to create, evaluate, and iterate on its processes. This isn't just about running smooth. The proverbial "well-oiled machine" isn't necessarily fast. It also needs to be well designed and well aligned. When you are intimately familiar with your normal processes, you know their inputs and outputs. You know their pace. If they aren't going to cut it, you know immediately that you need to try something else. When you finally get to

Fast, it's back into action, back to *doing*, with that same hunger to beat the competition and deliver the best product you've always had.

A Flash in the Plan

Here's the thing about Fast: Fast is flashy. Fast is fun-to-watch eye candy.

Stories of Fast inspire healthy aspiration, competitive ambition, even envy. They're memorable, too. Heroes and legends grow from stories about Fast.

Experiencing Fast is a rush. As in extreme sports, adrenaline plus endorphins can equal addiction. Coming down from Fast to fully engage in the next season of Slow takes discipline. But it's critical.

The jaw-dropping, ear-popping, eye-dazzling nature of Fast obscures all the careful, methodical, disciplined work it takes for anyone to execute Fast successfully. Scratch the veneer of any real-life underdog story, any rags-to-riches story, any *eureka!*-moment story, any overnight success story, and you'll see what I mean. These stories average between six and twelve *years* of preparation ahead of the big moment.

Velentium is right in the middle of that scale. We'd been in business for just under eight years before Project V. We'd been working with Ventec for five of them.

Hollywood pays token service to those years with the "training montage" scene. *Rocky* made this trope iconic, but couldn't save it from being parodied almost immediately, because audiences sense that the prep depicted undersells the hard reality. And yet we're still lulled into ignoring how much prep there really is. That's because the film industry exists to entertain us, not instruct us. It's more fun to watch the stalking cat than the curious cat. Even more fun to watch the pouncing cat than the stalking cat. But if that's where we focus, we miss the true nature of the beast.

Speaking of cats—if you know anything about cheetahs, you probably know they're astonishingly fast. You may have even memorized the fact that cheetahs can *run* up to 70 mph. That's fast enough to keep up with cars on the I-10 freeway near Velentium's Houston headquarters.

But you probably don't know that cheetahs sleep for twelve out of every twenty-four hours.

A cheetah can't live long on the spoils of one successful hunt. A few days later, it must perform at the same level again. And again, a few days after that. If it doesn't take time to recover between hunts, it won't survive.

Extraordinary performance depends equally on extraordinary preparation and extraordinary recovery.

The expression a *flash in the pan* means "a sudden, spasmodic effort that accomplishes nothing,"[21] or "a thing or person whose sudden or brief success is either not repeated or not repeatable."[22] It originates from the days of muskets, when unreliable firing mechanisms or improper shot packing could result in gunpowder igniting without propelling a bullet out of the barrel.

Big noise. Big fire. No impact.

I'm confident that every one-hit-wonder band is capable of producing a second hit. My hunch is, the Fast commercial pressure generated by that first hit short-circuited their ability to get back to Slow. Recording, touring, fan adulation, press appearances, public pressure, all conspired to rob them of the chance to review and turn the slow, steady years of development that yielded their first breakthrough into a reliable, repeatable process. They never gave themselves the chance to nurture the creative process into the re-creative process.

So, my question is: How are you going to stop that from becoming your story?

You prepped with Slow. A Fast opportunity came, and you pounced. Are you content to risk your "overnight success" going nowhere?

When your staff talks about what happened, a year or two later, is that how you want them to label it? A flash in the pan?

Or will it be a flash in the *plan*, just one of many, neither the first nor the last? One dazzling burst of speed that broke the ribbon at the finish line at one of dozens, hundreds, or thousands of races your organization successfully enters.

At Velentium, we have a mantra: "Go slow to go fast."

It means, tie your shoes before you try to run out the door.

It also means, stretch when you get back.

SLOW

Rest. Recover. Review. That's the cadence that follows Fast.

Rest

After an extraordinary challenge, the number-one job for you and your team is to rest. Give out comp time. Communicate an expectation that people will not work for a short period. Discipline yourself to honor that time.

There are phases to rest. The first phase is personal time. Sleep, a spa visit, a long bike ride or nature hike, curled up on a comfy couch with a good novel. Encourage everyone to make space and time for a day or more to themselves.

The second phase of rest is time with loved ones. Families and friends get neglected during Fast. Even your friends and family members who are colleagues. You might have been bumping elbows with them for hours a day, but if the context was an all-consuming work project, the other aspects of your relationship were temporarily shelved. Now it's time to dust those off.

Think of relationships like a savings account. When you spend quality time together, you're making a deposit. When you sacrifice that time to get things done, you're making a withdrawal. A period of Fast in your organization puts stress on your staff, but for them, it also comes with the thrill of a challenge and, if you succeed, the satisfaction of victory and pride in a job well done. But Fast puts equal stress on your staff's relationships, and the people on the other end of those relationships aren't getting those intangible benefits. All they get is less time with their loved ones while the organization consumes more time. That's a big withdrawal from the relational bank account. Spouses, partners, and friends have to do things like:

- Cancel plans at the last minute
- Pay bills
- Parent through tantrums
- Field the drama from your extended family

- Handle their chores *and* yours . . . and be bugged by the ones they can't get to
- Still go to work and do "life stuff"
- Maintain a semblance of "normal"

Alone. For more hours. Every day.

For as long as Fast persists.

Often, that extra burden comes with little to no warning. No chance to plan or prepare for all those specific "extras." And your organization is responsible for causing all that stress. Yes, that is part of what you and each staff member, and by extension, each staffer's family and social circle, "signed on for." But relationships need deposits to sustain withdrawals. And if your path to success as an organization involves repeatedly forcing yourself and your staff to make those withdrawals, it rapidly becomes unsustainable. Too-frequent demands without corresponding deposits erode everyone's psychological well-being. A relational check will bounce. And someone will either quit to go salvage their relationship, or they'll find themselves facing a separation, a divorce, or some other family crisis. From the organization's standpoint, this will happen at the worst possible time. It will be time again to move Fast, with all hands on deck, and key people are either bailing or radically distracted. That key person might even be you.

Respect the needs of your relationships.

Respect your own needs as a relational being.

Respect the same needs in your staff.

No human can sustain a healthy psychology and peak performance by doing nothing but work. The only way to get extraordinary performance from yourself and your team is to invest in extraordinary preparation and extraordinary recovery.

So rest. Rest alone, then rest with your loved ones. Incentivize, encourage, and, if possible, enforce rest across your organization. Communicate the expectation for rest, set the tone, and lead by example.

Then move into recovery.

Recover

Rest and recovery are not the same, but they are interdependent. Trying to recover without rest would be like running a half-marathon the day after running a marathon. You're basically inviting injury at that point. Your body needs time.

But if you take too much time to rest, your body will start to atrophy. Go one week without exercise and you may feel a little sluggish getting back into it, but your performance is unlikely to suffer. Go two weeks without exercise, and the losses of strength and endurance become quantifiable. Experts say you may require four weeks to build back up what you lose over a two-week sedentary period.

So, after rest comes recovery. Recovery is where you engage in a new training regimen, a new normal, designed to capture some of the performance capacity you developed during Fast and bring your organization up to a level above the one you were at before. It's moving base camp up to a higher plateau.

After the Fast of Project V, many aspects of how we work recovered to a better, stronger, new normal. Our purchasing process and team are far better. Our packaging and shipping practices are far better. Our operational logistics massively improved, with internal reorganization and promotions into middle and upper management and technical directorships paving the way for a bevy of new hires. Our marketing and PR surged forward as a result of people wanting to hear about Project V, which in addition to increases in exposure, market share, and sales, gave us the opportunity to write this book. The organization overall is larger, leaner, more efficient, and more capable. The institutional benefits are partly permanent, accruing through direct experience, as well as indirect contact.

Completing your first marathon is a big deal. It's worth celebrating. When you're training to run a marathon, your whole goal is to complete that marathon. After you've done it, you can elevate your goal. Now, maybe, your goal is to become a marathoner. If you gave yourself twelve months to train for the first marathon, your elevated goal can be to run the next marathon in eight months. But this time, your training regimen isn't starting from zero. It's not even starting from where you were at four months into your original training schedule. It's starting from "I just ran a marathon!" So you've got to exercise more cautiously at first, knowing you've just put your body under a lot of good stress. But you've also got to exercise diligently.

For most readers of this book, Fast will exercise and exhaust our minds more than our bodies. Mental recovery requires a slightly different approach. Having identified the new normal that moves the organization toward your elevated goal, you get to work. But you pay careful attention to what you do when you're *not* working.

In *Deep Work*, Cal Newport offers a tour of the research on mental rest and recovery, explaining: "Providing your conscious brain time to rest enables your unconscious mind to take a shift sorting through your most complex professional challenges." In other words, your mind engages in recovery on an *unconscious* level while you're *consciously* unplugged. But that only happens when you're truly unplugged, which needs to happen on a routine basis under normal conditions, as well as during recovery. "Decades of work from multiple different subfields within psychology all point toward the conclusion that regularly resting your brain improves the quality of your deep work. When you work, work hard. When you're done, be done." And the only way to "be done" well, Newport says, is to structure your leisure time. "Don't default to whatever catches your attention at the moment, but instead dedicate some advance thinking to how you want to spend your . . . evenings and weekends before they begin." Otherwise, your brain will be distracted by shallow activities that fail to refresh your conscious mind during your downtime.[23]

After rest comes recovery. After recovery, or sometimes during recovery, comes review. Review is where we reexamine the effort we're resting and recovering from.

Review

That culture of review that you've woven into every corner of your operations? After a burst of Fast, you're going to lean into it hard. You'll need to be prompt, because the blur of Fast isn't conducive to memory—especially after an adrenaline-fueled success. In the flush of a big win, it doesn't take long before the critical details, pain points, and near-misses with failure— even potentially catastrophic failure—get replaced with rose-tinted versions of reality, all throughout the organization.

One major thing that came up in review from Project V was how much we enjoyed and were impressed with one of our subcontractors, Oasis Testing. We'd worked with them many times before, but Project V was something else. As the schedule kept accelerating, we had to keep calling Demetri, then-VP of Engineering, with hard news: "We need it sooner." Demetri's team stepped up and made "it" happen, every time. They never said "no," never said "can't," but always found a way to get it done. They were putting test stations out the door within a week of coming on board. And they kept asking for more.

So we gave them more. Over time, Oasis ended up helping with thirteen different test stand types. Our engineers who worked closely with them said, "They took everything we gave them and made it better." That glowing post-project review led to us acquiring Oasis Testing six months later, allowing us to fully integrate their team into ours.

During Fast, when you were aggressively eliminating obstacles, piloting new processes, and experimenting with creative solutions under extreme pressure, the organization made some discoveries! Some of those things you tried are worth keeping around. Some will need refining. Some will have to be shelved for next time, or for when you have more resources.

On the other hand, some of that new stuff didn't work, and you need a way for your organization to remember that. Otherwise, someone might come up with the same idea again later, and the team might waste critical time trying again what you should already know won't work.

The pressure of Fast also exposes weak points in your operation. Under normal conditions, these suboptimal processes and risky behaviors may be tolerable (or at least tolerated), because the time and resources seem to exist to make up for them. Not so during Fast. The organization was forced to confront these weak areas. And now that you know they exist, you can't go back to tolerating them. That doesn't mean you have to adopt the stopgap solution implemented during Fast. That may not be optimal or practical. But thanks to Fast, now during Slow you have an opportunity to elevate your normal. And you must follow through.

Because, out beyond the horizon where your vision is hazy, the next wave is building. Around the bend in the gorge, the next rapid is coming up. You won't know what it will take to dominate those waters until you're in them.

Right now, though, the waters are calm. Take advantage of that. Get calm, too. Return to Slow. Rest. Recover. Review.

SLOW—FAST—SLOW

Master that rhythm. It's the cadence of shrewd preparation for upcoming opportunities, yet to be discovered. It's the secret to capitalizing that opportunity when it comes, turning its rewards into an elevated new normal: more efficient, more capable, more collaborative, and better resourced than ever before.

Section Wrap: Hatch

In this section, we focused on *identity*—on discovering your identity as a leader, and translating your identity outward so that it becomes the basis of *shared identity* in your organization.

Shared identity is culture. If culture isn't designed and guided, it develops blindly, based on your people's past experiences and assumptions, as well as the unconscious messages and signals you send as the leader and how those get interpreted.

To build culture, start with passion. Start with what motivates you personally, the macro- or micro-change that you care about so much that you'll assemble and direct a whole organization to do something about it. Proclaim that passion loudly and proudly as the reason for your organization's existence and the motive behind 100 percent of its activities.

Then, figure out your values. Values define *hows*—both how you will and won't pursue your passion, plus how you'll be known to clients, partners, vendors, the people you serve, and your staff's families and friends.

Values aren't a blurb for your website or marketing material. They inform, govern, and guide daily operations. Values are practical. Values are applied. Values enable you to resist "rule creep" and save your organization from devolving into bureaucracy, which drives away top performers. Values give freedom to your top performers, clear "culture fit" criteria for your recruiters and hiring managers, and a framework for mentoring, coaching, and, when necessary, firing your bottom performers.

Your principles are your passion plus your values. Principle violations cannot be tolerated. They must be dealt with swiftly because, "If you see something below standard and do nothing, you've set a new standard."[24] They must also be dealt with appropriately. Most violations are opportunities for training, mentoring, or coaching. Some violations should result in inviting someone to pursue excellence elsewhere. Remember that "what you do is who you are."

All the elements of your culture need to be refined until they are simple, easily communicated, and memorable. They can't inspire shared identity unless your people can grasp them and hold onto them. "Simple isn't easy, but simple is worth it."

One key practice that supports your principles should be a *culture of review*. Reviews must be welcomed and common across the whole length, breadth, and depth of the organization. Reviews are vehicles for curiosity, empathy, and process improvement. Their outcomes are lessons learned and initiative rewarded, never blame. Participating in reviews needs to be normal, not "extra."

The rhythm of a successful culture, and a successful leader, is Slow—Fast—Slow, because extraordinary performance depends on extraordinary preparation and extraordinary recovery wrapping extraordinary effort. Slow feels unnatural, but Slow is the discipline that enables your organization to pounce on opportunity when it comes. The work of Slow is learning to recognize an "opportunity match" that aligns with your principles, plus refining your processes and MO so you're ready to move Fast when the moment comes. "Go slow to go fast."

Fast is nothing held back, aggressively overcoming obstacles, going above and beyond as a team to succeed—even against overwhelming odds. It's about refusing to accept "business as usual" (if "business as usual" means failing to deliver) and embracing creative problem-solving to get the job done. And it's also about depending on the discipline and quality practices deliberately developed during Slow so you can react well and not be frozen by indecision or slowed by the unfamiliar when you need to move Fast.

After Fast, it's back to Slow to recover from the last extraordinary effort, solidify breakthroughs and insights to bring the organization up to its elevated new normal, and prepare for the next extraordinary effort. Post–Fast Slow entails three phases: Rest (away from work), Recover (easing back into it, but with loftier goals based on your accomplishment), and Review (look back at what you did and analyze it for lessons to apply going forward).

IMPLEMENTATION TOOLS

At the end of each section, we include tools to help you remember key takeaways and put them into practice.

Tool #1: Culture Grid

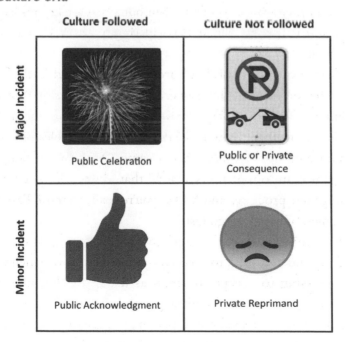

- Did someone follow the culture in a big way? Reward it. Talk about it. Turn it into a legend. Tell it and retell it so people know what happened, why it was awesome. Celebrate the person or team that made the right call and did the good work so everyone knows who they are and why they're being celebrated.
- Did someone violate the culture in a big way? Swiftly and dramatically correct the problem, heal the breach, and seize the opportunity to teach everyone why what happened was wrong and what should have happened instead. Do you need to name names? Maybe. Maybe not. Exercise your best judgment as to whether the *person* or merely the *situation* should be made an example of.
- Did someone violate the culture in a small way? Determine whether the situation calls for teaching, mentoring, or coaching. Assign the response to the violator's manager, mentor, or a peer with longer tenure. Keep it intimate. Nobody but those immediately connected to the situation needs to know what happened or who was involved, unless as an example you want to discuss what happened in general terms. Don't shame your people.
- Did someone follow the culture in a small way? Praise them. Give that positive feedback in front of their team. Give your managers freedom to issue token spot rewards at their discretion. Every time someone lives out your culture, take note and speak up. Never squander an opportunity to further the passion and reinforce the values. Publicly recognize individuals who do the right thing.

Tool #2: Problem Response Framework

Envision a problem that happened in your organization in the past week or month.

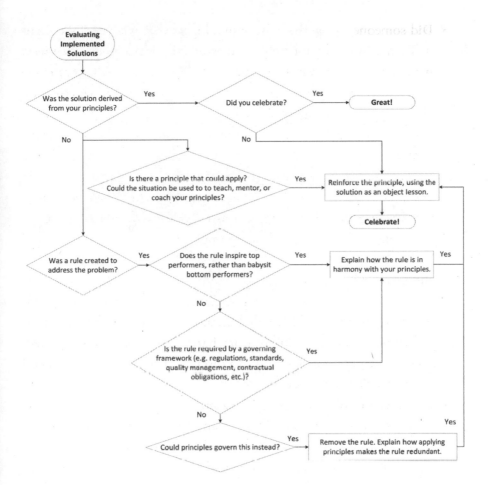

Tool #3: Slow Worksheet

Judge each day not by the harvest you reap, but by the seeds you plant.[25]

—*William Arthur Ward*

We recommend you do this exercise at least once each quarter. More often is better! This isn't time you're sacrificing, it's time you're investing. And your organization really will reap dividends. One of my CEO friends is fond of saying, "As the founder, some of the best work you'll ever do for your organization is in the shower." This pen-and-paper exercise probably isn't shower-compatible, but the point is to spend regular time alone, in silent thought.

The list of questions below is not a list to "get through." This is a list to dwell on. If you only work on two or three questions, that's okay. Schedule your next session and pick it up again.

1. Set a forty-five-minute timer.
2. Get a blank sheet of paper and answer the following:
   a. Looking Back
      - What's working?
      - What's not working?
      - Am I doing what only I can do?
        - What am I currently doing that someone could else do?
      - What has made me feel grateful?
        - What am I overlooking that I should feel grateful for?
        - Have I communicated my gratitude well? Have I left anyone "thankless"?
      - In what ways am I broken?
        - How do others experience my brokenness (closest colleagues, other staff)?
        - Have I hurt anyone because of this? If so, what should I do to make it right?
   b. Looking Ahead
      - What am I excited about?
      - What do I fear?
      - What do I dream of?
      - Given these sources of excitement, fear, and dreams, what needs to happen to set us up for success in the next quarter?

Tool #4: Cadence Visualization Tool

Your organization is on a river, and there is white water ahead. When you're on a calm stretch, you can choose not to prepare. You can choose to prepare ineffectively. After you've been through a rapid, you can choose not to rest, recover, review. It's up to you. But the next rapid is coming. What will you do?

Slow

Fast

Slow

NURTURE

Culture Takes Hold

Be Human

The section "Hatch" was about developing your principles. I invited you to explore who you are as a leader—your passion, your values—and apply those to forming a set of shared principles for your organization. Then, we talked about how to recognize opportunities that align with those principles, and getting yourself ready to pounce on those opportunities when they present themselves. In this next part, we're going to proactively nurture those principles into a shared identity.

Organizations are made of people, and people, including me, change slowly. No matter how much enthusiasm everyone feels for the principles, it takes time for them to take hold, fully applied in every aspect of the organization's life. But no matter what your principles are, they will take hold in your team when you nurture a human organization that is teachable and simple.

In this chapter, I'm going to urge you to Be Human. To care about your people *as people*. That person on the other end of your next Zoom call?

- Changed a diaper this morning
- Is grieving the loss of a parent
- Is wondering how they'll make rent this month
- Is terrified about drug use at their kid's junior high
- Has just landed an amateur gig at a local bar

That person is *human*. Why do we think we need to check our humanness at the conference room door? Are we even capable of that? I don't think so.

Organizations are made up of people: real human beings with dreams, goals, hopes, agendas, personal lives. Showing up to work doesn't change that.

It's all too common that "professionalism" leads us to treat others—and even think of ourselves—as functions, roles, steps in a process, cogs in the machine. As high-functioning, low-functioning, or malfunctioning assets, rather than as people. It's based on the idea that treating people like machines leads to better business outcomes. But "work life" isn't separable from "real life," no matter how hard we pretend otherwise. It's not OK to dehumanize people, by accident or on purpose, for the sake of productivity and profit metrics.

You work with real people. Take your principles from the first section and percolate them throughout your team. "People, meet the principles." Give your people time, and empathy, and love, and forgiveness when they screw up. Be human with them and allow them to be human with you. And watch as the principles move from words on a website to words in a story. A story about us.

Stories are what happens when your principles are wrapped in humanity. Stories are the harvest of principles practiced well. As culture grows, stories become legends. *Because people like us do things like this, we accomplish stuff like that.*

We survived the industry downturn. We said "no" to that client—and that led to this other opportunity. We won that bid that nobody thought we'd win. We pioneered that breakthrough, bringing a medical lab's worth of electronics into one coin-sized medical implant. We saved that supplier from closing shop. We sent that guy to go be with his family when his grandma was dying, even though the deadline was looming and we needed him. We pulled that team off that project and cross-trained them for this one over two days . . . and they nailed it! We hired someone we shouldn't have, the mistake was ours, and so we let him stay on for thirty days while he looked for his next job. We fired someone who needed to go, which created an opening, which is how we found her, and she's a total MVP. We've worked with that vendor for years, so it was only fitting that we attend his wife's funeral.

I didn't invent those examples—just changed the details a little. They're all stories that Tim and I, and other leaders at Velentium, have lived.

Being human together gives life to the principles through story. Then legend. Legends inspire ownership of the principles. Legend-level owner-ship of your principles, told by your team, will energize your group to dom-inate challenges. All because you, the leader, made a point of being human with your people, and gave them the permission and the challenge to be human with others, too.

Let's look at ten methods for being more human.

10 WAYS TO BE HUMAN

1. Be Open with Your Interests

When you are open with other people about the stuff you're interested in outside of work, it gives them a handle on your humanness. Sometimes it's hard for people to see you as anything other than the leader. Letting that misperception persist breeds the "we are assets" mentality.

My mom invested twenty-five years as a junior high math teacher. I remember once, when I was about high school age, being in the grocery store with my mom when we ran into one of her seventh-grade students there. My mom said hi to the kid. I remember seeing this strange look on the kid's face as he looked at me. Finally, he couldn't hold it in any longer.

"You're Mrs. Purvis's *kid*!???"

His tone spoke shock, horror, and disdain. He clearly couldn't cope with trying to imagine what it would be like to be raised by his math teacher. He couldn't picture his teacher as someone's mom. To him, she was merely the person that taught seventh-grade math. It reminds me of that *Calvin and Hobbes* strip where something similar happens to Calvin, and he confesses to thinking that teachers slept in coffins all summer.

As the leader, you have the same perception challenge. People will nat-urally only see you as the leader. Help people see you as human. Talk about what you're interested in. If that's your family, talk about your family. If that's sports, talk about sports. If that's your yard, talk about your yard.

Model openness about things outside of work. You'll become more human to them. You'll give your team ways to relate to you on a level other than as their boss. And in those conversations, there will come moments of connection that spark sheer delight. When people share interests, they end up talking freely. Not guarded. Not with invisible restraints holding them back. Suddenly that interaction isn't hard or forced or artificial. It's free and easy as you both reminisce on the model rocket that your kids built and shot off, that amazing dish that you had at that hole-in-the-wall restaurant nobody knows about yet, or the charity race you both ran, striving to achieve a new personal best.

As you open up about your interests and genuinely enjoy those connections, without trying to, you're modeling opening up and sharing interests throughout your team. You're proving that it's OK for people to bring their whole selves to work, that they don't have to pretend to only care about work stuff while they're working. You'll see that people with shared interests start to get to know each other better, start to enjoy being with each other on a whole new level, just like you do. There'll be more connection, more cohesion, more humanness throughout the organization.

2. Be Vulnerable About Your Situation

So much of how we feel, act, behave, react, and move has to do with the circumstances in our life. Circumstances happen at work; they also happen outside of work. And the ones outside of work impact us as much or more. Compartmentalizing these circumstantial pressures doesn't help. When we try to suppress that stuff long term, residual emotions tend to ooze out and filter unhelpfully into everything else.

So, learn to be vulnerable about your situation. You have to be careful here. You are still the leader. Not all of those circumstances are wisely shared with just anyone. But there are tons and tons of life experiences, situations, moments that you are going through that are familiar to your staff. Do you have a parent struggling with cancer? Chances are someone else at work has had that, too. They may even be going through it right now. But you won't connect with that person if you don't even know about it. And they are not going to open up about having had that experience unless they know that that experience is relevant to yours.

It's up to you to model vulnerability in your organization. You want an organization where someone comes to work ecstatic about the fact that their daughter won the spelling bee. You want people eager to come to work because it's a place where they can cope with the fact that they've just lost a loved one. You want people coming to work knowing that, in this organization, if they run out of gas or get into an accident at two in the morning, they have people who would come to their aid. Being vulnerable about your situation moves you from "leader" to fellow human. As humans, we are all equal.

This is a carefully navigated step. When you are vulnerable, it changes relationships. So make sure that you're sharing at an appropriate level for your position and the person that you're talking with. In my experience, most people don't struggle with over-sharing. Most of us struggle with having enough vulnerability to share at all.

Be willing to be vulnerable and show your weakness. It will make you the best possible leader. Through your willingness to humbly, accurately share where you're at, you inspire humble, authentic sharing throughout your organization and remind everyone that we're all human.

Early in my career at Velentium, I broke my leg. This was one of those crazy moments where, because I had broken my other leg five years earlier, I knew immediately what had happened. I was playing Wiffle ball in the front yard over a holiday weekend with a buddy and all of our kids. We had built a Slip 'N Slide in the yard earlier with some trash bags and hoses and soap. It made for a pretty muddy lawn. Hence when dodging a Wiffle ball, my leg stayed in one place, sunk in the mud, while the rest of my body twisted out of the ball's path. That led to seven screws and a plate in my right ankle. *Right* ankle. That part of your body that operates the accelerator or the brake when you drive. Suddenly, I was barely mobile. For the next eight weeks, I needed help from other people.

This kind of vulnerability is obvious. It's plastered right onto your appendage, a banner to everyone that you are not whole. And it opened up all kinds of relationships. Friendly employees smiling and opening or holding a door. Somebody bringing me a meal. For those eight weeks, my vulnerability drew me closer to others. But it shouldn't take a cast, a plate, a surgery, and some screws to make that happen. We can do it proactively, by sharing where we're struggling and being honest about what's really going on.

3. Be Alert for Empathy Opportunities

When you're listening carefully, you'll hear hints of humanity peppered throughout every conversation. Don't let those slip. When opportunities to dive in present themselves, seize that moment. Suppose you're in a meeting, and someone apologizes for the ringtone interruption because they got a call from their daughter. Carry on with the meeting, but make a mental note to ask them about their daughter. Make sure everything was okay. And just let the conversation happen naturally from there.

You'll find that in these moments of noticing and encouraging someone's humanity, you take people by surprise. They're not used to being invited past that barrier of "professionalism." By initiating a conversation, you've started to train them and your organization that being human is not only permissible, it is encouraged. Ask people about their lives:

- What do you like to do outside of work?
- How was your weekend?
- What's the next big thing you're looking forward to outside of work?

And as you get into these conversations, watch that person's face. In their expressions are the clues to deep pride, subtle fear, unbelievable excitement, sheer joy. Then speak to those emotions.

- "I can tell you're really proud of her. What did that feel like when she won the spelling bee?"
- "I could see how tough that would be. How are you and your spouse handling that?"

Deep, penetrating questions. They don't have to be terribly wordy. Simple is better. But they do have to be insightful, empathetic, and appropriate to the situation. After you ask, shut up. Lean into the silence. You have to be willing to handle silence because most people in the workforce are going to be so shocked that you crossed the "asset barrier" into humanity that they need an extra moment to process. *Did he really just ask me about my personal life?* Then you'll see their countenance change as they begin to consider if and how to respond.

Switch off your inner time-tracker. Once you've initiated this conversation, be ready to spend a few minutes and maybe more than a few minutes. You can't invite connection, then cut someone off right after they open up. Empathy takes time. Listen. Rejoice. Grieve. Try to experience emotionally what they're experiencing. Let them know with your posture, your attitude, your facial expression, and your words that they are not in those good or bad circumstances alone. And in so doing, you nurture a whole new depth of empathy in your organization.

4. Act on Situational Awareness

Some situations in life are more human than others. They are often personal to just one employee. In those moments when you hear about those things—they could be extremely joyous events or extremely traumatic events—step in. One of your employees has a new baby? Send a board book and a card and take the time to write something meaningful and specific in that card.

One time we sent an employee on a customer site for two weeks, and it turned out we needed him on a second project at a different customer site for another two weeks, right after the first concluded. That would've meant a month away from his family. That's no good! So we paid for his family to join him over those two weeks. It happened to be summertime, school was out, a great time to take a vacation, and the customer was located in a great city to visit. Our staffer was stuck working while his family enjoyed a vacation, but they had a good time on their own during the day and they all enjoyed evenings together as a family.

From time to time, we've brought a new hire to Houston to work a project or for extended training. Not everyone wants to live out of a hotel for weeks on end, and we happened to know that one of our local staff had turned the second story of their suburban single-family home into an

Airbnb, ten minutes away from the office. When visiting staff asked to stay somewhere that felt more homelike than a hotel, we arranged to rent out the Airbnb. The visitors got a host who could orient them to the area and the office, carpool if needed, and provide a better living environment. And we got to support our staff member's side hustle. We've enjoyed supporting other staff's side hustles as well, helping spread the word about music albums and concerts, custom shop builds for everything from furniture to vehicle mods, film releases, and world-class art. I love looking for ways to connect Velentium with our staff's passion projects outside of work.

Hard things happen in your staff's lives as well. We had an employee involved in a motorcycle accident on the interstate. He's single, so we sent him a DoorDash card and made sure he had a way to eat while he was recuperating. I'm thrilled to report that he didn't starve to death and recovered to full health! Another employee relocated across the country. The moving company's tractor trailer went off-road at highway speeds and tumbled down an embankment, turning the cargo trailer into a possession-crushing machine that destroyed almost everything he and his wife owned. We sent them Pottery Barn gift cards. Of course, we can't do that kind of thing for everyone, or even every time. But these were extraordinary moments of adversity that nobody would willingly choose, and at those moments, we had the means. Whenever we can, we do for one what we would love to do for all.

Be on the lookout for moments that are uniquely human—joyful or painful. Act to support them. Make people feel seen and cared for in the midst of those moments, and they'll do likewise for one another.

5. Stand Strong

Opposition proves our humanness. When you see culture violations, it's time to speak up. You've defined who you are. We talked about that in the previous section, "Hatch." Now, defend that identity with strong boundaries.

I can't tell you how hard this is, and I don't need to: You already know. We've all experienced the shame from walking away from a moment where we knew we should have intervened, should have spoken up, and we just didn't. Why didn't we? Because speaking into someone's life with a leader's critical tone, demanding accountability, hurts you. It hurts! It hurts like disciplining your kid hurts. But your organization will thrive for it. You owe it to the organization, you owe it to your top performers, and you owe it to yourself: *do not tolerate* violations in culture.

It doesn't mean that you go around pummeling people. You don't have to be mean, nor should you be, but you do have to be firm.

We had a situation where a new hire was talking about his experience getting his new driver's license here in Houston. If you've ever seen *Zootopia*—well, it's basically that, except with a three-hour wait before you even get to the desk. It is awful. Unsurprisingly, the story being told in the break room was filled with expletives.

I forced myself to interrupt the story. "Hey—we don't talk like that here. Ever. Even when there are no clients present. Humble Charisma applies just as much to who we are with each other as it does to who we are with clients and vendors."

I didn't like having to say that, having to deal with a violation immediately and publicly. But it sent a message that we're serious about our values. I can't tell you how many times when I've drawn a boundary with a staff person, made a statement that *we're not going to do it this way, because this company is going to be different*, where I've gotten knowing looks or a comment later saying, "Thank you for doing that; I really appreciate it. You don't see that in business often, and it's really great to know that our company truly is going to be different."

How is your organization different? How will your culture make you stand apart from the rest? I don't know! You're the one that worked through the exercises in the "Hatch" section and figured it out. Now, it's up to you to defend it. If somebody steps over a boundary that you've clearly defined, hold the line. Let that person know that they crossed it, and that's not okay. And when you do that, consistently, you give your staff permission to uphold that boundary on their own initiative, without needing to escalate, without needing special permission.

We're not perfect. We're going to overstep those bounds from time to time. I do it, too. I'm human. And when that happens, I have to receive that correction gracefully and model how this company responds to negative feedback. We want the best for ourselves, and getting the best requires opposing one another for the sake of culture, as well as accepting opposition in the name of culture and in the name of being human together.

6. Address Your Insecurities

I used to work at a company that had many regional divisions. Its headquarters were located in an area of the country that was not growing as rapidly as the division I was running in Houston. It caused some friction with management around raises. At headquarters, they didn't need to give raises very aggressively because the economy wasn't growing as strongly in that region. In Houston, things were booming, and my budget didn't allow me to keep pace with my competition. We had the ability to hire new graduates right out of college and advance them very quickly with our training and the experience they gained. It became a mantra around my division that three years here was equal to a decade in the industry. And we knew it was true because it was common for people after they'd been with our company, just three years out of school, to get offers for ten-year positions. It happened again and again and again. As a positive by-product, I got pretty good at university recruiting. But something else happened, too: I became very insecure that my people were going to leave the company. And that was something I had to work through. You can't lead from a position of insecurity. It doesn't work. It hurts you. It hurts your organization. It puts up emotional barriers between you and your team and turns fears into self-fulfilling prophecies.

So, what are you insecure about? Address that issue. Work with professionals. I am a huge fan of therapists. My family and I use them regularly. Therapy is great. We go to professionals to get our car's oil changed every few thousand miles, get the brakes checked out and the engine tuned up, but we won't take time to work on our emotions, our stress, our childhood issues? That's just silly. Work through things. Find someone you trust and get the job done. Because as you work through insecurities and become more secure in yourself, you become a better leader.

I'm very open about going to therapy. I want everyone in my organization to be aware that I do, and that I value and recommend it highly. We made sure that it was covered under our benefits package because I want my people to be able to take advantage of it. My openness about therapy has led at least one of the executives on our team to go get help themselves. That's vulnerability. That's humanness. That's a gateway to personal growth. And the organization benefits from that growth.

7. Highlight Human Moments

When work gets really tough, that's the time to proactively lean even further into humanness. When we were in the throes of Project V, working sixteen-hour days, seven days a week, it was important to remember that we were all human. There were family members making things possible by taking care of the home front while we worked. I spent ten days in Washington with Ventec. Then I came home for ten days. And then I was gone for three weeks in Kokomo.

Plenty of occupations require frequent travel like that. When you're home, how do you make it all come together? For me, it involved midnight basketball and runs to Whataburger with my high school boys. We would play basketball and eat burgers till one in the morning, then they would sleep until 10 AM. I would get up at six and get back to work. But those basketball games were sweet. They were worth less sleep. They let us connect during a time that was very, very hectic. They were necessary.

One of the things that we instituted in the midst of all of the chaos at work was—at the beginning of every meeting, we'd start with what I dubbed a "human moment." We'd go around the room and each person would tell a quick story about something that had happened since yesterday that proves we're human, not just a cog in a ventilator test system creation machine.

It could be that time where you lost your temper. I told several of those stories. It happened most when I was trying to get through to suppliers who refused to accept the urgency and importance of what we were doing. It could be that thing a family member did for you that touched your heart. I told a few of those stories, too! Really, it could be anything. Just something that's not a status report or work-related. It could be a moment from work, but it has to be interaction-based, human-based. It's remembering a moment with another person that wasn't transactional.

Those human moments kept us going. If you're up against some incredible challenge, deadline, or feat of accomplishment—I encourage you to proactively lead your team with human moments. That might mean 456 times a day if you're in lots of different meetings. It may be with the same people more than once in some of those meetings. Do it anyway. Connect as humans first. Then go change the world with your efforts.

8. Remember Names and Basic Facts

I really struggle with this one. What are the names of all of the people around you?

Velentium has experienced some very rapid growth. I was in a conference room recently, and I could see through the glass wall to the entry door. We don't have a front desk, so visitors have to come into the secure lobby and ring a bell to have someone come and get them. I saw someone enter the lobby and figured that I needed to go let them in. But before I could get up, to my surprise, the person reached for their wallet, pulled out a key card, tapped it, and let themselves in. I thought to myself, *Oh wow, that person works for me.* I was a little bit ashamed that I didn't know that person—didn't recognize them and couldn't even guess their name. That's new to me. But it's going to happen more and more often if we continue to grow rapidly, and I get that. We've more than doubled our full-time staff in the past twelve months.

I was truly alarmed, though, when over the next fifteen minutes the same thing happened twice more. Clearly, I have got some challenges ahead of me to get to know the people on our staff.

There is power in knowing someone's name. There is power in being able to look someone in the eye and say, "Hi, Raul. Hi, Sonya." Knowing someone's name matters. But don't stop at that. Ask about their families, their interests. Get to know them as people. Can you do it with everyone? Over time, if your organization gets big, no, probably not. Even then, can you still do it with some? Absolutely! And encourage them to do the same for others.

We have an opportunity each month for me to get to know someone at our company a little bit better. Our internal monthly newsletter includes a "Meet a Velentonian" segment, which I've deliberately chosen to be responsible for. I have an interview template on my computer, and I call a different staff member every month to ask them:

- "Tell me about your early years—school and hobbies. When was the first time in your life when you discovered your passion for building things?" I ask that one because we are an engineering company—we build things. If their role requires a different type of activity, I ask when they identified a passion for that activity.
- "Tell me about your significant relationships. How did you meet?"
- "What is a dream vacation?"
- "What do you like to do outside of work?"
- "How did you find out about us?"
- "What do you like most about this organization?"
- "What would you like to change about this organization?"

There are plenty of times during these interviews that we go "off the record." Where I stop typing, so they know I'm not taking notes anymore, and we're just talking, human to human. Those moments can get very emotional. I've heard employees talk about being abused as children. I've had employees talk about the fear of attempting to have a baby or potentially losing a baby through miscarriage. I've had people tell me stories of family strife that they were in the middle of right then.

Why do they tell me these things? I believe it stems from empathy, safety, and a desire to listen—then proactively creating the space and time to slow down and ask supportive questions. I try to be conscious of my body language, my words, and my facial expressions to show them that I care about whatever they're about to say. Engage, and you'll quickly move beyond knowing names and into getting to know people for who they are.

Now—how do you remember all of that? I used to resist relying on a "system" for remembering things. It felt artificial to me. But I've learned that with the amount of people in my life, it's important to take notes. To file those notes somewhere accessible. To study them periodically. To learn about what you've learned about, so that you can recall it the next time.

One of my favorite TV shows is *The West Wing*. It's common in that show to see President Jed Bartlet being briefed by someone walking with him down the hall until he's right around the corner from his next meeting, telling him all the details he needs to know so he can be personable with whoever he's about to meet. Do that for yourself with your notes. If you have an executive assistant, let him help. Get to know your people, learn about them, and connect with them through those details each time you interact. You'll be glad you did.

9. Consider the Human Angle

I've learned that, as the leader, my words have much more gravity around my company than most other peoples', even when I don't intend them to. For example, I have to be really careful not to accidentally end a discussion when my intention was simply to contribute an opinion. People easily misinterpret my ideas and suggestions as wishes and commands. So, if it comes out of my mouth, I'd better be sure that it's what I really mean.

My staff is second to none. I love them. I'm so proud of them. I'm amazed by their capabilities. So, when I find out something around the company that doesn't fit, doesn't seem to match that quality I know they usually exhibit, it confuses me and often makes me mad. *How could we have treated somebody like that? How could this be happening?* Chances are, I need to slow down and get more facts. Because if I jump to conclusions and respond in frustration, I will add to the problem so much more than if I understand it fully. I've learned how critical it is to never speak out of raw emotion. Once I understand a situation fully and have taken time to calm down, I can make a decision about how best to respond in a measured, calm, and, if necessary, firm manner. But then, I also have to ask the question: *Who is the best person to respond to this situation?*

Increasingly, the answer is not me. The answer is most often the supervisor closest to the situation. That's rarely me. If I circumvent the management chain, no matter how well I handle it, I've undermined other leaders and escalated the issue all the way to the top. Gone is any chance of addressing this casually. That more than likely means that if I step in, I'm going to cause as many problems as I solve.

When things are going wrong in your organization, take a deep breath, stay calm, stay measured, and make sure the right person is the one responding.

If something is going on that doesn't seem right, and you know the heart of the person that's doing this allegedly offensive or annoying or frustrating thing, dive deeper. Look for the underlying facts. There's usually something going on that you don't know about. We were having all kinds of productivity problems with one of our staff and we couldn't figure out what was going on, until someone overheard a conversation with him talking to his divorce attorney. Suddenly everything made sense. This individual's world was being turned upside down. Of course he couldn't perform to his top potential, because his attention was severely disrupted by dealing with a grueling, heart-wrenching personal situation. And what are we going to say in response to that situation? "Sounds like a personal problem"? "Deal with that on your own time"? Of course not. We're going to respond with empathy and support and recalibrate our productivity expectations for a time, because that is a tough, tough life situation.

Understand where your people are, and respond appropriately. That doesn't mean you accommodate everyone equally. Twenty-five years ago, I saw an interview with NFL coach and analyst Herm Edwards where he said something like (I'm paraphrasing from memory),

> Everything is fair, but not everything is equal. If you're on my practice squad and you show up late for my team meeting, you might very well find your bags packed and waiting for you on the curb by the time you arrive. On the other hand, if you're Peyton Manning and you show up late, I might stop the whole meeting to welcome him. "So glad you made it, sorry you're late—what happened, buddy?"

Edwards's point was that, as the leader, your level of understanding and accommodation for someone who is pivotal to the organization and has a long history with the organization is going to be much greater than it will be for someone who is new and less critical to the organization. And that's as it should be. There should be different levels of consequence, patience, and reward for different people within the organization, based on their level of contribution over time. But remember that everyone is human. Everyone. So, regardless of the consequences that you feel necessary to mete out when something goes awry, do it with dignity and respect. Respect humanity for humanity's sake. Treat everyone as human.

10. No Triangling

If Iggy does something that upsets Rey, Rey needs to talk it out with Iggy directly. But if Rey chooses to vent to Therese instead, and then Therese talks to Iggy, now you've got a triangle, you've got drama. The best way to keep this from happening is to refuse to be a third in the triangle. Instead of taking sides, Therese should send Rey right back to Iggy.

People try to triangle through a leader or supervisor because they're hoping to turn you into the big stick that goes and beats an apology or submission out of the other party in a perceived conflict. Don't be the stick! Most of the time, the conflict isn't even really a conflict. It's usually just a lack of communication. And your people need to communicate consistently, proactively, on their own, without recruiting others to a "cause." They need to drop that kind of competitive thinking and talk things out.

It happened again recently. One of my executives was upset about the actions of another department. I said, "Stop, I don't wanna hear about it. Go and talk to them." Turned out that it was a misunderstanding and everybody worked it out very quickly. But they wouldn't have if I had taken it upon myself to get involved on my executive's behalf, acting as a go-between from one executive to another and down into the other executive's department.

HUMANS AT WORK

Most of what's in this book are things you can do. Actions you can take to establish and reinforce your culture. This chapter describes someone you have to choose to be. It's a lifestyle, a way of being with your colleagues that brings ease and life to your business. You're not going to look back and raise a glass to signing off on that document. But when the project manager brings in a custom iced cake to celebrate the project close, you remember that! It's the human moments in the day-to-day life of your organization that gives energy to your passion, life to your values, and meaning to your daily effort. As much as we may feel fulfilled by a particular kind of work in the abstract, it's the connections with our colleagues that make any set of tasks worth doing, any milestone worth celebrating. Be human together.

Stay Teachable

If we're teachable, there's always hope."

Earlier in my career, we often recruited at universities. We were always looking for an edge, a way to attract the attention of students. One way that we did it was by plastering a flyer all over the engineering buildings. In big, bold letters, the top of that flyer read:

You Don't Know What You Need to Know to Work Here.

Then, in smaller letters right below, it said:

(Don't worry, none of us do.)

The flyer went on to talk about working on a team excited by continuous learning. A place where you are always a little bit overwhelmed. A place where you have to be teachable. A place where you can enjoy being stretched.

That flyer attracted a certain kind of person. Students who enjoyed delving into the unknown. Who wanted to find it, describe it, order it, and turn it into something interesting and useful. Those were exactly the people that we wanted on our team.

How about your team? Are they thrilled by learning? Are they excited to press into the unknown? And, most importantly, are you prepared to honor their mistakes when they do?

There are plenty of resources out there that explain why punishing mistakes is bad, while celebrating the right kind of mistakes is good. Organizations that are intolerant of mistakes stagnate. That's the best-case scenario. If your people learn they will be punished for making mistakes, they don't make fewer mistakes—they make more. And report them less often. They become secretive, fearful of collaborating, competitive with colleagues. Projects take longer and get released with more problems. And it's not their fault. It's the natural consequence of a mistake-intolerant culture.

My favorite illustration of this is actually a business parable from Cornell University's John Cleese. Cleese tells the tale of Gordon the Guided Missile, who, once launched, frequently finds that he has drifted off course. Yet, by signaling back to his controllers—aka admitting his mistake—Gordon obtains the crucial insight needed to correct his course, and ultimately hits his target. The parable concludes with a question: Should Gordon be criticized because he made so many mistakes? Or should he be celebrated for using those mistakes to avoid the one mistake that would have really mattered—missing the target?

In industries that are closely regulated like ours, mistakes and false starts are expected, especially during R&D. Quality controls are designed to manage them, limit them, and ensure their lessons get applied. Our Chief Quality Officer repeats this mnemonic: *fail-find-fix-fast.*

Mistakes in your organization are a sign of people stretching to their limits. Repeated mistakes in the same area are no longer mistakes; they are learning problems. Learn to discern between the two before you react, because how you react to missteps speaks volumes to your team about teachability. If you train your team to applaud people who swing for the fences, despite occasionally striking out, overall you'll score more runs.

In a teachable workplace there is an ease, a freedom, an intensity of striving, an outpour of positive energy. And this energy is collective, not individual. Teachable teams are eager to share their knowledge and learn from others. Teachability is what gives talent the freedom to stretch and strive to make things better.

Teachability flows from one source only: humility.

PROACTIVE HUMILITY

When we set the values at Velentium, we started by brainstorming all of the different traits that we really admired in other people. It took real effort to simmer that down into the three values that we have. We described the full process in "Hatch." We got down to twelve values, and that was not simple enough. Nobody was going to be able to keep twelve values in mind. The way we combined many of those values into one was the phrase *Humble Charisma*. Those two words really don't seem to go together.

When you hear the word *humble*, what do you think? You might think poor. You might think stricken. You might think oppressed. These connotations for *humble* involve lowliness of circumstance. Humble surroundings. Humble beginnings. But there is a second kind of humble. A self-imposed humble. When humility is self-imposed, it indicates high discipline. A willingness to self-regulate. A willingness to embrace silence. A willingness to reject coercion as a tactic and accept limitation. Not because that limitation has been thrust upon us, but because we chose it.

Why in the world would we choose humility?

I'm not sure you would if you were alone. But you're not alone. We're on this big spinning ball together. More to the point, you're in a group, an organization, a company, a team with other people. A community.

The presence of community implies opportunity. There's some reason why you've all come together. A community that lacks humility is a collection of individuals each competing to seize all of the opportunity. They see each other as obstacles to be worked around or tools to be manipulated. A community that embraces humility is a community able to come together and achieve the best outcomes with the lowest friction and least conflict. There is deep connection, value, enjoyment, and productivity when a community proactively embraces humility.

Let's dive into five aspects of proactive humility. My claim is that if you'll lead your own life and your team's life into humility, you will find that your entire organization realizes steep declines in destructive conflict and big gains in satisfaction. Will you be more productive? I think you probably will.

I think you'll especially benefit during Fast, when pressure is up, intensity is high, and interpersonal conflict is most likely to sabotage your shot at success. But even if you're not able to quantify the outcome, you'll have a lot more fun and be more effective working together when your egos are restrained.

1. Always Learning (Never Done)

If someone drops an acronym in my presence, and I don't know what it means, I'm going to interrupt them to ask. Recently I was in a high-powered conference room on the thirty-third floor with a dozen people in it, and I paused the meeting. "Hang on. Real quick, can you tell me what that stands for?"

The other person looked at me in astonishment. "Are you serious?"

I was! And I know from long experience that about 20 percent of the time, the person dropping the acronym doesn't know what it stands for either. Plus, I'm pretty sure that every time I ask, there's at least one other person in the room who doesn't know what that acronym means either. So, I'm not only helping myself, I'm helping that other guy in the room that wasn't willing to speak up.

Early in my career, someone told me that if you read a book every two weeks during your entire career, you will eventually be the world leader in your field, because your competitors likely aren't reading enough. So, my number-one tip for becoming an always-learner? Read! A lot!

Also early in my career, someone told me that I needed a mentor. Reading books was one thing, but I found the idea of recruiting a mentor to be very daunting. Not just intimidating, but off-putting. Getting through college with good grades had given me just enough hubris to feel like I could probably figure stuff out on my own. But careers and life are less about figuring things out and more about relationships, community, and making a difference together. When you pursue a mentor, you are, by definition, looking for someone who has gone before you. They've walked the path that you are about to walk. They know things and people that you don't. But I was young and immature and I fought the concept. For the first ten years of my career, I didn't act on it as others told me I should.

Finally, at a friend's urging, I arranged to meet a guy named Larry at a Starbucks. I went in with a PowerPoint presentation that presented my life, my goals, and my agenda for the future. I went on for almost an hour while he sat there and listened and a smile began to grow across his face. When I finally came up for air and gave him a chance to speak, he leaned back, folded his arms, smiled, and said, "You make me tired!"

I went into that meeting with an agenda for life. I hope you have an agenda, too. But if you feel like you have it all figured out and you haven't pursued someone who has gone before you, I can promise you that your agenda has some holes in it. If you think, as I did, that you'll be able to figure it all out, it's proof that you won't. People who truly have life figured out know enough to know that they don't have it figured out.

That first coffee started a relationship that continues to this day. Larry has been my mentor since 2005. I'm not saying this is what will happen to you, but that relationship turned into a lifelong friendship. Not only has Larry passed on to me many critically valuable lessons, he also became my first lead investor. I realize now how fortunate I was to connect with a great mentor on the first try. Typically, it takes more persistence, more trial and error to find a good match, and more self-discipline than I had back then to humble myself enough to go ask for help and let another person speak into my agenda, my goals, and my plans. But it's worth it.

2. Admit Mistakes (Never Perfect)

Can you laugh at yourself? Can those you love and those you work with laugh at you? It's a sign of true centeredness and confidence to be genuinely self-deprecating.

I like to say that I've got a gift for golf. Maybe not a rare gift, but a gift nonetheless. Here's how it works: We can go golfing, and without trying to, I will make you feel great about your golf game! I am literally that bad. When people ask if I like to play golf, I say I like to go out on a golf course with clubs and whack the ball around . . . not sure it counts as *playing*. But I have fun. Somehow, I find a way to screw up a round differently every time. But I love to compete, I love the game, and I don't mind laughing at myself. In certain situations, you can either laugh or cry, and laughing is more fun.

I had a situation several years back where I went charging up the stairs at home because I was furious with one of my older boys and I let fly some choice words that were beyond the standard of our family. My daughter was quick, in the midst of that enraged moment, to tell me it wasn't good to say those words. I got nose to nose with her and screamed, "Get out of my face!"

I could see my daughter wither right in front of me, but I went on to deal with the discipline situation at hand. What I didn't see was my youngest son go into my daughter's room, the place where she'd retreated from her dad's misdirected anger. He comforted his older sister, then proceeded to tell her how funny he thought it was that Dad had lost it. They started doing impressions of my distorted face, distorted words, and laughing like crazy at how ridiculous I had looked in that moment.

I finished the conversation with the older child, calmed myself down, and then regretfully, humbly, reluctantly began to enter her room. I opened the door expecting to find her buried in her pillow weeping, knowing that I would have to try to make things right for messing up like that. And what did I find? My two youngest children laughing like crazy, getting in each other's faces and mock-screaming at each other. Then they noticed me in the doorway, looked at each other, and started laughing all over again as they yelled in unison, "Get out of my face!"

I haven't lived that event down over the last half decade. From time to time, my kids will still get up in my face and yell, "Get out of my face!"

It made me really happy to know that kids are resilient. And to realize that I'm evidently the kind of dad whose kids feel perfectly safe making fun of in my lowest moments. And I felt perfectly at ease and relieved once I saw that they were laughing about it. I hope I won't ever lose it like that again. But I know that if it does happen, as long as I have the ability to laugh at myself, there is still hope.

Where have you screwed up? Chances are it has happened often and fairly recently. Always go to the person you offended and admit your fault. Tim and I have found that when we know we have let someone down, the best thing to do is set up a meeting and start that meeting with an acknowl-edgment, an apology, and a plan to make it right.

"I know we've let you down, and I want you to know that we're going to make it work. We have not wavered in our commitment; we've just wavered in our performance. Know that we have your back. Know that we will make this right."

A few years ago, we agreed to take on a project that included creating a mobile app. We'd never built a mobile app before. We radically underes-timated what it would take. We overran our budget by almost $1 million. But the project scope hadn't changed, it wasn't the client's fault, and we promise, *If we touch it, it will work.* So we sucked it up, ate that cost, and ultimately, delivered. We learned. And we kept that client, to the tune of another $6 million in lifetime business to date—because we admitted our mistake, yet refused to let the client down because of it.

It's not in the times when everything is going well that you get to show your true colors. It's when things are going wrong that who you are is revealed. Who you are as a person, and who you are as an organization. So the next time something goes wrong, be forthright and make it right. And if it's something you can laugh about, then laugh about it. I think you'll find that the marketplace is very responsive to someone who owns what they've done wrong and goes the extra mile to make it right.

3. Take Joy in Others' Success (Never Bitter)

A decade or so ago, I used to attend an industry conference in Austin every August. It was *hot.* But 104°F days were not what was most uncomfortable for me. This particular conference celebrated all the great stories from the past year in the industry. As the stories were told, I would get more and more uneasy. I felt like everyone else was accomplishing amazing things while I was being left behind. I had a fledgling business I was trying to get off the ground. And here were these "peers" who were just dominating. How in the world would I ever have a place amongst these giants?

When you're struggling with insecurity, it's really hard to genuinely enjoy the success of others. Insecurity can keep you from delighting even in the victories won by your closest friends, people you love. It can fill you with bitter envy toward strangers. But as you become more whole, your ability to celebrate the success of others—even direct competitors—increases dramatically.

Similarly, I cannot tell you how many times I've wanted to emotionally burn a bridge. Go in with napalm and just torch everything. *I can't believe you would treat me like that! How could you pick that company over us??? You have got to be kidding me!*

When we're disappointed, a sense of inadequacy and loss prompts us to lash out like a wounded animal. Or try whatever manipulation we can think of to force the outcome we want from the situation. Intercept that reaction with humility. Verbalize responses like "It'll be our turn next time," or "I guess we've still got work to do before we're ready for that." Demonstrate restraint. Find reasons to be glad that the opportunity went to someone else. Whether you were or were not hoping that project or that recognition would come to you, practice celebrating when others succeed.

And every so often, you'll be the one who wins something. Velentium has received a lot of recognition and attention in the last few years, both because of Project V and because of what we've done before and since. We've been delighted to celebrate those awards, talk to those interviewers, and address those audiences. And each time we're called out, I think about all the times I've been one of the dozens or hundreds in the crowd wishing it were me and my organization in the spotlight. About the effort it took for me to be happy for the person onstage. And about how a person acts when the spotlight is on them that makes it easier or harder for the audience to be happy for them. Because next week, next year, next time, it'll be someone else onstage, some other organization receiving well-deserved recognition. And I'll be in the crowd again.

When you win, don't gloat. Don't be smug. Don't tell yourself you had it coming. Don't act like the recognition was inevitable. Receive it as a gift, an unexpected gift, that could have gone to many others, most of whom are probably equally deserving. And to the extent that you did earn it, recognize that it was earned by many people's contributions—not just your leadership, not just your team's efforts. Velentium's streak of recognition is largely thanks to our PR team, whom we contracted to help us tell the Project V story. We may have qualified for the awards through our work, developed the expertise, and lived the experiences that give us a story and a perspective and insight to share, but we'd be getting none of that interest without their guidance and connections.

Thank the people who made it happen. Elevate the people who served alongside of you to put you in the place you're in. Be humble: Share the win. Help others to delight in your success, just as you've learned to delight in theirs.

4. Take Your Time (Never Hustled)

I've found that if you're feeling pressured, honest businesspeople will almost always give you more time if you're open with them about it. "Look, I really want to come to a solution here, but I'm feeling rushed. Can we work out a schedule that gives me time to consider all of the different variables and come back to you with a solution that might be better for everyone?"

Usually, people assume one of two things when you're asking for time: Either you're stalling because you don't have the guts to make a decision. Or you're genuinely looking for what Jim Collins, author of *Good to Great* and *Great by Choice*, calls "the Genius of the And." That's the magical solution where everybody gets what they want. You *and* me.

When I was working on my MBA, we were assigned an exercise where you and your team negotiated against another team for an orange. Then you all came back to the class and reported what percentage of the orange both teams ended up with. But, if you took the time to listen and not rush it, you would figure out that the professor had tasked one team with getting as much of the orange peel as possible, while the other team was tasked with getting as much of the fruit as possible. We were only going to discover that "Genius of the And" solution if we took our time, listened carefully, and refused to be rushed. There was actually a way for both teams to get 100 percent of what they really wanted.

This is a difficult thing as most of us leaders are hard-charging, fast-moving people. We want to be seen as go-getters. We want to be seen as decisive. We don't like the optics of having to say, "I'm not sure right now; I need time to think about it." But that pressure to appear like the stereotypical "Type A" leader doesn't originate from the other person. It's phantom pressure created by our own egos and insecurities. When we give in to that pressure, we end up hustling ourselves into a bad decision.

When you realize you're feeling rushed, ask to table the conversation and circle back later. When you're calm, centered, and assured, you're communicating respect for the importance of the decision, as well as respect for everyone involved, yourself included. Nine times out of ten, that respect will be recognized and returned.

5. Put Relationships First (Never a Loner)

Pride pushes us away from other people, toward the trap of self-reliance. Proactive humility opens up options by prioritizing relationships. I've had to learn to recognize and reject these self-defeating behaviors and mindsets:

- Winning / Being Right
  - *Stop thinking*: Zero-sum game (my success equals your failure and vice versa).
  - *Start thinking*: There's a way that all of us can leave with something we want.
- Fast Results
  - *Stop thinking*: Enforce rapid changes to hit metrics.
  - *Start thinking*: Make long-term investments in people.
- Insecurity
  - *Stop thinking*: How does this situation affect me?
  - *Start thinking*: How does this situation affect my team? My client? My supplier?
- In Control
  - *Stop thinking*: I'm the best! Results come from me making all the calls.
  - *Start thinking*: We're the best! Results come from delegating all the calls to the right people.

THERE'S ALWAYS HOPE

The mantra at the top of this chapter is, *If we're teachable, there is always hope.* We repeat that mantra around Velentium because we've come to believe that there is nothing more important than being teachable. Teachability is the prerequisite of progress. If I screw up every aspect of my life, professional and personal, yet remain teachable, I can still make progress and eventually get to a better position in life. Teachability is the measure of your potential.

Teachability is closely linked with flexibility. In Project V, we laid out a particular way of executing the project in the first few days. But the more we learned and the more we tried, the more we found ways to tweak and optimize. Send parts here, switch those assembly areas so those two systems are being built side by side and can share access to that specialized tool more accurately, give that subcontractor or that team a greater share of the workload. We had daily kickoff meetings, team-wide meetings, and leader meetings regularly throughout each day. We constantly reviewed what was working and what wasn't. A teachable team was immediately willing to stop and reconfigure. Nobody held dear the current way of doing things.

A teachable organization is one that can pivot quickly. Whether intra-project or intra-company, teachable teams are willing to let go and move. Openness to teachability makes you more human as a leader and makes your organization more human to clients. We're all on a journey. We never "arrive." If we stay teachable, we grow. No matter what happens along the way.

Reach Simple

HARD AND SIMPLE

Julie and I started doing jigsaw puzzles together during the pandemic, which I still find funny. I've always thought that puzzles were for little kids and "old people." We middle-agers are much too busy for things like puzzles! We've got places to be! . . . Until we don't, thanks to lockdown. We bought ourselves a two-thousand-piece puzzle with a border that looks like a picture frame. Every edge piece looks exactly the same as every other edge piece. The only way to find a match is to compare shape after shape after shape until you find that magic fit.

Julie is patient. Julie is deep. She takes life as it comes and seeks to understand and work with it.

I am not patient. I am not deep. I want to fit life into the shape I want, quickly.

Our personalities show up when we're puzzling. I want the puzzle to happen fast. When I find a piece that almost fits, I try to make it fit. That approach simply doesn't work. It doesn't matter how much I want it to fit. If there's a little bit of daylight showing, if the tab must be forced into the blank, it does not fit.

When I really want something to work, I decide that it's "right enough." I'll pass a pair of pieces to Julie and ask, "Is this a fit?"

We both know the answer before I ask.

Puzzles are hard.

Puzzles are simple.

Hard and simple are two qualities that seem like they shouldn't coexist, but I find that they are often highly correlated.

Simple is when the two pieces fit together. *Click.* It just works. It's tight. It's secure. It matches. And you know it. If you have to ask, you aren't there yet.

But if I force the piece? Not only is it not right, it messes up the whole section around it. Plus, it messes up another section of the puzzle that needs that missing piece. Force one piece into the wrong position, and the whole puzzle becomes incompletable.

When we settle for less than simple, whether designing an engineering solution, implementing culture, or overthinking a puzzle piece, the outcome is unstable. Something about the resulting system, even when it succeeds, either can't be maintained or can't be sustained. And since we can't control or predict the timing, that instability dominoes into cascading consequences for other aspects of life as well.

Yet in so many spheres of activity, professional and personal, we settle for less than simple. We force puzzle pieces into places they don't fit, only because they were the first pieces we found that seemed "close enough." We defer the hard work of reaching simple. And we suffer the consequences later.

Take a few minutes and do a Simple Audit with me. We'll look at simplicity across seven areas, starting from the inside and working our way out. When we're through, I think you'll agree with me:

Simple isn't easy. But simple is worth it.

SIMPLE AUDIT

Simple Character

A friend of mine describes the difference between conviction-level beliefs and opinion-level beliefs like this: There are certain statements that if somebody put a gun to your head and ordered you to repeat, you'd do it. At gunpoint, if someone wanted me to declare that the earth is flat, I'd say, "You know, now that I think about it, those globe people are crazy. I agree with you! The world *is* flat!"

But there may be other gunpoint commands where, instead of going along with them, you'd respond with your best Clint Eastwood impression. *Go ahead. Make my day.*

Some things aren't worth dying for. But some are. Only you know what those are for you. What do you believe in so strongly, so passionately, that you'll pay any price to support? What would you stand up for, no matter how unpopular, no matter how powerful the opposition? What would inspire a "lay down in front of the bulldozer and refuse to budge" kind of stand?

The things you won't abandon, no matter what, are the things that define who you really are.

When I formed Velentium, I was sitting with my mentor, Larry, and his lawyer. Larry was about to become my first investor, and we were working through the contract for the initial investment. Larry's lawyer pointed at him and said, "I would take a verbal agreement from this man over a written agreement from ten others."

Right then, I knew that I wanted to have a reputation for the same kind of integrity down the road. Which means I have to tell the truth and keep promises, even when it's painful, shameful, or costly.

Character is both aspirational and descriptive. I'd like to *be* the aspirational me. But I can't become that person unless my current self-description is accurate. There's always a gap between how I act now and how I aspire to act, and I need to know the dimensions of that gap if I'm going to bridge it.

This isn't a self-help book about character formation. Plenty of those exist already. Nevertheless, I'd like to encourage you to think through the aspects of character applicable to organizational leadership. Kindness. Optimism. Honesty with others. Honesty with yourself. Fairness over favoritism. Work ethic. Self-awareness and social awareness. Patience. Risk tolerance. Emotional intelligence. Listening.

You know who you want to be. What character traits are on your list? Rank yourself in two columns. Column A, description; Column B, aspiration. Where are the gaps?

This exercise isn't about character flaws. It's about development. It's about gaining insight into where your personality is limiting your effectiveness. Many times, it's about developing your strengths into greater strengths. You can do this in one-on-one reviews with your staff, and ask your peers or mentor to do it with you.

"I love that you can do the work yourself. You're incredibly capable. From now on, I want you to never do the work yourself. If you find yourself rolling up your sleeves, grab someone else to sit alongside you and teach them how to do it while you're doing it."

"You're very quick to spot a solution. I need you to hold off before jumping in—take time to see the whole picture before you start driving forward."

"I love how passionate you are. If you would be more careful about your language, it would help your colleagues. You use superlatives a lot, and it would help everyone stay calm and positive if you would use calmer words to describe events."

Simple Priorities

What really matters to you?

I've often been afraid to admit what I really care about, even to myself. It's too uncomfortable. It means confronting the mismatch between what ought to matter to me and the way I actually live.

The quickest way to find out what your priorities really are is to review your credit card statements, your calendar, and every time you overreacted or underreacted emotionally, over the past ninety days. Whenever I do this, I always find that things that may or may not be my "true" priorities have become my lived priorities. I see things like:

- It's become more important to impress my clients and fellow leaders, or to avoid looking like the least-committed person on the team, than to spend time with my daughter.
- It's become more important to be seen as successful, always risking everything down to the final penny to keep everything going as fast as possible, than to be out of debt.

- It's become more important to keep moving and check every box as fast as possible than to make regular time to reflect, think, and lead strategically.

I don't know about you, but I want to be in control of my priorities. I want to dictate to my life what my priorities are, not have them dictated to me by my passivity or reactivity, by advertising, by peer pressure, or by subconscious emotional needs. I want to determine what my priorities should be, then proactively live them out.

I find that's only possible when my priorities are simple. Having simple priorities leaves my options open when life throws a curveball. When my priorities are simple and few, I've got the margin to add in or swap out a priority when needed.

The way I keep my priorities simple is by having long-term priorities and next-semester priorities. I find it's easiest to think in terms of one, two, five, and ten years, plus fall semester, spring semester, and summer. Early in our marriage, Julie and I tag-teamed our way through grad school, and sometime in the midst of that, we had four kids in grade school. Our life rhythms seem to follow the school calendar. So, three times a year, I set aside time to ask, "What do I want to have accomplished by the end of next semester? What do I want to be true throughout the semester?"

Semester priorities must be stepping stones on the path to my long-term priorities. But they also need to be realistic for my current circumstances. For example, I have a long-term goal of being physically fit. It's a longevity goal—as much about health as appearance. So I have a long-term priority called "Different by Fifty." The specifics of Different by Fifty change from semester to semester. If it's a semester where I can spend significant time outside in nice weather, my priority might be focused on running. During an indoor semester, I might focus instead on diet.

This flexibility applies to every priority. Another long-term priority is "Be an Effective Father." So, one of my short-term priorities for last semester was to coach my daughter's basketball team.

I find that I can only focus on three things at a time. As Jim Collins says in *Good to Great*, "If you have more than three priorities, you don't have any."[26] So I pick three for the coming semester and work at them. At the end of the semester, it's time to reevaluate and pick the next three.

If your short-term priorities flow from your long-term priorities, and your long-term priorities flow from what really matters to you, then your priorities will be simple. Getting to that point isn't easy. But it's worth it.

1. Sit down in a quiet place and create a list labeled "What Matters Most to Me." Write down all of the potential candidates for your top priorities. Some of the things should include the aspirational character traits you considered in the last section. Some of the names should include your family members and your most important relationships. You may also want to consider including key staff and stakeholders in your organization.

2. After you have your list, sit with it awhile. Let the entries marinate. Do they seem right? Do any feel like a puzzle piece out of place?

3. If an entry doesn't seem right, don't remove it yet. First, ask yourself, "Why did this make the list?" Are you living with a priority placed on you by someone else? Your parents, your spouse, your community? Does it fail to resonate with your core desires?

4. Create a second list and label it "Others' Expectations (Competing Priorities)." Relocate the entries that don't belong with your top priorities to this list.

5. Once you've purged your What Matters Most list of Others' Expectations, it's time again for the Kill-Keep-Combine exercise. Determine the whos and whats you most desire to prioritize. Group them. Prune the remainder. Keep your life and your decision-making simple by keeping your priorities simple.

Simple Fitness

For many of us, life these days is so cerebral it can be easy to forget that we're dependent on our bodies. The human body isn't a single organism, but a complex ecosystem of cells in symbiotic relationships that affect everything from the quality of our moods to the quality of our thinking to the

quality of our work. Each of us only gets one body. Yet self-care often falls
to the very bottom of our to-do list. Nutritional needs get placated with
junk because the junk is convenient and accessible. Restfulness needs get
crowded out by busy schedules, endless entertainment feeds, and too much
caffeine. Exercise needs go unfulfilled in favor of sleeping later, running
errands and doing chores, or staying longer at the office.

But the condition of my body determines my capacity to do everything
else I want to do. Without good food, good sleep, and good activity levels, we
do not think well, judge well, feel well, emote well, relate well, or lead well.

Calories in vs. calories out equals trend. Minutes of activity vs. minutes
of sedentary equals trend. Hours asleep vs. hours awake equals trend. Good
trends equal health. Health equals maximized capacity to achieve goals. Bad
trends equal accelerated aging and reduced capacity to achieve goals.

We all know this stuff. It's simple.

It ain't easy.

In fact, it can be really, really hard. Julie and I had four kids in five
years. At one point we had ages four, three, two, and a newborn. About the
time you got one kid down, the next kid needed to go down. By the time
we got that kid down, somebody else needed a drink. By the time you got
that drink, the first kid wet a diaper or the bed. And on and on it would
go. Finally, you collapse, exhausted, around eleven thirty. And then around
two o'clock one of those kids wakes up from a bad dream and climbs in bed
with you!

How do you get enough sleep when that's happening? How do you make
regular time to exercise? How do you get healthy meals and not just suc-
cumb to an endless stream of frozen dinners, fast food, and delivery?

Whatever the situation is, strategize with your spouse, partner, or
roommates. Figure it out!

- Am I exercising as much as I need?
- Am I sleeping as much as I need?
- Am I eating what I need?

Your organization needs you to be at your best, and that can only happen when you take care of your body.

Simple Relationships

Because the most important relationships in our lives are also the most real, they're the rawest and most vulnerable. The people who matter to us, know us. Which means if you don't have your priorities straight and simple, your character straight and simple, then interacting more with those who know you best can be the most painful. So we often choose the dull, fading ache of letting our loved ones gradually slip away rather than risk the sharp pain of facing up to where we're letting them down.

Nurturing relationships with the people who matter most can sometimes be the hardest thing we do. But those are also the most meaningful, the most valuable, the most amazing relationships, if we'll fight for them. Those people are loyal to you. Those people are going nowhere, unless you drive them away. Those people are in your court. Those people deserve your full attention.

So let me suggest a different paradigm. Instead of trying to figure out who's "toxic" through trial and error, instead of avoiding negative relationships, fully limit yourself to the positive ones. The people who are good to you and for you, and whom you are also good to and good for.

Family matters. If you decide to join yourself to a spouse—if you decide to have kids—heck, if you decide to have pets!—you are irreplaceable in their lives. They are irreplaceable in yours.

I have a pyramid-shaped decision tree for the relationships in my life. At the pinnacle is my immediate family. The next level down is my family of origin, my in-laws, and my closest friends. Next level down are the people I'm mentoring, and the people who are mentoring me. Next level down are my colleagues at work. At the bottom level are those difficult people who do me little good, but who give me a chance to hone my character by getting to know them better and treating them well.

When the opportunity arises to spend time with someone on a lower tier of the pyramid, I start at the top and do a quick check. Before I say "yes" to this opportunity, have I appropriately prioritized the people above them?

Simple Leadership

What are the things that only you can do? If anyone else on your team can do it, they should. Do not do it for them. Simple leadership means you only do what only you can do, while ensuring that everyone else on your team will do everything else.

This shift is not easy to make. You'll be opposed. People will go to you because they see you as the best at something, or the only one with insight, or the shortest route to a binding decision. But just because that might be true doesn't mean that you should be doing it. If someone else could do it, they should do it.

You need to model this so that your senior leadership team follows your example, so that your management team follows their example, so that your specialized individual contributors follow their example. Aim the whole organization toward simple leadership. In a small organization, everyone has to wear many hats. As you grow, everyone from the top down should be shedding hats to focus on what their skills and role allow them to do best. Ultimately, everyone should do what only they can do. (We unpack this process further in "Launch.")

Simple leadership is how you level up your organization to self-reinforcing growth. My mentor, Larry, shared with me the principle that, at any given time, an organization should be capable of doing a project twice the size of the largest project it's ever done. Project V stretched that theory, but it still held true. And now that we've done it, we can look at tackling projects approaching eight figures. Because once you've pushed your limits, you can lock in those lessons and go after something even bigger and more challenging.

When you are doing only what only you can do, margin gets created in your schedule, energy, and attention. Having margin gives you optionality. Having optionality gives you the capacity to capture opportunity when it comes within range. Opportunities captured equals growth. None of that can happen if you're buried under tasks that someone else—anyone else—could be (and should be) doing.

1. Step away from the desk and phone for ten minutes.
2. Consider: What are the things that only you can do? Write down your answers.
3. Step back to your calendar and tasklist and compare it against your "only me" list. What are you doing that someone else could do? Write those down.
4. Make a ninety-day plan to divest yourself of those tasks, by delegating, hiring, and training others to do them. By next quarter, the only tasks on your schedule should be those that only you can do.

Simple Schedule

Your schedule from last fall is not going to work this spring. Your schedule from last year is not going to work this year. Why? Because life changes. Things happen. Each family member has different priorities and commitments. That kid who couldn't drive now can drive, which changes things. That kid who was on a local team is now on a travel team, which changes things. That kid attending the public school is now in the private school, or vice versa, which changes things. That spouse who was in a nine-to-five job is now going back to grad school, which changes things. The unexpected, both good and bad, happens at work, in your extended family, in your community, which changes things! You have to be willing to flex. So reevaluate your schedule regularly.

The only way to keep your schedule simple is to tie it tightly to your priorities. And that means taking risks.

It's a risk to tell your boss, your team, or your client that you need to start coming in at ten o'clock on Tuesdays, so the 9 AM meeting has to shift. The first time you do something like this, it feels like a huge deal. It feels like you're asking the whole world to bend just to accommodate you. You'll worry that your colleagues will see this as favoritism, like you're demanding preferential treatment. The truth is simply that you had the guts to go to your boss, team, or client and ask. If you're contributing like you probably are, you're worth that little exception. And that little exception makes it possible for you to take your kid to preschool on Tuesdays and go to music class with him. It's worth it. You'll both remember that for years to come.

Not only that, but by taking that risk, you've communicated what really matters to you. And if your team and your client can flex to give you that, they're thrilled to do so because it means you're more likely to stay. You've got a work situation that understands and accommodates your priorities.

On the other hand, if you get a lot of flak and pushback, maybe it's time to go find a different opportunity where they do understand. Because that music class with your preschooler is more important than anything.

Some leaders fear that offering flexibility to staff results in the organization getting taken advantage of. That attitude reflects a rules-oriented organization that wastes resources policing bottom performers. Workplaces that offer latitude and understanding inspire loyalty from top performers, who consistently reward that support with results.

Simple Culture

Your culture has to be simple.

Culture must flow from your passion. Why this organization? Why do we exist? What is our more-than-air purpose?

From *why* flows *how*. Core values describe how: How you will and won't pursue your passion. How you'll be known to clients, partners, vendors, the people you serve, and your staff's families and friends. These are the principles that facilitate your work and save you from devolving into rule-bound bureaucracy.

Whether you've designed this culture for your division, your team, or your entire organization, why you work and how you work needs to be simple. Your people can't identify and live out the passion and values if they don't know them. They won't know them unless they're easy to remember. So make it easy. Do the hard work to reach one simple passion and three to five simple core values.

Simple is still hard. With just a few governing principles comes nuance, apparent contradictions, situational conflict. Which principle is supreme?

Which are subordinate? Was that thing that just happened a principle violation, or not?

If there's a problem, seek a culture-consistent process that prevents that problem from reoccurring.

Simple culture is a beautiful thing. When the criteria for decision-making are memorable and actionable, when people can see how they function in practice, shared identity becomes self-reinforcing. Direct intervention from the founders is required less and less often as cultural consensus is reached. Soon enough, the leader's judgment is only needed for the most unusual circumstances. Culture lives on its own.

FORCE-MULTIPLICATION

Simple is a force-multiplier in your life and in the life of your organization.

"Almost simple" isn't.

If you fix the grade in your yard so that runoff flows away from the house as it should, your yard will stop breeding mosquitoes. Hallelujah! What a relief! That's one less unproductive distraction. But if you leave one low spot where stagnant water collects and lingers after it rains, you'll still have a mosquito problem.

If your car is in great shape, you'll maximize your fuel efficiency and won't have to stop at the gas station quite as often. Now your errands are simpler and take less time. But if you have one wheel out of alignment, you'll wear out that tire faster and burn extra gas getting around town.

Recall the two-thousand-piece puzzle. Until you go back and fix that misplaced piece—remove the bad apple from the team, cut the unnecessary rule, stop avoiding the difficult relationship in your family, streamline the complexity—until you do that hard emotional and critical work that no one else has the position, determination, or capacity to do, you will not reach simplicity.

This isn't a one-and-done deal. Reaching simple takes hard work. Keeping simple takes unwavering vigilance. Once you start reaching for simple, you quickly develop a gut-level recognition for it. You know it when you have it, and you know it when you don't. But when things are complicated, the path back to simple isn't obvious. And new complications show up *all the time.*

When you reach simple, it enables growth. Growth introduces complications. The ship that sailed so well to this trading port took on valuable cargo and added competent crew at the docks, but also, it's now dragging a bunch of barnacles. Speed is reduced. Agility is reduced. Timetables grow. Margin shrinks. Things that worked yesterday don't work today. And now the voyage is running behind, emotions are running high, and the crew's competence is sapped by anxiety and systemic conflict.

Everyone in the company used to send their expense reports directly to the finance team, who would handle those reports directly. That works fine when you have twenty people. Somewhere between twenty and a hundred and twenty, that becomes untenable. So now the expense reports have to get reviewed and approved by project managers before being passed upward. When you have twenty people, everyone knows everyone; hence everyone knows who the go-to person is when you have a particularly thorny problem to unravel on a particular subject. Somewhere between twenty and a hundred and twenty, everyone stops being familiar with everyone else. Therefore, we created a technical director position over each major discipline, so people can check with a glance who they should go to with that tough question.

Do not tolerate complexity.

Clean off those barnacles. Eliminate the drag. What no longer clicks? Work on it! Revisit that Simple Audit. Double down on that culture of review. Keep after it until it's smooth, until it's clean, until everything is in the right place.

Sometimes, to get all the barnacles off a hull, the ship must be taken all the way out of the water. But that extra day in dry dock more than pays for itself with fewer days at sea during the next voyage.

Simplicity creates margin.

Margin makes room for options.

Options make room for opportunity.

Opportunities make room for growth.

Section Wrap: Nurture

In this section, we focused on translating your principles from phrases on a website into the living experience of your organization. The best techniques for moving a crafted culture from words on a page to words in a story are humanity, teachability, and simplicity.

Stories and legends are what shared identity is made of. For identity to be deeply shared, not just jargon to which your people pay lip service (or can't even remember), leaders must pursue humanity, teachability, and simplicity. Personal connection, proactive humility, and memorable simplicity are the most effective ways to ensure each person in your organization understands and owns the passion and values.

Below are some worksheets and tools to help you internalize these concepts and put them into practice.

IMPLEMENTATION TOOLS

Tool #5: Human Stories Worksheet

Get a blank page and a pencil and write down your responses:

Think back over the last few days, weeks, and quarters. Think about the human stories in your organization. These might be interpersonal with colleagues; inter-organizational with clients, partners, and suppliers; or personal to a single staff member and something that happened in their life unrelated to work. These stories should exemplify your culture and evoke deep emotion. Jot down the first five stories that come to mind. If you come up with more than five, keep going and writing them down until you can't think of any more. But don't stop until you have at least five.

(If coming up with five stories is a struggle, you already know your next action item: start working on the 10 Ways to Be Human!)

Once you have at least five, ask yourself the following:

- Have we obtained permission to share these stories? Have we determined the right people to share each story with? Who is the best person to share this story?
- Have these stories been commemorated?
  - If so, how? Do we have photos, write-ups, video?
- Have we made space to tell stories like this? Good avenues for sharing stories around an organization include:
  - During regular weekly or monthly meetings
  - In an internal newsletter or company portal
  - On the company blog or social media
  - At social events, parties, and off-sites
- Will it feel natural to tell and celebrate these stories, or will it feel like a big shift that came out of nowhere? What's the best way to ease into storytelling as a regular and normal "thing" around the organization?

Sharing deeply human stories that relate to your passion and values on a regular cadence forces the organization to remember and articulate the culture in a connected, personal, relatable, memorable way. There's no more powerful way to cement shared identity and multiply satisfaction than with stories.

Tool #6: Know and Be Known Survey

Use a blank page and a pen to answer the following. After reflecting on your own responses, adapt these questions into surveys you can roll out, team by team.

- Leadership team
  - Management team
    + Organization-wide

1. List your "spheres of activity" within the organization. This should include project teams, cross-team discipline or interest groups, business or management units, regular meetings, and any "extra-curricular" groups or activities where you engage in things that are tangential to or outside of your regular job description.

2. Consider the activities listed above. In which activities are you limited to being a "hand," expected to do and talk about nothing but your tasks and functions? In which are you allowed to be your whole self?

   For those activities where you can be more than just a "hand," is doing and talking about things outside your specific tasks and functions:
   - Discouraged?
   - Tolerated?
   - Appreciated?
   - Encouraged?
   - Proactively welcomed and supported?

3. Fill in the statement blank with "None," "A Few," or "Many": "I am known, really known, by _____ of my colleagues."

4. True or False: People I work with could name my family members or other members of my household.

5. True or False: If I needed help at 3 AM, I would consider calling someone from this organization.

6. True or False: I am curious about my colleagues as people. I've initiated conversations with them where I've asked about their personal passions, hobbies, families, and activities outside of work.

Tool #7: Humble Pie Chart

Rank yourself honestly on each aspect of proactive humility using a 5-point scale (0–4). Then, without revealing your self-ranking, ask three to five people who know you best—your spouse, your closest colleagues and friends—to rank you on each aspect as well. See how the scores compare (and brace yourself to humbly accept that others may not perceive your behavior to be as teachable or as humble you do)!

Average these rankings to give yourself a final score. Shade out the pie chart segments corresponding to your score. What's left? Use the results as a way to visualize where you need to double down on your pursuit of teachability.

Tool #8: Simplicity Sign

*Visit velentium.com/craftingculture to download a
high-res, printable version of this sign.*

LAUNCH

Culture Lives on Its Own

Defend

Your culture must permeate. Completely. It must be universal.

Every division.

Every leader.

Every team.

Every action.

All must come into alignment.

Project V only succeeded because all sixty-plus Velentonians, all sixty-plus temporary contractors, and everyone at both subcontractor companies completely bought into the culture and the priority of the moment. This fact was eloquently summed up by one of our engineers, a new hire who had been with us less than six months, whom I was pushing into yet another sixteen-hour day and about to send across the country, away from his family, amidst the pandemic. I told him, "Under other circumstances, I would never ask you to do this."

And he said, "That's good, because under other circumstances, I would never do it!"

I absolutely stand by that attitude.

When something's not quite right, everyone knows it. It's a splinter, a paper cut—not in itself catastrophic, but a distraction and a detriment. If it persists, if it multiplies, it becomes intolerable. *If you see something off-culture and ignore it, you've created a new culture.*

Deep down, I just want my days to go well. But things that are going well get handled by my staff. It's the novel problems, the knotty, thorny, sticky, painful problems, that get passed up to me. That's the price of leadership. The hard problems are yours. The blame is yours. I fully understand that it is lonely and it is hard. It is our job to be hypersensitive to those things that aren't quite right. Get to the bottom of those issues. You have to root out and defend your culture. The signs are subtle, so amidst everything else you're doing, you have to stay alert.

Plenty of your staff know exactly what is happening, and they can't figure out why you aren't doing something about it. When you're not defending the culture you say you care so much about, they start to doubt. If head tilts at your level are train wrecks three management levels down, and you don't deal with it, you now have issues. Your top performers' online resumes get ten hits a day from recruiters—they don't have to stay! Unaddressed culture violations read as promises you aren't keeping, and that casts doubt on the whole organization, past, present, and future. Can you and your leadership team be trusted?

Too many organizations lose their culture to alteration by a thousand cuts. Every culture violation represents an opportunity with massive leverage, because everyone is watching. Your response matters. You must be endlessly creative, positive, and uncompromising. When irritations are eliminated, when everything aligns, your organization surges forward with new energy. Whenever there's a "culture win," celebrate. Loudly! From the rooftops! It's what makes you and your organization unique and difficult to copy. It's why your staff stay instead of taking a $10K raise from your competitor. It's why your clients happily refer you and come back for repeat business.

It's impossible to overcommunicate culture. When implementation feels done, when you start to feel like a broken record, find a fresh angle and start anew. You're only just beginning!

Defending your culture is as simple as addressing *every* culture violation. Never tolerate a culture violation without leaning in.

When you start digging into "head-tilt moments," whatever you culture is, you'll generally find seven kinds of root causes. Each requires a different approach. Nuance is key here. You're looking to salvage the situation by reaching the best possible outcome while involving the narrowest circle of people possible.

SEVEN ROOT CAUSES OF CULTURE VIOLATIONS

1. People

You may already be familiar with the Right Person, Right Seat (RPRS) paradigm. The right people in the right seats on the bus was popularized by Jim Collins in *Good to Great* and further developed into RPRS by Gino Wickman in *Traction*. RPRS helps you think more clearly about people vs. roles. A Right Person is someone who resonates with the organization's culture. She's motivated by the passion. She shares the values. She's comfortable navigating and applying the principles. A Right Person is in a Right Seat when, as Wickman explains, they "GWC" the role that that seat requires. That is, the person Gets (as in *understands*) the role, Wants the role, and is Capable of performing the role. A person is in the Right Seat when all three, GWC, are true of that person in that role.[27]

A Wrong Person, or a Right Person in the Wrong Seat, is the toughest root cause to address emotionally. It's also the one causing the most collateral damage. The biggest problem with a Wrong Person or Wrong Seat is that top leaders are often the last to know about it.

It's been our experience that a Wrong Person is almost impossible to correct. Your "Wrong Person" staffer is not aligned with your passion or your values. People will either resonate with your principles, or they won't. Ideally you catch those misalignments in the screening and interview process, but from time to time someone will slip through. Once you realize what's happened, you have to act. You have to remove the Wrong Person. You won't want to remove the person—firing is hard when you're human—but you must. Their colleagues already know the person is a bad fit, and they are working overtime to make up the Wrong Person's shortcomings. As a friend put it, "Invite them to pursue excellence elsewhere." Post the job opening and move on.

Be patient with a Right Person in the Wrong Seat. When you have a Wrong Seat issue, there's a lot you can do. You can train. You can reassign. You can mentor. And those investments will be worthwhile because a Right Person is going to work hard at it. They will put in all of the effort they can muster.

After training, reassignment, and mentoring, you may get to a point where the Right Seat issue is just not solvable. This is super painful. You love this person. But perhaps you don't have room in the budget to fill the role that would suit them best. Or perhaps they just can't do the job. They, too, have to go.

You cannot hire perfectly. You can fire perfectly. Hard? Yes. Necessary? *Yes.*

2. Ethics

I hope that one of your core values is related to integrity. Leading an ethical organization is less stressful and far better for your mental health than the alternative.

This root cause has the added risk of prison, lawsuits, and fines. And the person going to prison over a major ethics violation is the big fish that everyone else can cut a deal to deliver. That's you! So, whether you want to or not, you have to deal with ethics issues proactively and decisively.

Unfortunately, unethical behavior will likely manifest at some point, somewhere in your organization. Under pressure, the temptation to cut corners or do something dishonest can be very strong. You have to step in and show your organization, yourself, and your clients that anything that threatens to compromise your integrity cannot and will not be tolerated.

3. Negativity

Ever been to a booster club meeting? They have two flavors, depending on how successful the school team is. If the team is lousy, everyone has an opinion about what needs to be fixed. And that opinion is almost always about their kid getting more playing time or that coach being fired. I don't know about the parents at your school, but when it comes to our parents,

I'm pretty sure we're not as skilled at coaching football as the coach of the football team!

I've seen some terrible behavior at booster club meetings. Instead of focusing on bringing in support and resources, the whole meeting gets consumed by loud discussions of everything the parents think is wrong. What really makes me shake my head and chuckle is that the whole charter of a booster club is to boost! Not to critique and tear down!

Negativity is way more subtle than RPRS or ethics issues. If RPRS and ethics issues are a deadly rattlesnake, negativity is the mosquito. Mosquitoes are annoying. Mosquitoes that carry disease can be lethal. But more than anything else, mosquitoes are voluminous. You let them breed and you won't have a mosquito, you'll have a swarm.

Negativity is like that. It swarms, because everybody has negative thoughts. The issue is whether or not we exercise restraint and audience awareness. Restraint is when we all use self-discipline and keep our mouths shut most of the time. It's just like your grandma taught you: If you don't have something nice to say, don't say anything. That should be default encouraged behavior. When one person says something negative, it encourages everybody else to check their self-restraint at the office door. Everybody's tongue gets loose. A little bit of negativity feeds on itself. Don't be that organization! Exercise self-restraint. When feeling negative, everyone should first ask themselves, "Does this really need to be shared?"

And if it does, the second question we should ask ourselves is, "Who is the right audience?" At Velentium we talk about "grumbling upward." Don't complain sideways to your peers. Don't complain outward to a client or a vendor. And don't complain downward to those who report to you. If something is really bugging you, go to your supervisor. Or if it's an HR thing, go to HR. If your supervisor *is* who's bugging you, and you've already gone to them (no triangling, remember), then go to *their* supervisor.

And if people aren't willing to take it on themselves to do that, then guess what? It must not really be a big deal to them. If it doesn't bother you enough that you're willing to take it to HR or to your supervisor, who can address the issue, then you need to recognize that what's driving you to voice that negativity is nothing more than a desire to make yourself feel a little bit better. Complaining sideways, outward, or downward produces at best short-term relief, because deep down you know that the people you're grumbling to can't enact the change you feel is needed. All you've done is unleash a round-robin of negativity that will make its way around the team and come right back to you, raising and reinforcing your original frustration all over again and eating up everyone's time and attention along the way. Grumble *up*—or not at all.

Meanwhile, leaders—yourself included—need training, coaching, and mentoring on how to receive complaints. One of the greatest challenges leaders have is not knowing what's really going on in the trenches *but believing that they do*. When a report from the front lines comes up the chain of command, and it's positive, managers tend to believe it. But when that report is negative, or includes a complaint, managers tend to downplay it, disbelieve it, or dismiss it as exaggeration. And to the extent that they do believe it, they're often reluctant to pass it upward to *their* supervisor.

In "Slow—Fast—Slow," we mentioned Dorothy Winsor's analysis of the two years of communication failures that led to the *Challenger* shuttle explosion. Winsor writes, "Research has repeatedly shown that bad news is often not passed upward in organizations . . . even when bad news is sent, people are less likely to believe it than good news." Regarding *Challenger* specifically, she notes that at six months ahead of launch, "Managers and engineers were beginning to disagree over the seriousness of the O-ring problem, and engineers had a difficult time communicating their view upward." When the concerns finally found a hearing in January, just before the scheduled launch, recommendations were "split along role lines. The engineers continued to argue against launch." And when the fateful decision was finally made, the vice president who had initially recommended delay reversed his decision when a fellow VP asked him to "take off his 'engineering hat' and put on his 'management hat.' When [he] changed his role, he changed his position, and the four managers voted unanimously to launch."[28]

At every level, nobody wants to be known as the bearer of bad news. And so rather than listening carefully, treating it seriously, and—this is key—*responding gratefully* when someone brings us something negative, all too often our first instinct is to ignore it, reject it, or bury it. And, because we've all had the experience of sticking our neck out and bringing a complaint to the powers that be, only to be patronized, punished, or ignored, we've learned to instead seek out that tiny hit of temporary relief we get from grumbling sideways.

Your organization has to be different. Otherwise, no matter how great it is in most respects, negativity will multiply rapidly around its shortcomings, and before you know it, morale is down, suspicions are up, distraction abounds, and communication falters. When your people grumble to the right audience, the response must be teachable and humble ("I recognize that I don't know what I don't know, and this person is trying to communicate something I don't know") and grateful ("I recognize that the person complaining is closer to the situation than I am, and has a perspective on its challenges that I don't"). When complaints are received in that spirit and dealt with appropriately, negativity is minimized and transformed into upward-flowing constructive feedback. When a complaint rises successfully, hope rushes in and takes its place, boosting morale and energizing the whole organization. Grumbling upward actually creates opportunities for positive change.

Sometimes, though, negativity shows up for reasons unrelated to work, or about situations that the organization has no power to change. This is unconstructive or random negativity. It shouldn't result in an upward complaint and can't be turned into constructive feedback. What's the best antidote to random negativity? Be human together, and show each other empathy and grace.

Significant leaders under significant duress exhibit significantly positive attitudes in negative circumstances. And that starts with you! Do you show up with a smile on your face every day? There could be horrific things going on in your personal life. But it is your job when you come through that door for everybody to read your expression and know that, at this organization, things are OK. If you enter the office or the conference room wearing a worried or angry frown, their first thought won't be that you're upset over last night's parent-teacher conference. They're going to think that they did something wrong or that the company is in trouble. And the rest of their day is going to be distracted and emotionally off-kilter because of that assumption. Take a few extra minutes outside. Compose yourself. Then come in, and be genuinely glad and grateful to be there. With your countenance, give your people good, solid reasons to believe that this place is the greatest place on earth. Then, make it true!

4. Blame

At Velentium, one of the problems we have is everybody going the extra mile to take all of the blame. In consequence, sometimes a Wrong Person ends up staying at the organization longer (or a Right Person stays in a Wrong Seat longer) than they should, because everybody else is covering for them. Our staff are loath to hang anything and anyone other than themselves.

Another problem with blame is that mistakes are frequently due to overenthusiasm. Sometimes we make a mistake because somebody wanted to go the extra mile. We had a client living near one of our remote offices who would show up unannounced to talk to our engineers about the project. They would talk shop and brainstorm together, and the next thing you know, that young engineer is implementing something on the client's behalf without a change order, to the great surprise of their PM. Suddenly, we're doing pro bono work, sometimes trying to implement new features without an appreciation or understanding for how that awesome new feature will impact the agreed-upon features that we're under contract to deliver. I love the enthusiasm! I love the desire to serve the client. It's not appropriate to blame that engineer for the client getting free work or running the project into problems because they didn't go through the proper channels and a controlled process. Yet the problem underlying the lack of process remains.

People welcome accountability when they feel safe sharing lessons learned by getting something wrong. People avoid accountability when they fear its consequences.

Blame as a root cause shows up most egregiously in triangling, which we talked about in "Be Human." Triangling is dangerous because you're not blaming somebody to their face; you're blaming somebody to someone else. That takes far less courage. It may make you feel better briefly, but it solves nothing. What takes courage is to go directly to a person and say, "Hey, you screwed up and we need to address it." This allows a situation to be addressed with the least drama and the least collateral damage by involving the fewest people. If it's an interpersonal issue, honest confrontation is the shortest route to healing the relationship. Confrontation doesn't have to be emotional, loud, messy, angry, or violent. But it does have to be direct. And there will be some tension. But it doesn't have to be contentious.

When you go to someone other than the person who caused the problem and talk about what happened, it does not allow the relationship to be healed, it does not address the root cause, it sucks up more people's attention and emotional energy, and it causes further harm to the situation, making it harder and more expensive to solve with each extra person that gets involved.

5. Inauthenticity

Where is the line between confidence, chutzpah, boldness—and a shell game? It's really quite simple: results. Results speak for themselves. If you declare, "*X will happen*," and it does happen, that's not inauthenticity. That's boldness. But if you proclaim something that then doesn't happen? Now we've got problems. Because other people are making plans based on what you say. People inside and outside the organization are trusting you to be right. And everyone is going to judge your organization as an extension of you, its leader. As your organization goes, so you go. When a football coach calls a fake punt on his own 25-yard line, it's gutsy and ingenious when it works. It's foolhardy when it fails. It's your job to assure others that your organization is authentic. Step out on a limb? Absolutely! Often! But then you must deliver.

6. Comparison

In "Stay Teachable," we talked about the importance of enjoying and celebrating the success of others, including your competitors. In a capitalistic society, we have to emphasize that, because everything about our economic environment screams competition at us all the time. I have no doubt that you have the will to fight, to win, to dominate a challenge. If you didn't, you probably wouldn't be leading your organization. But remember that we are all human. Change the terms in your head. Fight . . . for better work and better careers for your people. Win . . . opportunities for them to advance. Dominate . . . the challenges that are keeping your industry and the people you serve from blazing that trail to a better world. And when you compare yourself and your organization to others, maintain perspective!

Comparison is dangerous when it leads you to look down on yourself. As the leader, that has been a serious struggle for me when I've looked outside the organization. For your staff, it will probably also be an issue within the organization. Nobody in your organization can be as good as your top performer. By definition, only one person can be your top performer. So how do you make sure everyone else knows they're appreciated and that their contributions are valued? Sure, you may have several top performers in different disciplines. But everyone who isn't at the top needs to know that they are OK. They need to be taught that it's not about comparison, it's about team. Stress fractures start to appear in the culture when people feel like they have to compete and jockey for position internally. I'm aware that some management theories consider a certain amount of internal competition to be healthy and fruitful. I don't completely disagree, but in my view, internal competition very easily gets out of hand and siphons energy, time, and attention away from serving the customer, solving grand challenges, and moving the organization forward.

Competitive rowing is a good illustration. If each member of a crew team is competing with their fellow rowers to pull hardest or to squeeze in the most strokes, the boat is going to go all over the waterway. Time and effort are wasted because instead of traveling straight on to the objective, the craft wiggles back and forth as everyone tries to outdo everyone else. The crew team that competes with itself loses out to a team that maintains a steady, even, synchronized effort from start to finish. The internally competitive team might even have stronger, faster, more experienced rowers. But they're still going to lose ground to a team of less-skilled individuals that consistently pulls together. And the farther the race, the wider and more apparent that gap will become.

The real problem with comparison is that it lacks perspective. At the conference, I was comparing myself to the five biggest stories of the year in our industry. That lacks perspective. A junior employee comparing himself to your lead engineer who has twenty-five more years of experience lacks perspective. We got beat out in a key deal by the industry leader, who in our industry happens to be a multibillion-dollar publicly traded firm. I'm frustrated about that, but I've got to be careful, because my frustration lacks perspective.

Kids fall into this trap all the time. If you're a parent, how many dozens of times have you been asked some variant of, "Why does Victor get to do that?"

"Well, Son, because Victor is five years older than you."

Or, "Why do you spend so much time with Amanda and not with me?"

"Because Amanda is three months old and right now she needs my constant attention to survive."

What's weird is that we really don't seem to grow out of this naturally. It gets more subtle as our critical thinking develops, sure. We don't get as hung up on obvious mismatches as we did when were kids. But I find that plenty of adults, myself included, still fall prey to inapt comparison. Thinking with perspective isn't something we mature into. It takes intentionality and discipline.

As a leader, take it on yourself to root out comparison. Be careful not to create a compensation-and-reward structure that incentivizes internal competition. And when you hear unhealthy or unhelpful comparison being expressed, lean into the conversation. And what you may find is that all you need to do is dole out a little perspective, and the problem will solve itself.

7. Burnout

Your best people are very resilient. They are strong of mind. They are "pop their shoulder back into the socket and get back in the game" kind of people. The problem with resilient people is that even resilient people eventually break. And, with your top performers, when it finally happens, it happens swiftly and without much warning. Because they've been taking it and taking it and taking it and taking it.

You usually see it on their face. You smile as you walk by their office, and you don't get much of a response. Or, it shows up in bags under their eyes. They're just exhausted. The organization's productivity flywheel is spinning faster and faster, and they will try to keep pace forever. You have to give those people a break.

Make a point of kicking them out for a two-week vacation on a regular basis. Many top performers won't take initiative to do this on their own—not often enough. You'll have to insist and pressure them through their protests, reassure them through their reluctance.

Why two weeks? Because it takes them three to five days to stop thinking about their job. Only after that mental wind-down period can they truly start vacationing. So, in order to give them one week off, you really have to get them out of the office for two.

What are the rhythms in your company that give your best people the time they need to recharge? We need to work at our company to force people to take better care of themselves. Work is a marathon, not a sprint. If we're going to be sustainable, it's crucial that we run like it.

LETTING THE RIGHT ONES IN

Not everything that undermines your culture is rooted internally. You'll face threats from outside the organization, too. Some of them will be super obvious and not very tempting, like trends in management theory or incentive structures or even office layouts that just aren't a good fit. However, threats to your culture that *are* tempting always come disguised as opportunities.

When I left my previous employer to start Velentium, I let them know that I would honor the non-compete clause in my employment contract. I spent the next twelve months waiting to get Velentium up and running. I took on zero client work that whole time.

We weren't swimming in startup capital. To ensure that we would retain a controlling stake and have complete freedom to build a culture-forward organization, Tim and I accepted less than $1 million from friends and family in initial investments. We pooled the rest from our own savings, 401(k)s, and home equity loans.

One week before my non-compete expired, I got a call on my personal cell phone from a former client, whom I'd met through my ex-employer. It was about a new project that they wanted my help with. A six-figure project. I could have explained my new position and bid on that project. Probably nobody would have known. Or, just to be safe, I could have said, "Call me again next week and let's talk." But a big part of what I'd spent those twelve months doing was crafting principles for this new company. And our number-one value was Honorable. So I simply said, "I appreciate the call, but I don't do that for [my former company] anymore. I recommend you give my replacement a call, and they'll get you taken care of. Let me give you his contact info."

Tim made several similar choices. In the last few weeks he spent at his old job, including after he'd given notice but before he officially joined Velentium, Tim estimates that he sold hundreds of thousands of dollars in new contract work on behalf of his soon-to-be ex-employer. Most of it was work that Velentium could have bid, and badly needed. We've always grown rapidly, and always devoured cash just as rapidly. But if we'd compromised on Honorable right at the beginning . . . well, there goes the culture. We can't enforce values we're not willing to live. We can't build shared identity we're not willing to buy into, even when it's costly.

Sometime after we were clear of non-competes and Velentium was up and running, a friend and longtime customer whose projects we'd worked through a former employer invited us to lunch. He brought his current contract with him and pointed to its exit clause.

"Look," he said. "It says here that I can cancel this contract with fourteen days' notice. So why don't I just do that, and transfer the work over to you guys?"

"No, no, no, no," Tim replied, earnestly and immediately. "Thanks very much, but no. You'd be well within your rights to do that, and we truly appreciate the offer—but we care about our culture, and our first value is Honorable. They'll do a great job for you, and we want you to stay with them. Give us the opportunity to bid on future work. We want you to pick the company that can serve you best."

Remember the accordion effect of growth and cashflow I mentioned? That was our consistent experience during each and every one of the first nine years we were in business. From a 2-person operation with less than $1 million in startup capital in 2012, we've bootstrapped our way to over 120 staff and $20 million in annual revenue. We've averaged 40 percent growth every year since inception. Growth gobbles cash fast, so we've experienced that "accordion squeeze" of being cash-strapped multiple times a year. Yet, we've still turned away business when it isn't principle-aligned.

Do external threats to culture always come with a sizeable paycheck riding sidecar? Not necessarily. But they do come with a clear upside. There's something good and valuable they're offering, or you wouldn't be tempted to say yes. But your culture is an investment worth protecting, even when it hurts. It's what makes your organization unique. It's why your best people stay. It's your competitive advantage in the marketplace. So remind yourself: It doesn't pay to be "penny-wise and culture-foolish." Say no.

A GOOD OFFENSE

What's the best defense? Yep—a good offense. So let's talk about defending culture by supporting the good, rather than rooting out or fending off the bad. Finding those great culture moments, then celebrating and rewarding them.

Celebrating Good Culture

Our monthly all-hands meeting is driven by an agenda on a shared server. Anyone in the organization can get to that document, and everyone knows they have permission to add to it. Have an announcement you'd like to share? Add it to the Headlines. If your project is selected as the Project of the Month, get ready to talk about what you and your team are working on. But by far, my favorite part of the meeting is a section called Values

Celebration. Anybody in the company can name a colleague that they saw living out one of our company's core values:

- (Jimmy) Results⁺⁺ to Krishna for the way that he handled the customer in a difficult situation. He really went above and beyond to get them exactly what they needed.
- (Anya) Humble Charisma to Matt for taking time to help me work through an unexpected challenge, even though it wasn't his project.

When we get to this part of the meeting, each person who added a Values Celebration briefly tells the story of what happened and why they nominated their coworker. We have so many nominations, it typically takes about twenty minutes to get through this section. That's twenty minutes of the most expensive meeting in the organization because everyone is present and nobody's time is billable. But it's also twenty minutes of people celebrating our principles in the lives of their colleagues, teaching each other what they look like in practice, being honored for role-modeling the values we all aspire to. In our book, that's twenty minutes well spent.

What are some ways you can celebrate good culture in your organization? Do you have regular off-sites? Division happy hours? Team huddles? Think about the ways you could include recognition for people who live out and embody your principles into those routines. Try different things until you discover what works. It's worth it!

Rewarding Good Culture

In "Be Human," we talked about those unique moments where you can step in and care for your people. "Do for one what you wish you could do for all" when something extraordinary happens in their lives. But there are also moments that happen outside the organization that present opportunities to uniquely reward individuals. As you get to know your people as people, you get to know what excites them outside of work. And from time to time, an opportunity will catch your eye and you'll think of that person. Set aside some reserve in your budget for not-so-random gifts and seize those moments for the sake of staff who love your principles and live them out well.

And then, there's stuff that you do for all. In 2020, we couldn't gather for a company Christmas party. How do you appreciate a staff that worked so hard right through the pandemic when we're not allowed to gather? Well, every year for Christmas we send our clients a box of high-end chocolates from a local, family-run Venezuelan chocolatier. It's swanky and delicious. So we decided to send a box to each of our staff in addition to their year-end bonus. But, while nice, money and chocolate alone still wouldn't have gotten us the personal touch that really matters. So I handwrote dozens upon dozens of personal notes to accompany each one of those gift boxes.

We also play a game at our company every quarter. The game changes every quarter, and its objective alternates between cultural objectives and operational objectives. The culture games are about improving the "softer side" of the organization, while the operational games are about improving the "hard numbers" of the organization. It's always a team game—all of us vs. the objective. We win or lose as a company. Each quarter that we meet our objective, everyone in the company gets $100. I got this idea from Gordon Bethune's book, *From Worst to First*, describing the turnaround of Continental Airlines. It's been great for our company. Twice a year, we reward good culture. Now, is an extra hundred bucks a big deal? It's a bigger deal to some than to others. But it's something everyone wins together. Hence it promotes good culture and incentivizes positive peer pressure to earn a team-wide reward.

One other way to celebrate and reward at the same time is to set up moments where your team or your partners get recognized for living your principles. This creates massive "wins" all the way around. Help a vendor get some positive local media attention for the good work they do. Enter a contest with a client and make sure they stand front and center to claim the trophy. Serve in the local community and publish internally and externally pictures of your team serving. Elevate others when they live out the principles and shout their accomplishments from the rooftops. There are few things more enjoyable than being someone else's number-one cheerleader. Finally, celebrate culture yourself by living out the principles privately. Behind the scenes, do for one what you'd like to do for all.

Catch that? Your actions in private. Your team's and clients' and partners' actions proclaimed. That's celebrating and rewarding culture. You'll find that heavy doses of both defense and offense create massive internal momentum in your organization. When we know what we're about, and we reinforce that certain knowledge with meaningful actions and passion-fueled experience, everyone is energized to keep pressing ahead.

Grow

Organizations like yours can make a lasting and meaningful impact on the world. When your culture challenges and improves on the status quo, its ripples are felt far and wide. In this chapter, we look at how to bring all the elements of culture together to fuel your organization's growth and magnify that impact.

I don't only mean increasing your annual intake or staff head count and doing more of what you already do. I also mean innovating ways to do your existing stuff better, so you serve your customers better and more efficiently. Plus, expanding your current offerings, developing new products and services, and adapting what you do so it can reach and serve people you're not currently reaching or serving well.

IDEATE

Think back, for a moment, to "Slow—Fast—Slow." Think back to "Reach Simple." In those chapters, I argued for the importance of slowing down and devoting time to silent thought and reflection. I laid out why you need to deliberately prepare your organization to pounce when the right opportunities appear. I encouraged you to build margin into your schedule so you have the flexibility to evaluate and respond to unexpected opportunities and unanticipated problems. I encouraged you to set yourself the goal of "only doing what only you can do." And one of the things that only you can do is select the ideas that will shape your organization's growth.

Coming up with new ideas is not straightforward. It requires discipline. That discipline is different from many of the things you've done in the past. It begins with the discipline to slow down and think. It includes the discipline to be secure enough in yourself to consider outside-the-box ideas that your brain will naturally reject as unfeasible. It includes the discipline to see the world that *could be*, as opposed to the world that is.

Ever had that experience where you're considering buying a new car and you've narrowed the choice down to a particular vehicle, and suddenly that model seems to be everywhere? It's not that they weren't around all along, it's just that now that you are considering buying one, you notice them wherever you go. Your focus has changed, which changes your perception of your environment. The environment did not change. Your awareness did.

Ideating is no different. The key is to open your perspective to actively look for things in your field or your market that aren't as great as they could be. This could be driven by new technology, or new regulation, or a change in the financial landscape. It could also be driven by the untapped abilities of your staff. Your people have experience and skills with applications beyond the role you recruited them for. Lots of things can lead to opportunity—if you're constantly on the lookout for it.

Now, you won't be the only source of ideas in your organization. Your staff are engaged with the broader field and industry, reading the news, participating in working groups and other organizations and institutions on the side. So are your mentors. So are the best and brightest thought leaders whose books you read. Ideas come from many places. A lot of them will be better than what you would come up with on your own. Or, they'll provide a key modification or augmentation that gives a so-so idea some real value. So leverage those habits of silence and thoughtfulness and personal development to shape yourself into someone who can listen openly and teachably—with humility, with curiosity, and with an eagerness to give someone else credit for the next great idea that drives the next new thing in your organization.

Coming up with ideas and evaluating them is something that you should do. But it isn't something that *only you* can do. What only you can do is select which ones to pursue. As the leader, you have access to the full breadth of organizational information needed to determine whether the organization can and should get into a position to develop that idea. Nobody else has quite that same vantage point. And only you have the right to authorize pursuing a new initiative. Of course, you might share that right with other senior leaders. And as you grow, you will likely delegate and duplicate that right to several more . . . but I'm getting ahead of myself!

There are more than a few resources out there that address ideation and brainstorming, so I'm not going to spend more time covering idea generation. But I've observed that a common shortcoming in leadership materials is that you don't hear much about the ideas that flamed out. People talk about their story when the idea works. Or, occasionally, because the idea flamed out spectacularly. But that 80 percent in between, where an idea kind of just didn't work, didn't generate strong enough results to justify continuing, or never gained momentum and just petered out, is 80 percent of the ideas you're going to be sorting and selecting. Most of the ideas you consider are not going to work out. A few of them will work really well. Figuring out which to test, and how to test them at the lowest viable cost so you can tell whether or not to keep going, is a little bit art, a little bit science. Try stuff. Double down on what works. Don't get too attached to any one idea, or any one source of ideas, along the way. Do entertain lots of ideas, all the time, so you can develop the skills and intuition for sorting through them. And, like that vehicle you're thinking about buying that is suddenly everywhere on the road, you'll soon find that ideas worth pursuing are everywhere, too.

THE GROWTH CYCLE

From time to time, an idea will come across your radar that sends you into a Growth Cycle. The Growth Cycle is how you spin up a new, ongoing initiative in your organization. It's fed by a constant stream of ideation, but only a few of those ideas will be strong enough to power the Growth Cycle through all four stages of a full revolution. Those stages are PIONEER → STABILIZE → TRAIN → DELEGATE.

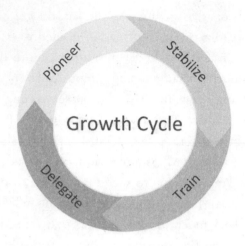

- **Pioneer:** Evaluate promising ideas
- **Stabilize:** Get the new idea rolling with a documented process
- **Train:** Mentor and coach others to manage the new process
- **Delegate:** Hand the developed process off to competent people

Now, you might look at that cycle and experience mixed reactions. You might feel a thrill of freedom and potential as you realize what implementing this cycle could mean for you and your organization. You might also feel a sense of unease or even a flash of panic over the loss of control and the amount of trust those last two stages entail. That's OK! This chapter and the next are designed to address those concerns.

This chapter looks at the first three stages of the Growth Cycle. Delegate is reserved for the next chapter, because you can't successfully delegate until your culture aggressively develops independent decision-making throughout the organization. Think of this chapter and the next as a two-parter.

The point of the Growth Cycle is to give you a formal process that:

- Frees you from having to actively oversee everything your organization does,
- Gives you a road map and clear objectives for raising up new leaders,
- Sets those new leaders up for success, and
- Ensures that the faith and responsibility you place in them is justified.

Without this growth-supporting structure aimed at setting up and spinning off initiatives to others, your organization can't grow beyond what your desk can handle. All activities bottleneck at the topmost decision-maker. The only solution to that challenge is to divvy up activities and appoint new decision-makers to lead them. But if you don't prepare your processes to be handled by others or your people to take them over, the organization will be plagued with false starts and sunk costs and abandoned initiatives. When ideas fail, you won't know whether the problem was the idea or the lack of structure supporting it. And you'll risk burning out key people on a succession of under-supported, ad hoc initiatives that "seemed like good ideas at the time."

That last one is especially dangerous if you're a dreamer. That's me at times. Some leaders need to focus on the discipline to ideate and take pioneering risks, to get over fear and indecision and try new things. Other leaders need the discipline to evaluate ideas more selectively and realistically and put other ideas on hold until a well-chosen idea has been pioneered far enough to judge its merits.

So let's look at how to select a promising idea from the ideation cloud and spin it up into new growth.

Pioneer

Pioneering is really a culmination of most of the book to this point. Does the potential opportunity align with your principles ("More than Air," "Principles over Rules")? Are you ready to pounce on it ("Slow—Fast—Slow")? If you did, would it engage the full humanity of your team ("Be Human")? Can your organization stretch itself to learn what needs to be learned to succeed at this opportunity ("Stay Teachable")? Is it a simple, straightforward next step ("Reach Simple")? Is there anything you need to prune out of your organization in order to capitalize on this opportunity ("Defend")? Missing any of these previous steps makes it much harder to pioneer.

Pioneering is an exploratory process. If an idea is a stream you're trying to cross, you're not so much asking, "Can I personally get across this stream, and is this the best spot to do it?" as much as you're asking, "Can I lay some stepping stones across here? Can we then use those stones to help us lay a log bridge from bank to bank? Can we then replace that log bridge with a sturdy, even, well-made bridge that a large group can cross together?" Evaluating ideas is less about "Can we do this?" and more about "Can we learn to do this well, repeatably, sustainably, and at scale?"

Those aren't the kind of answers you can derive with guesswork and thought experiments. Once you think you've identified a few viable crossing points, you've got to go right down to the stream and see if any of them will work. That's why this has to be done by a leader. For now, only you bring enough insight and institutional knowledge with you to make the call of how far to pursue a possible route—whether to keep going or turn back, and when.

In *It Doesn't Have to Be Crazy at Work*, Fried and Hansson devote a chapter to the idea that what appears to be low-hanging fruit can still be out of reach.

> Declaring that an unfamiliar task will yield low-hanging fruit is almost always an admission that you have little insight about what you're setting out to do . . . any estimate of how much work it'll take to do something you've never tried before is likely to be off by degrees of magnitude.[29]

When you're confident because you've experienced a measure of success, it's easy to underestimate the difficulty of the new and unfamiliar. It's easy to underestimate because you actually don't have enough data to estimate it. But you do know yourself and your team, so in the absence of real information about the effort, you overestimate your ability to succeed. And there's a lot to be said for optimism plus stubbornness. That combo will take you far. Often, they're your ticket to success. But when it comes to pioneering a trail into new territory, they can also be expensive.

In "Stay Teachable," I told you about that project where we overran our budget by nearly $1 million because we promised to deliver a mobile app that we had no prior experience developing. That was one expensive learning opportunity! Has it paid off? It sure has. Although we didn't realize how much it would take when we bid on the project, we included that work in our proposal because we'd already carefully evaluated it and identified it as a strategically important offering that we needed to get good at. And now, we know how to build those deliverables and we've done them for lots of projects.

In Jim Collins's book *Great by Choice*, he talks about bullets before cannonballs. It's a great concept. Bullets before cannonballs means that you have lots of bullets that you can spray around and then, when you acquire a good target, you put more effort and resources in that direction by chasing the most successful bullets with cannonballs. Fire lots of pioneering bullets. Use the cheap ammo. Take many shots and see what happens. Does it seem like it might be successful? Does it seem like it might fit your organization? Run the target through the different parameters of the previous chapters. If it passes, then that could be a signal to break out the heavy ordnance.

Let me give you an example. In 2018, the FDA clarified its expectations for cybersecurity in medical devices. Essentially, they declared that, from now on, medical devices have to be made secure. Velentium saw this coming, and recruited and invested in cybersecurity competence early on. It's been one of our core offerings for years. But that announcement from the FDA signaled an industry shift. So we began thinking about what to do about it. Lots of ideas got tossed around. We considered launching new marketing campaigns, offering new services, developing new products, even looked at acquiring a couple of companies. We had to reject or slow-play a lot of very strong ideas because we didn't have the resources to plunge into them. How do I know they were strong ideas? Because a lot of them have since been brought to the marketplace by other companies! But at the time, they weren't right for us. We needed to pursue an idea that was right for us.

So I went to Chris, my medical device cybersecurity expert, and Jason, my marketing guy, and said, "Why don't you two write a book?" Between them, they had the experience and expertise that made writing a how-to book feasible. We already knew there was a serious lack of in-depth resources on the subject. Cybersecurity for medical devices isn't like IT cybersecurity. Very few people are knowledgeable about it, and Chris knows many of those people personally.

Our team liked the idea and created an outline for the book. They planned to develop the outline into a proposal to pitch to publishers, but before they got the chance, Chris was contacted by one of his industry peers . . . who had been offered a contract . . . to write and publish a book on medical device cybersecurity. And he wanted Chris to be his co-author.

Not only did that invitation validate our choice of ideas in a big way, it saved us significant investment in late-stage pioneering. We were able to capitalize quickly on the opportunity because we'd already begun to pioneer the idea. When Chris got the email asking if he'd consider working on such a book, he was able to respond immediately with an outline and significant groundwork for the project. That external interest and confirmation made it an easy decision for me to clear their schedules so they could follow through. As the first rumblings about COVID-19 were beginning to circle the globe in late 2019, they wrote *Medical Device Cybersecurity for Engineers and Manufacturers*, the world's first comprehensive how-to book on the topic. It was released the following September, enjoyed a few weeks as an Amazon bestseller, and was heralded as 2020's "Cybersecurity Book of the Year."

When you're pioneering, resist the feeling that all the ideas you select must be good or somehow "proven" before you pursue. Often you won't know until you try—so try them and see! Likewise, resist the inertia that says all the ideas you pioneer have to then be implemented. Don't cave to the sunk-cost fallacy—turn back and try something else. But do get into the habit of pioneering. And then, over time, notice which of the ideas you pioneered have the most staying power. The ones that won't go away deserve more attention. And, eventually, you may find that it's time to financially support that idea, flesh it out some more, and test it in the marketplace.

The more you do this, the better at it you'll get. You'll fire fewer bullets before acquiring a promising target. You'll get better at picking crossing points just by studying a creek's contours. Once you've been around the full Growth Cycle a few times, you'll recognize false starts and bad fits earlier. You'll shift focus sooner to even better ideas, the ones worth advancing to the next stage: Stabilize.

Stabilize

Stabilizing is codifying what you've pioneered into a documented process. As you work out how to do something for the first time, take notes to remind yourself of what you did and what you'll do differently next time. Then, expand and develop those notes into a process others can follow.

This is not a trivial activity. Your aim is to create a set of instructions that someone with *no specific knowledge* of the new process could follow successfully, *even if they never talked to the original pioneer.* That's the level of clarity your documentation should strive for.

In "Reach Simple," I said that the path forward is found by asking yourself, "Am I only doing what only I can do?" That's part one of a two-part question. Whenever and wherever you identify something that you're doing that someone else *could* do, you need to follow up with the second half of the question: "What needs to happen so that someone else can do what I'm doing?" When the time comes to pass a project or process on to someone else, our focus is more typically on ourselves—on winding down our involvement and ramping up to whatever we're transitioning to—than it is on setting up our successor for success. Very few people have practiced and gotten good at answering the question, "What do I know that the next person won't?" Under pressure, this question becomes even harder to answer, and is often never asked at all. So-called "tribal knowledge" can run deep on even the most basic tasks, and most of the time, the first person to realize it is the newest person to join the project or go through the process. That's the person who finds everything missing from your handoff and gets slowed or outright blocked until they can fill in the blanks.

One of the things we did in the wake of Project V was to look at places where the stress of moving Fast had made gaps and weaknesses in our operations glaringly apparent. That review prompted us to hire a number of key people, including a VP of Operations named Mark.

Mark came to us from a large multinational medical device firm. The group he led for them incorporated hundreds of people. Thanks to that experience, Mark has been able to add some serious stabilizing discipline to our organization. Over the course of his first several months with us, he mapped out our entire design and development project cycle. As part of that effort, Mark worked to meet with every single person on staff, both to get to know them and to interview them about their pain points. Then, he used those interviews to color-code his project map according to the following scheme:

- Stuff we do well that has a well-documented process
- Stuff we do well that does not have a well-documented process
- Stuff we don't do well that has a well-documented process
- Stuff we don't do well that does not have a well-documented process

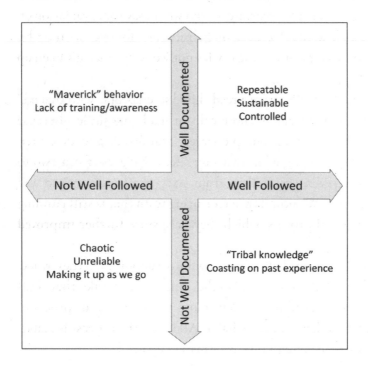

That gave us a quick visual diagnostic into where everything stood—what was stable and well established, and what was not yet stable. It also gave us an immediate and actionable road map to improvement.

We've found that documenting our processes makes our principles easier to follow. What's the difference between a documented process and a rule? I think it has to do with the attitude or the posture of that thing. A rule is placed upon you, and sends a message about punitive effects if it's not followed. A process is placed under you, and seems to have a supportive or boosting effect if it is followed. A rule pressures you to avoid failure, whereas a good process points you toward success.

When Velentium first started to grow in earnest, I had point on all our recruiting. I quickly realized that vetting candidates was not something that only I could do. I worked to map out a recruiting process, train someone else to that process, and turn it over to him to manage.

As part of that process, we put out ads on all of the major job sites. I would repeatedly get calls from recruiters, who would say some variation of, "I see that you have an ad that has been on [jobsite.com] for over six months. We can help you fill that position. Clearly it's not working since it's been up there so long."

And I'd respond: "Actually, we've already hired seven people with that ad."

Every time I answered one of those calls, it made me smile—because I was reminded of how much our pioneered, stabilized, and delegated recruiting process was saving us in recruiters' fees. We grew from two to sixty-five staff over seven years. Then from sixty-five to a hundred and thirty in the next three. We now have a recruiting team that is still running a variant of the original process, which they have since further improved over time.

Pioneer, then document. Follow your own instructions. Do they work? Are they clear? Test them on others. Do they understand? Take that feedback and revise. Repeat. And repeat some more. Over time, your processes will gain maturity and slowly become habit. And once the process is stable, it's time to train someone else to take over managing it.

Train

There are two elements to training: mentoring and coaching. We've mentioned both before. Mentoring puts into you something you don't already have. It's teaching a new concept, a new skill, a new process, a new paradigm, a new way of thinking, or a new way of seeing the world.

Coaching takes what's already in you and makes it better. Coaching makes you faster, leaner, more productive, all with greater ease. The point of coaching isn't to squeeze more out of you, but to show you that you're more capable than you currently believe. Some flow research suggests that to get into a flow state, you have to push yourself as little as 4 percent past your current level of comfort.

When they turn ten, each of my kids gets to go on a one-on-one trip with me somewhere awesome. The catch is, going on the trip isn't free. They have to earn it. The price of the trip is a series of things I want them to do that will make them a better person. These year-ten trips are an excuse not only to get some quality time with my children, but to mentor them into new skills. Once they learn them, they'll have the rest of their lives to develop those skills and be coached into something more.

One of my son's challenges is to run a 10K to develop his endurance. I know the importance of this only because a high school coach cared enough to force me to develop it. That mentoring has benefited me ever since and made it much easier for me to stay in shape into my forties. But at the time, I was not interested. I tried out for the varsity soccer team in high school. When the coach called to tell me I made the team, he said, "Welcome to cross-country."

"Uh . . . I tried out for soccer."

"That's correct. Welcome to cross-country."

Oh no. You've got to be kidding me! Sure enough, when you made the varsity soccer team at my high school, you got enrolled in cross-country, too, whether you liked it or not. Although this did create some of the most painful training moments in my life, it also put "distance runner" into me. Just as friends who played football in high school have a base of muscle on their bodies, I have an ability to run longer distances. So now, I'm able to further that skill, which does double duty by furthering simple fitness and giving me time to go slow and think, or helping me stay teachable and learn by listening to audiobooks, during extended runs.

The more you mentor people, the easier they are to coach because there's more there to coach. So get proactive about things that have been pioneered and stabilized that can be "mentored into" others. Leveling up everyone around you a little bit further than what they would do on their own is the mark of a good coach.

Coaching and being coached aren't always pleasant. But pursuing the right kind of discomfort leads to improvement over time.

My whole career has been in the technical world, working on or leading engineering projects. For whatever reason, a high percentage of engineers don't seem to be comfortable with public speaking. There's enough truth to the stereotype that people have often been pleasantly surprised when they hear me give a talk. I knew it was an area of opportunity for me in my early career, so I chose to push through the discomfort and got mentored and coached by joining a Toastmasters club at my first workplace. It took several years of practice, but now, I'm comfortable and competent in front of audiences.

Most of us prefer to avoid conflict. Conflict avoidance impacts organizations negatively, because course-correction often requires conflict. Conflict doesn't have to be rude, violent, loud, or abrasive, and rarely should be. But leadership often requires principle-based opposition to something happening that should not be, whether within the organization or between the organization and another entity. Conflict-avoidant leaders allow their organizations to drift and founder. Not only am I naturally inclined to avoid conflict, but I have struggled, in both personal and professional areas of my life, to overcome people-pleasing. There exists within me a gut impulse to try to make those around me happy, short term. And that's no good, because in leadership and in life, you achieve neither success nor satisfaction through short-term happiness. So I have worked and gotten coaching and mentoring, including from therapists, to develop my ability to embrace productive, principle-based conflict for the good of myself, my family, and my organization.

Growth requires discomfort. And a certain degree of risk.

If you don't take that hike, you won't turn your ankle . . . and you also won't summit.

If you don't call that acquaintance, you won't be rejected . . . and you also won't start your next relationship.

If you don't say yes to that opportunity, you won't fail miserably . . . and you also won't be in the running for the next promotion.

If you don't force yourself to let go of that Great New Idea that you pioneered and got so excited about, stabilizing the process, training up new leaders, and turning it over to them completely, you won't experience the pain and anxiety that comes with surrendering control . . . and also, you'll bottleneck not just this new thing, but all future new things by not freeing your time to *only do what only you can do*. Which, if you've done your job right, no longer includes the Great New Idea you've sweated, coaxed, and pushed to reach this stage in the Growth Cycle. And growth will plateau.

To keep your organization growing, you've got to keep yourself growing. You've got to proactively pursue your next source of discomfort.

Discomfort is not the same thing as pain. Pain drives people away. Nobody is eager to plunge back into pain. Pain results in inconsistent practice, which isn't beneficial. What you practice is what you perfect, so you've got to practice well and ambitiously. If your form is off, no amount of repetition will get you to the next level. Earlier I joked about my golf game. Not only do I not practice very often, when I do practice, I'm sure I practice bad habits. Which leads me to 105: my score, every round. If I decide to get serious about improving, it will take coaching from someone knowledgeable, serious effort on my part, and significant discomfort. Correcting a habit never feels natural. It involves doing something over and over the right way to reprogram our muscle memory into the proper form.

When you're stabilizing and training people to take over something new, it's the same. Mentor your staff into the skills and perspective they're lacking. Coach those skills to the level needed to take on the new thing. And be ready to share in their discomfort, because overcoming institutional muscle memory and getting your team away from how "we've always done things" is going to be uncomfortable. It's going to take consistent effort that pushes everyone past their current capabilities. And it's going to take time. But it's worth it, because that's how you'll grow.

Delegate, Part I

The last stage of the Growth Cycle is Delegate, which is where you completely turn the new initiative over to the people you've trained. Pass it on and let go. From now on, it's theirs to carry forward. It has to be theirs, because as the leader, it's your job to get back to ideation and pioneer the next thing. You've got to find the next idea that will power the next cycle of growth. It is not your job to run the new thing; it's your job to keep the whole organization moving, growing, developing, launching.

But as you delegate, there's something else about your organization that has to be true. Everyone has to be prepared to Think.

Think

"WE DON'T HAVE AN F-KEY FOR THAT!"

When Julie and I were pursuing the adoption of our first son, we had a tiny mountain of paperwork to fill out. Most people in the country we were adopting from did not have bank accounts, so the adoption dossier required a letter from our bank that simply stated, "Dan and Julie are account holders in good standing." It didn't make a lot of sense to me, because most adults in the United States have bank accounts. But the requirement is the requirement, so I headed to my bank, part of a major national chain, to get the necessary letter.

"Hi! I need a letter on bank letterhead that says I have an account here."

The bank officer shook his head. "Unfortunately, that's not something we can do."

"I don't understand. Why not?"

Bank officer: "We don't have letterhead here at the bank. The only forms I can print are from the preapproved set that comes up when I press one of these twelve F-keys on my keyboard."

"So, if I need something custom that your F-keys won't create, I'm just out of luck?"

"Yeah, that's about right."

OK, I try to be a kind person. But that proverb that warns you not to get between a mama bear and her cubs hints at a ferocity I was suddenly beginning to understand. *Don't get between a father and his son . . . who is waiting for him . . . on the other side of the globe!*

I tried to stay pleasant. "I understand. But that's not good enough, because I need the letter to complete this adoption dossier."

Bank officer: "But, sir, I don't have letterhead. I don't have the ability to do what you're asking."

"Hmm. Does your computer have Microsoft Word?"

"Yes."

"And do you have a printer that has paper in it?"

"Yes."

"And does your computer have access to the internet?"

"Yes."

"Great! Go to www.yourbank.com. Copy the logo and masthead off of the webpage, paste it into a Word document, and write a sentence that says I have an account here!"

"Sir . . . I can't do that."

Here's one of my top pet peeves in life: I hate bad business. Bad business makes me crazy. And one of the things that I dislike more than anything else in bad business is when people say, "I can't," when they actually mean, "I won't." If someone says, "I can't," it may mean that they truly can't. It may mean that they don't have the autonomy, the authority, or the ability to do it.

- **Autonomy:** Your company has trained you to think for yourself and make a decision on your own.
- **Authority:** Your company has given you the right to make decisions on your own.
- **Ability:** You have developed the talent, skill, and experience to make the right decision.

I have no idea which of the three was in play that day. All I know is that bank officer looked at me like I was from Mars. Yet the request was incredibly simple. I was not asking him to put on letterhead some statement that I had a right to access $100 million in cash anytime I wanted. Literally all I needed was a letter stating, "Dan and Julie have a bank account in good standing at This Bank."

And despite the "F-key limitation," the solution was so plain to me. Take a chance, change the process just a little bit, and grant the customer his extremely simple, quick, harmless request.

After about forty-five minutes of me getting more and more infuriated as the bank officer resisted, protested, and generally acted like he was bending over backward to do me a massive favor in response to my unreasonable request and let me know *in no uncertain terms* that he was making a special onetime exception to do this thing for me *and would never do it again*, we finally got to the point where he did create the letter.

Needless to say, Julie and I found a new bank.

"YOU DECIDE!"

You decide. Powerful, powerful words. It's my favorite mantra at Velentium, directly inspired by that experience at my old bank. These words launch your organization to a new level. Uttering them is fearful, even painful, because they mean you're giving up control. You'll have to back people who choose to do something different than what you would've done. When you speak these words, you hand the proverbial car keys to someone else.

But each time you speak them, you develop your organization a little further.

Each time you say, "You decide," your life gets:

- a little bit messier,
- a little bit easier,
- a little bit more wonderful, and
- a little bit more terrifying.

Embracing "You decide" forces bravery to flow from you into your whole organization. "You decide" comes at this point in the book because, before you can use it effectively, you have to have already laid the foundation for decision-making. People have to know what you're passionate about. They have to know what the organization's values are. They have to understand what it means to be human and teachable and simple. You've given your team all of these constructs to create a framework for decision-making.

Now launch them! Launch them into the world of uncertainty and ambiguity that you as a leader have known from day one. Kick them out of the nest, just as you kicked yourself out of the nest. Teach them that forging ahead into uncertainty will develop their abilities. Soon, you'll see them soar.

Soaring doesn't happen overnight. Everyone makes bad decisions. I've made hundreds of bad decisions. You must champion a culture that forgives bad decisions, as we discussed in "Stay Teachable." That's how your people learn and grow.

Sure, there'll be a few folks who don't or won't learn to make good decisions. They continuously make decisions in their own self-interest, or they lack the smarts to do what's needed, or they possess too little emotional intelligence to read a situation. In the "Right Person, Right Seat" paradigm, this is a "Right Person" problem. There will often be a few "Wrong Persons" around, because no organization has figured out how to hire perfectly. Fortunately, you can fire perfectly. And you owe it to your team to fire "Wrong Persons" without dithering or delay.

A great thing about "You decide" is that once you've onboarded new hires and exposed them to implemented culture, it becomes pretty obvious pretty quickly which people are eager to embrace the culture and do the work you need the way the culture demands it to be done, and which people aren't. We screen candidates for culture fit at least as rigorously as we do for technical competence. That's how we build a stellar team. And once you have that stellar team, trust them. Allow them to flap their wings. Let 'em flap, fail, even fall, and very soon, they will soar. That means giving them autonomy, authority, and ability.

Autonomy

Autonomy is based on a sense of self. It is inner confidence in decision-making capability. It's a person's deep belief in her capacity to make the call that must be made to accomplish the goal. Leaders must teach and train to autonomy. How? By getting out of your team's way, then rewarding their actions.

Getting out of the way requires more than resisting your temptation to lay out a step-by-step path and constantly check to make sure they're walking it. Not micromanaging is just the first half. The second part is *stubbornly refusing to step in and rescue* when they get stuck. You cannot make the decisions for them. You cannot respond with the answer when asked.

When someone comes to my office with a problem, I say, "Tell me what's going on." And I listen. Then I say, "So tell me what you think." And right about then, they start to realize what is happening. Those who've been with me awhile either start to smile or scowl, because they know what's coming.

If they are struggling to clarify what they think, I may ask them, "How would this decision align with our passion and our values? Which principle should take precedence here?"

Ultimately, they get to a recommendation. "Here's what I think we should do." And don't miss this, because it's key: *Do not agree with them!* Agreement from the leader lets them off the hook. And, unless it's gonna lead to some catastrophe because that person sitting in your office lacks full perspective or experience or crucial information, *don't disagree with them, either*! Just smile and drop it on 'em . . . "You decide!"

As you model "You decide" and autonomy grows, make sure that all the leaders working under you are doing likewise. You should see "You decide" happening at every level of your organization. Each decision should be made by the person closest to that situation. And the only way that that can truly work out well is when everyone owns the principles and understands what the organization is fundamentally about.

Whenever someone makes a decision, exercising their "You decide" autonomy, unless it conflicts with the passion or the values, *you have to back that decision!* This can get sticky at times. People are going to make decisions that are different from the decisions that you would make. Back them if you possibly can. If the decision is being challenged by others, if you don't like the decision or its consequences, search ardently for a way to justify that decision against your culture and use that justification to defend the decision—to yourself and others. If you can't figure out the justification, if the decision is truly puzzling and carries negative consequences, the decision-maker's supervisor needs to go to that person in a spirit of curiosity and a posture of listening and simply say, "Help me understand why you made that decision. How does it align with our principles?"

Even when that decision costs the organization in the short term, I'm gonna support that decision both publicly, to others in our organization and to our clients if appropriate, as well as personally with that person. A culture-aligned staff person who is closest to the situation where the decision needs to be made is always the best person to make that decision.

Nurturing autonomy is about building up your people's confidence in their decision-making ability. You do that by forcing people to face just how committed you are to "You decide." They have to make the decision! You *will not* make it for them.

Authority

Now that people are making decisions throughout the organization, you have to support those decisions. Celebrating decisions once they're made is very important. It shows your staff that they have the authority that goes with the calls they made. They exercised autonomy. If you undermine, reverse, or scold their decisions, you're withholding authority. The aggravation of that blatant contradiction will drive your people crazy. They'll eventually jump ship. And it will be your best people jumping.

That doesn't mean there can't be teaching. It's common for me to pull someone into my office and say, "Hey, thanks for making that decision. I appreciate that you took the initiative and kept us moving. When I was in a similar situation, here's what I did. It was different than what you did. Neither is right or wrong—I just wanted to give you some of my thinking. Now, tell me about what you were thinking." And we analyze together and celebrate together. The important thing—*more important than what was decided*—is who made that decision and how uninvolved you were. You are celebrating the real-time building of less of you and more of them in their workday, projects, and processes. You are proactively supporting the authority that your staff person exercised.

Where autonomy is a person's intrinsic confidence in their ability to make decisions, authority is the external, public affirmation of that person as a capable team member. It is your stamp of approval. This person made the call. That means we're going all-in with them.

This is an investment. During Slow, it's a moderate-risk investment, but during Fast, it's a volatile one. Near the start of Project V, we designated owners of each test system type. We then tasked them with evaluating delays caused by those systems. The systems had been designed for a factory load of a few hundred units a month, so the operation speed of each test had not been of paramount concern. Now it was. Could any of these designs be upgraded? Does the test itself require this time to complete properly, or is there downtime because the test system isn't fully optimized in terms of cooldowns, mechanical reset, operator procedure, or the like? Can we accelerate test times without sacrificing results, or do we have to build more systems to achieve the target production rate? That was the question each system owner had to answer. It meant changing procedures, designs, and parts—on top of parts changes already being driven by supply chain issues. Neither Tim nor I, nor our project managers, could make those decisions. It had to be made by the people whose job it was to own the creation of those systems, start to finish, within the timetable. And once those final decisions were made, everyone else, from managers to purchasing team to build team to support team, had to promptly accept and roll with them. There was no time for back-seat driving or second-guessing. Were mistakes made? Of course! Mistakes get made by the best people on the simplest tasks under ideal circumstances. Mistakes were made, discovered, and dealt with. And we kept moving.

Even—maybe especially—during Fast, it's critical to support people over circumstances. When a decision is different from how you would do it, ask yourself, "Is this going to lead to utter catastrophe?" If not, let it be. The person and the reinforcement of autonomy through publicly blessing (or at least not criticizing) the authority of that decision is worth more than the decision going the exact way that you would have wanted.

I've been at entrepreneurial conferences in the past where there were entire tracks of sessions around overwork. The sessions get mobbed with people who look exhausted. Inevitably, a group forms and people start to talk about their last time off. People end up bragging about how long it's been.

It happened in my first job, too. I was around a group of people and they were boasting about months, even years, since they had had a vacation.

I guess it was a shorthand way to signal how essential they felt they were to the company. I remember thinking to myself, *You've got to be kidding me. Who wants to live like that?*

Teaching autonomy and then celebrating authority when those people make decisions on the organization's behalf is the recipe to a balanced professional life. If you have to make every decision, you will be on-call 24/7 and you'll never get that critical time away we discussed in "Slow—Fast—Slow" and "Reach Simple." If you have to make every decision, every leader under you will mimic your example or go even more extreme into micromanagement. Every project will be constantly bottlenecked by management attention. Individual contributors won't be free to serve the customer, even when it's as simple as making some letterhead and writing a quick sentence underneath it. Everyone will be continuously stressed, and nobody will be satisfied. Nobody will achieve a healthy work-life "fit." However, if you support principle-aligned autonomy by delegating authority *and* responsibility, everyone wins.

Ability

Give staff the autonomy to make the call. Support them with the authority to make the call. Then watch as ability grows throughout your organization. Every time you grant autonomy and celebrate authority, you are building ability.

Ability is only forged through practice. And practice isn't practice without freedom to fail. If you've created a punishing organization that hammers bad decisions, your people will never develop the ability to handle autonomy and authority. It is in decision-making itself that people learn to make good decisions. And they learn most from the decisions that don't turn out perfectly.

In our company, we've got many staff with twenty to thirty years of industry experience. Many decisions are made not because of complete hard data, but because of intuition. And that intuition is forged by decades of experience. Many decisions around here have one, two, or even half a dozen stories behind them. And it's from the accumulated experience of those stories that wisdom is born. Wisdom is forged in the furnace of experience. And your people can't get that experience if you don't enable them to make decisions. Without autonomy and authority, ability dies on the vine. Paradoxically, staff who are never given autonomy and authority never develop the competence and effectiveness that would justify you trusting them with autonomy and authority. Ability doesn't just magically appear from nothing. You have to give them room to grow.

That's why it's so important to celebrate failure. In one of my previous companies, every week in our company meeting we had a "failure of the week" competition. I would pass out a gift card to the person who'd made the biggest mistake and created the best learning opportunity. And the team would compete to show that mistakes are OK and we would talk about them so we could all learn from them.

I'm not sure that a reward system that proactively encourages mistake-making is the best idea for organizations, since people will ultimately do what gets rewarded. You don't want people taking unconsidered risks or fabricating mistakes just to win a prize. But you get the idea: failure has to be permissible so that it can be learned from, and evidence of learning from failure deserves celebration.

When I talked to my son the other day about pitching, I asked him why he doesn't throw as hard as he's capable of in games. He told me that he gets results at about 60 percent power and it gives him way more control. It allows him to place the ball more accurately and pace himself through the game.

All of that makes great sense. But my intuition tells me that if he's going to level up his pitching game, he'll have to learn control when he's throwing closer to all-out, and along the way he'll have to learn to be emotionally and situationally OK with the occasional walk and occasional hit batter. Sometimes he'll plunk someone, sometimes he'll leave a fat one out over the plate. It happens. He'd have to be OK with that. But what he'd get in return is the joy and the results of performing at his peak, elevating his peak over time, and pitching successfully against ever more skillful players.

As ability grows in every person throughout the organization, your staff collectively and individually become capable of handling more and more difficult situations. Lots of decisions are not cut and dry. What about those gray-area moments? What about when two of your principles seem to conflict?

Honorable is our first value at Velentium. We talk about how that doesn't just mean dealing ethically with others. It also means dealing ethically with yourself. It means being internally honorable, true to yourself. Self-honor demands candor—you have to exercise your voice when there's something wrong. So, Honorable can mean to not lie, cheat, or steal from someone outside the organization. More commonly, and just as importantly, it means that you have a duty to yourself and to your organization to be honest with yourself, which is the only foundation for being honest with others.

Our second value is Results⁺⁺: we do the job and then some. So, when we end up in a situation with a client who wants more than the original contract outlined, maybe on a tight turnaround that would entail working extra hours, Results⁺⁺ prompts us to say, "Yes, I'll do it." Meanwhile, Honorable says, "No, that's beyond our agreement. If I just give that to you without a change order, I'm stealing from my employer. And if I do that on the timetable you're requesting, I'm stealing time already promised to myself and my family."

What's the right answer? Do we hold the line and demand a change order and a calmer schedule, as Honorable would suggest? Or, do we say, "Sure, we can do that favor for you this time," as Results⁺⁺ would suggest?

You may have guessed where this illustration is headed. I'm not gonna tell you the "right" answer. Why? Because I'm not the person closest to that situation. It's not my project to manage. I don't have a relationship with that client who's asking for something extra. It's not me who will have to work through the short-term consequences of that decision.

It's you.

It's *all* you.

So I'm going to smile and drop it on ya:

"You decide."

"YOU DECIDE" CULTURE

"You decide" culture is how your organization resists the slide toward "F-key" culture. Pressures from the drive toward efficiency, from the desire to maintain close control, from the need to manage risks, all join forces to drive organizations toward "F-key" culture. In "F-key" culture, frontline staff are only authorized and enabled to respond to customer needs with a short menu of the most common preapproved actions. Any request that doesn't appear on that limited menu gets denied . . . or escalated up the management chain until it gets stuck in a queue and bottlenecks . . . and is still effectively denied through sheer untimeliness. The needless bureaucracy of "F-key" culture frustrates and drives away the customer, and wastes the time and attention of every employee who comes into contact with the off-menu request.

"You decide" culture is the antithesis of "F-key" culture. In a "You decide" culture, staff are empowered and expected to seek out the resources they need to problem-solve. To exercise their own judgment. To take principle-aligned actions on their own initiative.

"You decide" culture demands autonomy, authority, and ability throughout the organization. Without a culture that culminates in "You decide," your organization is forever tethered by the amount of bandwidth that your desk can directly handle. "You decide" requires the groundwork that precedes it throughout this book, because "You decide" is based on mutual trust: You trust your staff to make decisions without micromanagement, and your staff trusts you to evaluate, support, and reward their decisions according to the principles you have all bought into. And that provides a firm foundation for the final stage in the Growth Cycle: Delegate.

Delegate, Part II

Once upon a time, when Velentium was very small, like most founders, I wore almost all of the hats at least some of the time. As we grew and hired more staff, I started passing out those hats two and three at a time as new hires got comfortable in their roles and we worked out new processes together as a team.

Then we grew some more, and the people who'd taken on three or four hats would get to pass one or two off to somebody new. We're still looking forward to the day when every person on staff only has to wear one hat.

In the meantime, nostalgia builds around progress. A few short years ago, my job looked and felt very different than it does now. People like you and me gain the experiences we get and start the things we start because we have a serious bent toward action. As organizations grow, founders and leaders get more and more removed from the action. There are days I miss the action. I look back fondly at when we were together in the same room, all pulling together toward production.

But I didn't found Velentium for the action. I founded it to change lives for a better world.

If I were here for the action, I could change maybe four hundred lives. That's about as far as my reach can go if I'm the one doing all the reaching.

If I were here for profit, I might be able to pocket more with a smaller, hyper-elite team charging much higher rates.

But if I want impact—tens of thousands of changed lives impact—it can only be through others. We have to grow. And I have to delegate.

So, I hunt through the hat-warehouse that is Ideation for a new stack of hats—a new set of roles. I Pioneer the stack. I Stabilize it. I Train others to it. And then I pass out each and every hat. "Here. This is yours now." And back to Pioneering I go.

In "Grow," I told you about how we co-authored the world's first comprehensive how-to book on medical device cybersecurity, in response to an industry shift started by the FDA. That book was lauded as 2020's "Cybersecurity Book of the Year" and became an engineering bestseller. It's helping to shape the future of healthcare for the better. It's enhanced our reputation. And it's brought lots of new business our way.

So we took that success right back to the Pioneering stage and kicked off a new Growth Cycle. If outlining the book was laying stepping stones in the stream, and signing on to write the book was the log across the creek, it was time to build a footbridge. Our industry changed, so it was time for us to change again. I went back to my team with a new idea. "Why don't we create a set of training courses and certification exams based on the book?"

Again, they liked the idea . . . and they took it and ran with it. They've delivered that training course a few times now, both to corporate clients and as a full-semester university program. From the book to the training was a natural progression. Pioneering it was rapid. Stabilizing it has been more challenging. The team tells me they were literally developing the final touches of the course the night before it was first offered. There have been numerous challenges to navigate, including supply shortages and delays for training materials, plus competing demands on instructors' time for other projects. The training has not yet matured to the point of becoming rote and repeatable. But it has become a normalized part of our company's services.

New things feel normal after they cease to be new. Then they seem obvious, even expected by others. *Of course Velentium has a cybersecurity book and suite of training courses—they are leaders in embedded medical cybersecurity.* But that was not the perception before we spun through the Growth Cycle twice—once to create the book, and then again to create the training program.

Old Hat, New Hat

If you were keeping track of all the hats in my overdone hat-warehouse analogy, you probably noticed that the people who got trained and delegated to each ended up with an extra hat. There are the hats they were wearing already. And now there's the new hat they just got handed.

How's that supposed to work?

Well . . . it's not gonna work. Not for long.

Not unless they hand off some old hats, too.

The more you run through the Growth Cycle, the less you have to be involved in the cycle each time. Eventually, you can delegate the entire growth process. This takes Think to a whole new level. What if . . . the thing you are Pioneering, Stabilizing, Training, and Delegating is the Growth Cycle process itself?

Push your organization. Push others to start this cycle within their group in the organization. Work to free staff at all levels to *only do what only they can do.* Everyone must think. Each person should pioneer a new function, stabilize the change, train a replacement, delegate, and move up and grow out.

"What do you think?"

"I think . . . that you're going to make a great decision!"

You have to let go.

And they have to launch.

Section Wrap: Launch

This section was all about the final prep needed so your culture can launch and live on its own, embraced and lived out by every individual in your team. Culture must be regularly reinforced, championed, and taught.

Threats to culture emerge organically from within the organization, and must be weeded out. Threats to culture appear from outside the organization, always offering a strong incentive (such as financial reward) to compromise on some aspect of culture, and must be reckoned with. Examples of great culture, applied and embodied by members of your team, will abound! Team members who champion culture must be personally rewarded and publicly celebrated.

Once culture is established and lives on its own, you can begin to develop new ideas to drive future growth. The Growth Cycle is Pioneer → Stabilize → Train → Delegate. After you spin up a new initiative and delegate it, it's time to go back to ideation and pick the next thing to pioneer. Expect that most of the ideas you pioneer will not work out, so try lots of ideas, but don't get too emotionally attached to any one idea, and don't invest too many resources into an idea until it proves its worth. Determine the minimum investment needed to see whether that idea is worth taking further.

Stabilize what you successfully pioneer by documenting the new thing with enough clarity that someone with no specific knowledge could take over the effort without ever talking with you. Then, train a successor to take over the new thing through mentoring and coaching. Set them up to win. After you identify a thing that you're doing that someone else could do, fully answer the question, "What do I know about doing this thing that the new person won't?"

Get everyone in your organization to think. Give them autonomy, authority, and ability, so that whoever is closest to any situation can be trusted to personally respond to that situation. Don't provide answers; coach each person to make their own decisions using all of the decision-making tools established by your culture. Then, support their decisions and celebrate that they made those decisions, even if you would have done things differently. The long-term investment of having an organization filled with people who think will ultimately be far more profitable, efficient, and satisfying than having every decision go exactly the way you want.

When the organization is filled with people who think, you'll have no trouble seeing new initiatives through to the final stage of the Growth Cycle, Delegate. People who think can be trusted to take ownership of new initiatives and make them even better. And you'll be able to propagate the Growth Cycle to every corner of the organization. Over time, every person in the organization will be able to follow your example by asking, "Am I only doing what only I can do?" They will be able to pioneer and stabilize their role, train a replacement, delegate to that replacement, and move up or over into the next role.

IMPLEMENTATION TOOLS

Tool #9: Head-Tilt Exercise

1. On a blank piece of paper, write down the seven root causes of internal culture threats: people, ethics, negativity, blame, inauthenticity, comparison, burnout. Leave three blank lines under each one.

2. Rank the seven causes from most annoying to least annoying (or most serious to least serious). Think about which troubles you personally, which probably make the most trouble for your team, and which are the most incongruous with your culture.

3. Under each root cause, what are the top three culture threats that come to your mind? Write them down. (It's fine if you can't think of three for each category—but I bet you won't have any difficulty coming up with at least one!)

4. Make a plan to phase out and purge the top threat in each category from your organization as soon as possible. If you can't figure out how to get rid of a threat because it's too entrenched, set it aside for now and revisit it after you have time to ponder. Involve other senior leaders in the challenge. Use your best judgment. But don't let the threat go unaddressed. There is something you can do, if not to eliminate it completely just yet, at least to keep it in check. Do that.

5. Repeat this exercise once a quarter.

6. Keep this worksheet confidential. It is highly sensitive.

Tool #10: Culture Threat Visualization Tool

This ladder looks OK at a glance, but notice the cracks. It won't hold weight for long.

Tool #11: *Ideation Worksheet*

1. Pick a day and set aside a five-hour window.
2. Spend the first three hours like this: Set up thirty-minute one-on-one meetings with three customers and three staff members. Use the following interview to guide each conversation:
   a. What's going well in your job? Because of our organization and/or in general?
   b. What's not working well in your job? Because of our organization and/or in general?
   c. If you could solve one problem or challenge in your job by waving a magic wand at it, what problem or challenge would it be?
   d. What companies or product lines/brands do you admire and why?
   e. If nobody could do what we do, what would your substitute/alternative/workaround be?
   f. What other products/services do you use that are parallel or in tandem to what we provide you?
   g. What's your greatest pet peeve at work?
   h. Is there anybody else you think I should talk to about this stuff?
3. During your fourth hour, pick three industry journals or major websites and spend up to twenty minutes perusing each one. What catches your attention? What ideas are sparked by what you read? Write down some thoughts to follow up on.
4. Spend all five hours reflecting on your conversations and research and see what comes to you. If you had to follow up on one of these, what would it be? If nothing sparks you as worthy of follow-up this time, schedule your next five-hour period and repeat this exercise. The goal of the exercise is to train yourself to seek out inspiration, come up with ideas, select ideas, and begin the process of exploring and developing those ideas for the Growth Cycle.

Tool #12: Process Growth Visualization Tool

Tool #13: "Only You" Worksheet

Quick Exercise:

1. Review your calendar and your inbox for the past week. On a blank piece of paper, bullet out everything you do.
2. Highlight each thing you did that only you can do. There are two elements to this:
   a. Personally: What am I really good at and enjoy?
   b. Strategically: What does the business need that only I can do because of my position?
3. Using different colors, highlight each thing you did that:
   a. Someone else could have done (can be trained to and delegated)
   b. Did not need to be done (stop doing it!)

In-Depth Exercise:

1. Review and list your activities for the last four months.
2. Highlight and consider . . .
   a. Things you did that you should have done, are glad you did, and need or want to keep doing.
   b. Things you did alongside someone you're training.
   c. Things you did that you shouldn't be doing because there is someone else who could do it or who could be trained or hired to do it (read chapter four, "The People Component," in *Traction* by Gino Wickman).
   d. Things you did that you shouldn't be doing because you don't enjoy the task.
   e. Things you did that you shouldn't be doing, but had to do because there isn't anyone else who can be trained to take over and you don't have the resources to recruit an additional team member. As a counterargument, consider the additional resources you could bring in with the time you freed up by recruiting someone else to manage this thing (read: *Who Not How* by Dan Sullivan and Benjamin Hardy).
   f. Things you did that you shouldn't be doing, but feel like you need to be seen doing it (by your staff, your customers, or

someone else). Does that feeling reflect reality, or does it stem from within you? Is it a good and valid feeling about setting a tone or a positive example, or is it about avoiding a sense of guilt or shame?

g.   Things someone else did that you should have done.

3.   Write one thing that anyone in your organization could do, but that you will periodically do, visibly but without making a big deal out of it or drawing attention to it, to set an example of humility and initiative. For many years, for me, that activity was unloading the communal dishwasher in Velentium's office kitchen. Each person is responsible for dealing with their own dishes, but someone has to choose to do that little bit of extra lift to run the dishwasher when it's full and unload it when it's clean. I think it's good for my staff to see that their CEO isn't too bigheaded to be the guy who takes five minutes out of his busy day to do a menial task that serves everyone. I hope it inspires them to pay it forward by doing the same thing next time, or serving their coworkers some other way.

Tool #14: "You Decide!" Visualization Tool

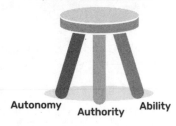

"You Decide!"

Autonomy   Authority   Ability

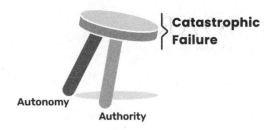

Catastrophic Failure

Autonomy   Authority

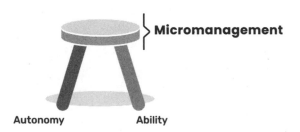

Micromanagement

Autonomy   Ability

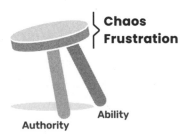

Chaos Frustration

Authority   Ability

SOAR

On April 17, Day 28 of Project V, I stood with marker in hand, poised over a box of finished ventilators, wrapped and ready for delivery. This box was about to become part of the first two shipments to leave Kokomo, headed straight to hospitals to save lives. Factory workers had been invited to grab a colored marker and leave a quick note of encouragement on the outside of the box. It felt a little like the grown-up version of signing a friend's arm cast in elementary school.

I didn't have the full scope of our effort at my fingertips right then. All the members of our team, all the parts ordered, money spent, hours worked, hours of sleep missed, miles driven and flown. Symbolically, all of that was boiling down to this—signing the box for a team of heroes working a hospital ICU somewhere, whom I would likely never meet. How to capture everything in just a few words?

"Excited to partner with you to change lives for a better world."

—Velentium

Amidst the chaos, our culture remains a fixed point of reference. We're founded on it. It grounds us, guides us, and sustains us.

I hope this book helps you implement a culture that does the same for you.

You've identified your organization's basic principles ("More than Air," "Principles over Rules").

You've readied your organization to pounce when an opportunity presents itself. You know you'll need to rest, recover, and review afterward ("Slow—Fast—Slow").

You're applying these principles humanely, because an organization is made up of real people ("Be Human").

You've cultivated a culture of learning throughout your organization ("Stay Teachable").

You have honed every aspect until it's simple ("Reach Simple").

When you find culture violations, you treat them with urgency and priority ("Defend").

You're Pioneering, Stabilizing, and Training. Growth is happening ("Grow").

Everyone who works for you understands that they have the authority, autonomy, and ability to think for themselves. You've incorporated "You decide!" throughout your organization ("Think").

You're doing great! Now, it's time to fledge the final flight feathers that will help your organization soar. What you need is a clear, powerful picture of where you're headed. And that picture should evoke powerful emotion.

VISION

I recently read Barack Obama's memoir, *A Promised Land*. Around the same time, I binge-watched the entire *West Wing* TV series. Both the fictional *West Wing* and the factual memoir depict the same reaction when people encounter the Oval Office for the first time: awe. There is just something about the office of the president of the United States. It is charged with history, prestige, and power. If you get asked to serve in the White House, you pretty much say yes. Because it's an awesome, once-in-a-lifetime opportunity.

How do you begin to shape your organization into that kind of institution? With *vision*.

Vision is an evocative picture of the organization's future—a future the organization will work to make real. When that vision is authentic, realistic, and inspiring, your team will eagerly adopt it. And you'll get to see something that hatched as a fuzzy dream in your head take on real life of its own, out in the world.

I have many, many journals. I've written in a journal for decades. The first page of every journal is what I call "the state of the Dan address." It's fun to look back thirty-plus years ago and see me eager to someday find a spouse. Then, twenty-plus years ago to see me dreaming of kids. We had four kids in five years, at which point the spaces between my journal entries mysteriously grew much farther apart than they were before. And I wouldn't trade it for anything!

In the first pages of my 2005 journal, I wrote, "I dream of running a $250 million medical device firm like Cyberonics." (Following an international merger, Cyberonics is now called LivaNova.)

A decade later, a few years after founding Velentium, I was invited to attend a benefit for epilepsy. At the benefit was the former CEO of Cyberonics, and by then the chair of LivaNova, whose name also happens to be Dan. Some people want to meet Michael Jordan or Derek Jeter. I wanted to meet Dan. I had watched as his team assumed leadership of Cyberonics amid deep financial trouble and turned the company around. I knew from his reputation that he shared my values and that he ran a company in my industry the size of the company that I dreamed of building. And I knew I needed his mentoring.

I found Dan at the benefit, handed him my card, and asked if we could have coffee. Six months of persistent follow-up later, I got my meeting, which happened to kick off a friendship.

Fast-forward several meetings. Dan and I are having beer and pizza and talking about the culture at Velentium. At that point, Velentium was tentatively describing its vision as "One thousand staff." As Jim Collins describes it, every organization has a key metric, and its vision should be expressed in terms of that metric. Velentium's key metric is "revenue per developer," which annually comes to $250,000. Therefore, to become the $250 million medical device firm that I'd journaled about in 2005, we needed one thousand developers on staff.

The problem with that vision, especially the way I just described it, is that it's monetary. Monetary goals aren't motivating. I was looking for a way to connect our key metric—revenue per developer—to our passion—changing lives for a better world.

The conversation went like this:

Me: "I really want our vision to pop. I like that we're talking about staff and not about dollars, but it's just not there yet."

Dan: "Hmm. But you're as passionate about your family and the families of your staff as you are about the staff themselves."

Me: "You bet I am. Nothing's gonna get in the way of me being there for my kids during the 'critical decade.'" (The "critical decade" in parenting is those ten years from six to sixteen where kids go from kids to almost-adults. I don't get a second chance at the critical decade!)

Dan: "So, if your goal is one thousand staff, and you're so passionate about family, why wouldn't you express your vision as one thousand families?"

Click. Perfect fit.

I still get chills thinking about that moment at the pizza joint in Indiana. The phrase "one thousand families" combines the dream from my journal with Velentium's passion for changed lives and translates them into an actionable image for the future. If I can offer one thousand staff the opportunity to invest their careers toward the passion, and teach them to work according to the values, it will change their lives. It will change how they are not only at work but at home, in their communities, in their next job if they move on, in their volunteer activities, in their kids' schools, heck, at the dog park. It will change the world. And that's what we're about. So one thousand families is our vision for Velentium's future.

And guess what? Our staff are excited about it, too! Not so surprising, because we recruit for culture. As soon as Dan helped me clarify our vision so fittingly, we put it into our recruiting, onboarding, and routine cultural messaging.

One thousand families. Simple. Authentic. Emotional. Human. *Let's go!*

So what's your vision? And how do you communicate it to your team in a way that evokes emotion and inspires action?

Paint the Future

What does the future look like at your organization? Dream. Big.

Describe it. Write it down. Maybe it's words in a free association. Maybe it's a bulleted list. Maybe it's a description in a paragraph. Maybe it's a picture. And mull it over. Let it marinate. Accept that this takes time. Get away from it for a while, then return.

When you think you might have it captured, run it through this filter:

1. **Is it doable?** SpaceX has the extremely ambitious goal of enabling human colonization of Mars. Could I do that? No. Do I want to do that? Again, no. But could a private company do it? Maybe! I think they've at least proved that it's within reach—their vision is doable. On the other hand, your vision shouldn't include something that's probably impossible, like time travel. It might be worth doing, but it almost definitely can't be done.

2. **Is it worth doing?** This is the emotional side. Only you can decide if it's worth doing. And you will know deep inside of you. Is this "you"? If it is, it will elicit a deep emotional response. And once you know it's "you," don't apologize! It *is* worth doing. For you, and for anyone who signs on with you.

3. **Do I have the drive to accomplish it?** Count the cost. What will it take? You will have less time. Less freedom. As you look at the cost, do you have friends or family who are gonna be there beside you no matter what? Knowing that you are not alone in the corner is huge. If you do get cornered, you know you'll be fighting your way out against the circumstances that threaten to crater your dream alongside those who have committed to you and love you.

4. **Do I have the team that can accomplish it?** Do you have the team right now? Do you have to go recruit that team? Have you recruited before? Do you have someone on your team who has recruited? Learning how to articulate your dream and showing people how they can be a part of that dream is one of your prime directives.

5. **Will I know when it's accomplished?** Your vision needs to have a very clear definition of the finish line. It gives you and everybody else something to shoot for. Plus, it makes clearing the final hurdle easier.

6. **Can I articulate it in three to five seconds?** Package your vision so that people "get it" right away, or are challenged and intrigued enough to ask questions. Work on this with meticulous stubbornness. Do not be satisfied until it clicks. Until it sends a chill down your spine. You must know in your core that *that* vision, expressed like that, will motivate you every day for years.

Do you have six yeses? Bam! Nailed it! Now go and make it reality.

CLIMB WITH BOTH WINGS

There are two wings to every leader's role. With one wing you define the principles. With the other, you continuously, creatively champion those principles into practice. And *that*, together, is culture. Before you can soar, you have to gain height. And the way you do that is by flapping both wings together.

First Wing: Define the Principles

Leaders define the organization's daily reality by setting the *tone*, painting the *target*, and deciding the *tactics*.

> **Tone:** Work to ensure that the day-to-day experience of being at work for your staff is in harmony with your core principles. If there's a clash, a violation, a head-tilt issue, and you don't deal with it, your culture will slip. And it will take shared identity down with it.
>
> **Target:** Show everyone where your organization is going with a simple yet evocative vision that gives everyone a "heart lift" from being two parts inspiring, one part terrifying. Spotlight the hill (mountain?) you want them to charge—and start running!
>
> **Tactics:** Always be Pioneering, Stabilizing, Training, and Delegating. Make a decision in the face of extreme ambiguity, then do the work to ensure that decision is the right decision. Coach everyone to Think—level them up, by refusing to step in. "You decide!"

Second Wing: Champion the Culture

When you start pitching what you want the culture to be, you're hoping that someone (anyone?) will smile, nod in recognition, and buy in. As more and more do, they attract people like them. As more and more join, and you do more and better work together, you begin to curate a collection of the most powerful teacher of culture and wisdom there is: stories.

Over time, the best stories develop into legend. And the growing group attracts even more people who are attracted not so much to what you're doing, but to how you're doing it, and most importantly, to why you're doing it.

The secret to keeping this momentum going is, never get weary of championing culture. It feels to you like redundancy. But nobody else hears the message as clearly as you feel like you're saying it. Nobody else remembers it as well as you do. Every person on staff needs a slow drip of cultural messaging over years to fully own it and consistently apply it. Everyone who joins your organization likes what they see on a conscious level. But on an instinctive level, everyone (including you!) is bringing with them unconscious programming from previous cultures. It takes time—and *lots* of reinforcement—before shared principles fully mature into shared identity.

Culture is impossible to overcommunicate. Incorporate new ideas and initiatives carefully to ensure that your culture and messaging stay consistent. Try new things; double down on what sticks. Eventually, with enough consistency and critical mass, culture takes hold and becomes self-sustaining. Once you build it in enough places, duplicate it to enough people, it just feels natural. Culture soars on its own.

Soar

Your culture is inimitable. Is culture "soft," squishy, complicated, emergent? Yes. Does it give you lift, clarity, energy? Yes. Is it effortless to maintain? No. But once you have it, it can't be copied. It becomes a competitive advantage. It inspires people to work for you and other organizations to work with you. You will see the impact on your bottom line.

You craft the core: passion, values, vision.

The core attracts people. People live out new stories, with the culture's core for their theme.

You cement those stories into legend by retelling, showcasing, and rewarding them.

The exponential result is energy, growth, and increasing resources to pursue your shared vision and achieve your shared passion.

It's been a long time since you asked yourself "Why not me?" and left the nest. Since then, you've had practice learning to flap, to fall, to fly. You've

defined a new identity. You've defined a new vision. You've found and nurtured a team that embraces that identity and is eager to achieve that vision.
Together, you've grown.

Now it's time to spread those wings, and soar.

Acknowledgments

Authoring and publishing a book is a massive effort. There are more contributors who deserve mention than can be acknowledged here, and everyone, mentioned or not, deserves to have more said about them than there is space for. So here's my "short list" of those without whom this book would not exist.

First, our publishing team:

- John: Thanks for seeing the potential in our book pitch, taking us on, and coaching us to the next level. *28 Days to Save the World* would have gone nowhere without your vote of confidence and expertise!
- Matt: A genuine pleasure working with you. Thanks for believing in this project and nudging it back on course whenever we began to drift.
- Katie: Thanks for keeping track of all the moving pieces of the publishing effort and for making sure they all found their way to the right spot at the right time.
- Camille: Wow. Your insightful criticism and experienced editor's eye gave us some of the most encouraging feedback we could ever have hoped to receive . . . alongside incisive revision recommendations that made us groan, grumble, and acknowledge that you were absolutely right! Thanks for helping us make this book so much better than we would have managed on our own.

- Nate: Quickest turnaround on an independent manuscript review ever, man! Your comments and reactions made it much easier to swallow all the good medicine Camille dished out.

Next, mentors, family, and friends:

- Trae: You've always believed in me. That belief has fueled me more than you know.
- Larry: Since 2005, you have taught me, challenged me, invested in me and in Velentium, led our initial board, and been my cheerleader. Thank you for taking the time to share the lessons you learned from Bill with the "next generation."
- Dan: Your leadership inspired me to create an organization like yours. It has been a dream come true that I now not only admire you from afar as I have for many years but can also call you mentor and friend.
- Tim: This is our story—as much yours as mine. From that first lunch in a Tex-Mex diner, to the countless breakfasts at Cracker Barrel, to the decades in the trenches, I've been fortunate to be partnered with someone so genuinely great. You are one of my favorite people.
- My kids: Thank you for your patience as you tolerated countless hours of Dad on the phone talking about this book with Jason while driving you to school, practice, food runs, and even trick-or-treating. I love you all!
- Jason: For me, the best part of working on this book is summed up by that innocuous phrase on the front cover: "with Jason Smith."

Finally, everyone from the Velentium team—staff, contractors, suppliers, vendors, and volunteers—who contributed to Project V: You accomplished this. You proved that the impossible was actually possible. Tens of thousands of people are alive because of what you did! Thanks for making Velentium culture your own, and for making this place what it is. Together, we're changing lives for a better world.

Josh Aguilar
Randy Armstrong
Malcolm Barnes
Ananya Bhattacharya
Soumendu
  Bhattacharya
Jennifer Brough
Devin Carroll
Randy Carroll
Sean Carroll
Stacy Carroll
Tim Carroll
Jon Cedillo
Juan Cedillo
Ryan Clingan
Paul Cochran
William Cochran
Seth Dunn
Gilberto Flores
Ron Flores
Tim Grogan

Levi Gustin
Blane Hearn
Navor Hernandez
Chris Jensen
Jessica Joslin
Girven Kissell
Mahdi Koubaa
Mark Kraft
Caylin Kuenn
Matt Kuss
Hamilton LaRee
Jonathon Leaverton
Matt Leaverton
Alberto Lin
Jennifer Martinez
Steve Martinez
Mohita Minocha
Larry McKormack
Corey Morgan
Frank Newcomb
Caleb Oliphant

Chris Oliphant
Cole Oliphant
Denise Oliphant
Paul Oliphant
James Ortega
Forrest Palmer
John Pergande
Steve Powell
Julie Purvis
Santiago Sanchez
Christian Schaffler
Robert Schaffler
Jason Smith
Nathan Smith
Jason Swoboda
Ben Trombold
Craig Underwood
David Weng
Chris Wolf

Acopian Technical
Alicat Scientific
Allied Electronics
ARCS Diversified
Ashcroft
Blackstone Global
BriceBarclay
C&M Machining
Cole-Parmer
  Instruments
Conroe
  Manufacturing
Dataforth
  Corporation
Digi-Key
Fictiv
Grainger

Hartfiel Automation
Hatfield and Company
LEVO Technology
Maxon Precision
  Motors
McMaster-Carr
Mensor
Michigan Instruments
Moore Control
  Systems
Morris Export
  Services
Mouser Electronics
NI
Newark
Norgren
Oasis Testing

Omega Engineering
OnLogic
Oxigraf
Praxair
PrecisionBlend
Pride Printing
Protolabs
Scientific Glass &
  Plastic
Setra Systems, Inc.
Sunstone Circuits
Uline
UPS
Wholesale Electric
  Supply
Xometry

Endnotes

1. Brett Samuels, "Trump Presses GM, Ford over Ventilators," *The Hill*, March 27, 2020, https://thehill.com/homenews/administration/489849-trump-lashes -out-at-gm-ford-over-ventilators.

2. David Welch, Shira Stein, and Josh Wingrove, "GM Forges On Without U.S. Ventilator Contract After Trump Attack," Bloomberg Law, March 27, 2020, https://news.bloomberglaw.com/pharma-and-life-sciences/trump-threatens -to-force-gm-to-move-faster-on-ventilators.

3. Neil Gaiman, "The Neil Story (with Additional Footnote)," *Journal* (blog), May 17, 2017, https://journal.neilgaiman.com/2017/05/the-neil-story-with -additional-footnote.html.

4. Marc Randolph, *That Will Never Work* (New York: Little, Brown and Company, 2019), 273.

5. *The Fellowship of the Ring*, directed by Peter Jackson (2001; New York: New Line Cinema), Movie.

6. Seth Godin, "Reject the Tyranny of Being Picked: Pick Yourself," *Seth's Blog* (blog), March 21, 2011, https://seths.blog/2011/03/reject-the-tyranny-of-being -picked-pick-yourself.

7. Seth Godin, "People Like Us Do Things Like This," *Seth's Blog* (blog), July 26, 2013, https://seths.blog/2013/07/people-like-us-do-stuff-like-this.

8. *Office Space*, directed by Mike Judge (1999; Los Angeles: 20th Century Fox), Movie.

9. Ben Horowitz, *What You Do Is Who You Are* (New York: HarperCollins, 2019), 5.

10. Dorothy A. Winsor, "Communication Failures Contributing to the *Challenger* Accident: An Example for Technical Communication," appearing in *Strategies for Business and Technical Writing, Sixth Edition*, edited by Kevin J. Harty (New York: Pearson Education, Inc., 2008), 350.

11. Amy Edmondson, *Teaming*, quoted in Brené Brown, *Dare to Lead* (New York: Random House, 2018), 36.

12. Brené Brown, *Dare to Lead* (New York: Random House, 2018), 67.

13. Larry E. Senn, *The Human Operating System: An Owner's Manual* (Los Angeles: Senn-Delaney Leadership Consulting Group, 2005), 4–7, 21–22.

14. Cal Newport, *Deep Work* (London: Piatkus, 2016), 158–159.

15. Jason Fried and David Heinemeier Hansson, *It Doesn't Have to Be Crazy at Work* (New York: Harper Business, 2018), 54, 63.

16. Paul Graham, "Maker's Schedule, Manager's Schedule," *Essays* (blog), July 2009, http://www.paulgraham.com/makersschedule.html.

17. Fried and Hansson, 62.

18. Ibid., 178.

19. Ibid.

20. Newport, 157, 165.

21. *Merriam-Webster.com Dictionary*, "flash in the pan," Merriam-Webster, accessed February 14, 2022, https://www.merriam-webster.com/dictionary/flash%20in%20the%20pan.

22. *Farlex Dictionary of Idioms*, "flash in the pan," accessed February 14, 2022, https://idioms.thefreedictionary.com/flash+in+the+pan.

23. Newport, 154, 212–213.

24. Horowitz, 5.

25. William Arthur Ward, quoted in *Oklahoma City Star* (Oklahoma City), May 17, 1963, M-110.

26. Kimberly Weisul, "Jim Collins: Good to Great in 10 Steps," *Inc.*, May 7, 2012, https://www.inc.com/kimberly-weisul/jim-collins-good-to-great-in-ten-steps.html.

27. Gino Wickman, *Traction: Expanded Edition* (Dallas: BenBella Books, Inc., 2011), 99.

28. Winsor, 350, 355–359.

29. Fried and Hansson, 91.

Index

About the Authors

A serial entrepreneur and the founder of six companies, **Dan Purvis** has deep experience with small business. An engineering graduate of Texas A&M with an MBA from Rice University, Dan brings nearly thirty years of practical know-how in creating corporate environments that people love to work in and clients want to engage. Dan realized that if you seek revenue first, relegate "culture" to a poster slogan, and shoehorn in customer care, you'll reap dysfunction. But if you make promises you keep, put client success ahead of your own, protect your people, and keep operations human—then loyalty, referrals, growth, and profit will follow. And the way you do that is through culture.

Velentium, Dan's current firm, began as a two-person operation in 2012. Ten years later, it ranks thirty-second on the Inc. 5000 list of fastest-growing engineering companies nationwide and has averaged 50 percent annual growth for nearly a decade. Dan's purpose in writing *28 Days to Save the World* is to share his insights, mistakes, and experiences in building successful cultures with other leaders so that, together, we can make the world a better place to be human.

At age fifteen, **Jason Smith** founded his first company, a residential landscape design and installation service, thanks to mentoring from other entrepreneurs in his community. By the time he graduated from college, his company had helped pay tuition for a dozen staff, each recruited away from passion-crushing employment in big-box stores or fast-food restaurants. Fueled by polymathic curiosity, Jason subsequently worked in a variety of industries: real estate, property management, nonprofits, trade associations, higher education, and now medical device development. Jason's wide-ranging experience enabled him to recognize something rare at Velentium: most organizations lack the combination of insight, empathy, and budgetary guts required to do right by their staff, clients, and investors alike. He believes that *28 Days to Save the World* will show leaders how to harmonize these "competing" interests, resulting in more effective, resilient, and positive organizations.

During Project V, Jason spent his days buried in the "Multi-BOM" spreadsheet, maintaining data integrity while coordinating parts and supply orders between the Friendly Neighborhood Purchasing Team and system owners.

28 Days to Save the World is the tenth published book he has helped author.